Evaluation for school development

David Hopkins

Open University Press
Milton Keynes · Philadelphia

This book is dedicated to Marloes,
for being there in the beginning,
and to Jeroen, for joining us at the end.

Open University Press
12 Cofferidge Close
Stony Stratford
Milton Keynes MK11 1BY

and

1900 Frost Road, Suite 101
Bristol, PA 19007, USA

First Published 1989

British Library Cataloguing in Publication Data

Hopkins, David, *1949–*
    Evaluation for school development.
    1. Education. Evaluation research
    I. Title
    379.1'54
    ISBN 0–335–09241–1
    ISBN 0–335–09240–3 (paper)

Library of Congress Cataloging-in-Publication Data

Hopkins, David, 1949–
    Evaluation for school development/by David Hopkins.
        p.   cm.
    Bibliography: p.
    Includes index.
    ISBN 0–335–09241–1   ISBN 0–335–09240 (pbk.)
    1. Educational evaluation – Great Britain.   2. School improvement
    programs – Great Britain – Evaluation.   I. Title.
    LB2822.75.H63   1989
    379.1'54 – dc20
                                                                    89–8807
                                                                    CIP

Typeset by Scarborough Typesetting Services
Printed in Great Britain by
Biddles Limited, Guildford and King's Lynn

Art is knowledge realised in action.

Rene Daumal

Methodological confusion can always be traced to ideological error.

Paulo Freire

With the institutionalisation of 'new wave' evaluation, I think we have produced a situation in which there is some danger that evaluators create their own establishment and glamorise it as an elite. Let's keep hold of the idea that it is mostly a matter of commonsense and learning from experience. That is not entirely true but it keeps us from going technical or theological; and a little modest oversimplification is better than a lapse into jargon or pretentiousness.

Lawrence Stenhouse

Contents

Preface

A few years ago the Open University Press published my *A Teachers Guide to Classroom Research* (Hopkins, 1985a). The purpose of that book was to make an argument for a teacher-based approach to classroom research that had improvement as its main aim and to provide a description of the skills for so doing. With a few notable exceptions, the book was well received, particularly by teachers, which is how I had hoped it would be.

Since completing the first draft of that manuscript the educational scene in the UK has changed dramatically. We are, in this country, in the midst of an unprecedented era of change; and although the main lines of the debate are becoming increasingly clear, the pace will continue for some time. These changes, besides being substantive, i.e. relating to specific innovations, also reflect an emerging national educational policy that is increasingly centralist, instrumental, accountability-oriented and embodies the values of the marketplace. Consequently, evaluation features large in the rhetoric of these changes and current policy. Although evaluation has been forced centre stage of late, it is a form of evaluation unfamiliar and antithetical to those involved with the development of the 'new wave' of curriculum evaluation in the 1970s. That approach to evaluation was concerned to illuminate educational processes and issues; we are now in an era of 'performance indicators', 'needs assessment' and 'product' evaluation that has a concern for, but limited view of, quality in education. This tension will be a continuing theme of this book.

One of my main regrets with the classroom research book was that it did not give enough prominence to the ways in which teachers could work together or how teacher-based classroom research could lead to school, rather than individual, classroom improvement. In short, the book lacked a 'classroom exceeding' or school improvement perspective. Over the past 5 years I have been fortunate enough to be involved with the OECD's International School Improvement Project (ISIP) with a particular emphasis on school-based review (SBR) or whole-school evaluation. My contact with schools and authorities in a variety of cultural contexts, and consequent discussions with colleagues, has taught me a great deal. Over the same period of time, I have been involved in this country with a series of local and national evaluations of 'categorically funded' educational projects. 'Categoric funding' refers to the current practice of finance-led curriculum development, whereby LEAs and schools bid for funds to initiate specific educational innovations in accordance with a time-limited brief from a central authority. This experience has been instructive because the evaluation style in all these projects (despite the ethos and rhetoric of various governments and authorities) has had a developmental focus which also took into account factors operating at the national, LEA and school organization as well as classroom levels.

It was this combination of factors – the growth of evaluative activity in this country, which at a policy level at least often espouses accountability rather than developmental values; a dissatisfaction with the lack of a school improvement perspective in the classroom research book; and my own involvement in a variety of evaluation activities that have a development orientation – that encouraged me to put pen to paper again. There is also another reason: although the literature on evaluation is burgeoning, it is often fragmented (located in academic journals or reports) and technical (written for academic evaluators). There is little written for teachers and practitioners and yet it is this group who are increasingly being required to 'do' evaluation.

Although the book had been planned and written in my head for some time, it took the discipline of an editorial deadline and the opportunity of a Christmas vacation to complete the manuscript. It was also during this time that our son Jeroen was born. This miraculous event may go some way to explain the optimism that pervades the pages that follow. I hope that the book will, in the same way as its companion volume did with classroom research, serve to make an argument for an approach to evaluation that is developmental and formative, and which is of some practical help to those teachers and others who find themselves in the position of doing evaluation, and improving the quality of education in our schools and LEAs.

Acknowledgements

I could not have prepared this book without the formative influence of three groups of people: those who contracted me to work as an evaluator on a variety of local and national projects and so gave me the experience; colleagues in this country, in the OECD and North America who in discussion helped to develop and broaden my understanding; and students on my evaluation and change courses whose scrutiny of the ideas forced me to clarify my thinking and so sharpen my practice. But it was Marloes Hopkins de Groot who in her own inimitable way encouraged me not only to have the experience but also to explore the meaning by allowing me space to write it all down. My thanks to her too.

I am most grateful to Mel Ainscow, Rob Bollington, Julie Howard, Marilyn Leask, Jean Rudduck and John Skelton who took time to read the manuscript and whose perceptive comments have improved immeasurably what is here. My thanks also to Angie Ashton and Gill Abbott who typed the various drafts of the manuscript, and to Barbara Shannon who exercised a fastidious yet caring eye over its production.

Finally, I am most grateful to the following authors for allowing me to quote from their work in this book. Each contribution is also acknowledged in the text and appears in the Reference List. They are: Ron Abbott, Robert Bollen, Rob Bollington, David Bridges, Per Dalin, John Elliott, Rob Fiddy, Carol FitzGibbon, Wynne Harlen, Peter Holly, Michael Huberman, Bruce Joyce, Stephen Kemmis, Marilyn Leask, Susan Loucks-Horsley, Colin McCabe, Robin McTaggart, Matthew Miles, David Nevo, Fergus O'Sullivan, Beverly Showers, Robert Stake, Ian Stonach and Marvin Wideen. I am also grateful to ACCO (the publisher of the ISIP books), Evaluation and Research in Education, The Journal of Staff Development, the National Development Centre, the OECD, Sage Publications, and the SCDC for allowing me to quote from copyright material.

It goes without saying that the views expressed here do not commit the aforementioned, any other individual, or organization; they, like the errors of fact or interpretation, remain my own.

List of abbreviations

ACAS	Advisory Conciliation and Arbitration Service
ACSET	Advisory Committee on the Supply and Education of Teachers
APU	Assessment and Performance Unit
CARE	Centre for Applied Research in Education
CERI	Centre for Educational Research and Innovation
DES	Department of Education and Science
DESSI	Dissemination Efforts Supporting School Improvement
DION	Diagnosing Individual and Organizational Needs
ESG	Education Support Grant
FOCUS	Framework for Organization Change and Underlying Style
GCSE	General Certificate of Secondary Education
GIL	Guide to Institutional Learning
GRIDS	Guidelines for Review and Institutional Development in Schools
GRIST	Grant Related In-Service Training
IDP	International Development Programme
ILEA	Inner London Education Authority
IMTEC	International Movement Towards Educational Change
INSET	In-Service Education of Teachers
ISIP	International School Improvement Project
LASS	Library Access and Sixth Form Studies
LEA	Local Education Authority
LEATGS	Local Education Authorities Training Grants Scheme
LOU	Levels of Use
MSC	Manpower Services Commission
NFER	National Foundation for Educational Research
NDC	National Development Centre (for School Management Training)
OECD	Organization for Economic Cooperation and Development
R & D	Research and Development
SBR	School-Based Review

SCDC	School Curriculum Development Committee
SDG	School Development Guide
SIGMA	Self-Initiated Group Managed Action
STP	Situation Target Plans
TRIST	TVEI Related In-Service Training
TVEI	Technical and Vocational Education Initiative
TVEI(E)	Technical and Vocational Education Initiative, Extension

Section I
What is evaluation?

1
Evaluation for school development

The central theme of this book is that evaluation needs to be linked to development. Educational evaluation has utility only in so far as its outcomes enable LEA officers, heads and teachers to improve the substance of their educational programmes and the quality of the teaching learning process in their LEAs, schools and classrooms. This is particularly the case in the UK at present, where the proliferation of 'categorically funded' change projects, centrally initiated curriculum innovations and government legislation tend to have an evaluation brief attached to them. Unfortunately, the consequent evaluation reports have a notoriously short half-life, and even their limited usefulness is often squandered through bureaucratic delays and a style of presentation inimicable to those for whom they are intended. This creates particular problems for those of us concerned with the developmental aspects of evaluation.

This point is particularly poignant in the current climate of change in the UK where many of the recent developments are contentious. Evaluation, which has an improvement perspective, provides a structure for teachers and others to subject a particular curriculum change to their own professional judgement and, in so doing, to improve the programme and make further plans for implementation. In this way an evaluation can provide a means for translating an educational idea into practice as well as monitoring and enhancing curriculum development.

Defining evaluation

To many this may seem an idiosyncratic interpretation of the word evaluation and indeed it is somewhat at odds with mainstream definitions. Ralph Tyler (1949: 105–6) originally defined evaluation as 'the process of determining to what extent the educational objectives are being realised'. Most evaluators,

...arly those working in North America, are in accord with this ...ition. As Nevo (1986: 16) points out, 'there is a considerable consensus ...garding the definition of evaluation as the assessment of merit or worth', or as an activity comprised of both description and judgement. There are, however, some dissenting voices. Here is Nevo (1986: 16) again:

> A major exception to that consensus regarding the judgmental definition of evaluation is represented by the Stanford Evaluation Consortium groups who defined evaluation as '(a) systematic examination of events occurring in and consequent of a contemporary program – an examination conducted to assist in improving this program and other programs having the same general purpose' (Cronbach *et al.*, 1980: 14). Cronbach and his associates clearly reject the judgmental nature of evaluation advocating an approach that perceives the evaluator as 'an educator (whose) success is to be judged by what others learn' (p. 11) rather than a 'referee (for) a basketball game' (p. 18) who is hired to decide who is 'right' or 'wrong'.

Cronbach's interpretation is closer to the image I tried to convey earlier and more in keeping with Stenhouse's (1975) view when he argues against the separation of programme developer and evaluator and in favour of integrated curriculum research. Although the aspiration of this book is broader than curriculum research, the argument remains the same. As Stenhouse said (1975: 122):

> Evaluation should, as it were, lead development and be integrated with it. Then the conceptual distinction between development and evaluation is destroyed and the two merge as research. Curriculum research must itself be illuminative rather than recommendatory as in the earlier tradition of curriculum development.

In the same way as Stenhouse used this argument to elaborate his definition of curricular research and the teacher as researcher, I regard the fusion between evaluation and development as defining new opportunities for the educational process and the roles of those involved.

Although I am arguing for a developmental approach to evaluation, this does not imply that evaluation is not about making judgements. Developmental efforts are facilitated by clear analysis and criteria. Consequently, much of what follows is about how to ensure that one's conclusions are valid and about articulating standards against which judgements can be made. It is also necessary to make the basis of one's judgements open to scrutiny and to be clear about the derivation of one's criteria.

Another idiosyncracy to my view of evaluation is that it is not an act committed by one person on another. Nor is it an activity confined to those in a hierarchical power relationship. As Stake (1986b: 89–90) points out, evaluation is a serious business: 'We deal with people's lives – not only the lives of young people, but of teachers and other adults. . . . We interfere with their lives convinced we are helping them toward something better.' So convinced are we by the altruism of these motives that we often ignore the moral implications of such interference. Implicit in this book, therefore, is a democratization of evaluation roles. As will be seen in Chapter 6, the concept of the external evaluator as the only person able or suited to undertake evaluation is becoming increasingly unrealistic. This, however, is not to underestimate the importance of an expert or knowledgeable perspective. But, by its very nature evaluation for development requires collaboration between the range of stakeholders in the educational enterprise. An important feature of the recent spate of curriculum innovations is the increasing involvement of teachers in educational evaluation. Many of the new curriculum initiatives (e.g. TVEI) insist on local evaluation, and for other innovations it is a natural expectation. Increasingly, LEAs are seconding teachers to perform the evaluation task or expecting it to be done in school. Although these teachers have the connection with the field and an intimate knowledge of the innovation, they often lack specific expertise in evaluation. This book is designed specifically for teachers – whether primary, secondary or further education – who are, or will be interested in becoming, curriculum evaluators. Thus the *raison d'être* for the book: the elaboration of an argument for evaluation as development and a description of the skills for so doing.

The evolution of curriculum evaluation in the UK

The context for any debate on curriculum development or evaluation was set by Ralph Tyler with the publication in 1949 of his book *The Basic Principles of Curriculum and Instruction*. Dismayed by the sloppy approach to curriculum development that he witnessed in the United States in the 1940s, Tyler proposed as an antidote a systematic and beguilingly simple approach to curriculum planning based around four questions:

1 What educational purposes should the school seek to attain?
2 What educational experiences can be provided that are likely to attain these purposes?
3 How can these educational experiences be effectively organized?
4 How can we determine whether these purposes are being attained?

The so-called 'Tyler rationale' is often expressed in an even more simplified form:

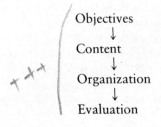

Objectives
↓
Content
↓
Organization
↓
Evaluation

Tylers' approach, often called the objectives model, has been enormously influential, so much so that many claim that it is the *only* way to develop curricula. The model has also had a profound impact on curriculum evaluation because the logical way to evaluate this type of curriculum scheme is through discerning some change in behaviour that signifies achievement of the objective, usually a test score or examination result, on the part of the student. In turn, that objective has to be expressed in behavioural terms so that the achievement can be observed and evaluated. It is a very instrumental and outcome-oriented form of evaluation.

Much of the post-sputnik flurry of curriculum development and evaluation in the United States, some 30 years ago, was based on the objectives model and it also influenced curriculum developments in this country during the 1960s and early 1970s. The first British publication in the field of curriculum evaluation, a short book by Wiseman and Pidgeon (1972) entitled *Curriculum Evaluation* and published by the NFER, was firmly located within the Tylerian tradition. They say, for example, that: 'Only by the evaluation of aim—achievement can we ensure that curricula remain flexible, and responsive to new demands and changing circumstances' (1972: 90).

At about this time the Schools Council's programme of curriculum development and evaluation was well under way and many of those involved in these projects were concerned at the instrumentality and ubiquity of the objectives approach. This concern was given focus by Lawrence Stenhouse, Director of the Humanities Curriculum Project, in his seminal paper 'Some limitations of the use of objectives in curriculum research and planning' (1970–71) and later in his influential work *An Introduction to Curriculum Research and Development* (1975). He summarized his concerns about the objectives model as follows (as quoted in Rudduck and Hopkins, 1985: 77–8):

1 It does not draw on, nor is it in accord with, empirical studies of the classroom. Those studies which exist suggest that for the most part this is not how students learn nor how teachers teach. Teaching and learning at their best unfold, are built up and do not aim at a goal: they build as high as they can.

2 Analysis of curriculum content into behavioural objectives is not in accord with the nature and structure of knowledge – with epistemology. Knowledge cannot be reduced to behaviours. In particular it cannot be expressed in terms of pre-specified performances for it is the function of knowledge, as opposed to mere agglomerations of facts, that it does not determine behaviour but liberates it. Knowledge is a basis for diversity of performances characterised by understanding.

3 Normally, the objectives formula sidetracks and blurs the ethical and political problems associated with the control of education, its aspirations and its individualisation. Whose objectives are these to be: those of the State, of the curriculum developer, of the teacher or of the student?

4 All this leads me to the assertion that the objectives model over-

estimates our capacity to understand the educational process. It may increase the clarity of our intention but it does little or nothing to improve its quality.

The reason for discussing the work of Tyler and Stenhouse is to suggest that, on the one hand, Tyler's model set a direction for and imposed a straitjacket on the field of curriculum evaluation. Stenhouse's critique and intellectual leadership in the 1970s, on the other hand, was to inaugurate an alternative approach to curriculum evaluation in this country and elsewhere. Working from within the crucible of the Humanities Curriculum Project at the Schools Council, and later at the Centre for Applied Research in Education (CARE) at the University of East Anglia, Stenhouse exerted a profound influence. His critique of the objectives model led to the formulation of a process model of curriculum research and development, exemplified in the Humanities Curriculum Project and described in his *An Introduction to Curriculum Research and Development* (1975). Similarly, his critique of the instrumentality of a behaviourist approach to curriculum evaluation led to the creation of an alternative approach. In this case, however, he was not the author but exerted more of a 'godfather'-like influence on, and intellectual leadership over, this new wave of curriculum evaluation which was nurtured in and continues to be associated with CARE.

The most important single contribution to this new wave of curriculum evaluation was Malcolm Parlett and David Hamilton's (1972) paper 'Evaluation as illumination: A new approach to the study of innovatory programmes', where they critique the dominant 'agricultural-botany' approach, as they call it, to evaluation with its insistence on prespecified objectives, experimental designs and statistical analysis. They proposed in its place an approach based on the methods of social anthropology that they called 'illuminative evaluation' that takes account of the wider contexts in which educational programmes function. Its primary concern is with description and interpretation rather than measurement and prediction. A number of conferences were organized during the 1970s to explore the implications of this alternative approach (e.g. MacDonald and Parlett, 1973; Adelman *et al.*, 1976).

Some years later, a number of the leading figures on the 'new wave' evaluation scene published a book of readings whimsically entitled *Beyond the Numbers Game* (Hamilton *et al.*, 1977), which as a description of the alternative approach remains essential reading. Although the Cambridge conferences and the associated publications are significant milestones, the road to the establishment of an alternative tradition was more mundane, and was travelled by a number of others who over a period of a decade contributed to a firm foundation. Two groups of evaluators are of particular importance – those involved with the evaluation of the Schools Council curriculum projects and those involved centrally or less formally with Stenhouse at CARE. These, however, are only loose groupings and often the actors' roles intertwined.

The evaluation of the Schools Council curriculum projects gave an enormous impetus to new wave evaluation, mainly because there were so many of them (Stenhouse, 1980). Also, because many of the curriculum projects adopted some form of process curriculum and enquiry–discovery teaching strategy, traditional forms of evaluation were soon found to be wanting. Arguably, Barry MacDonald's work in developing a case study evaluation methodology for the Humanities Curriculum Project was the most influential (e.g. MacDonald, 1978). MacDonald's 'political classification' of evaluation models approach to reporting evaluation data has been equally important (MacDonald, 1976), as will be seen later. The Schools Council evaluator's group published a series of books on aspects of their work which, taken together, given an invaluable background to the development, both practically and theoretically, of the alternative approach to curriculum evaluation (e.g. Tawney, 1976).

The second group were those working with and influenced by Stenhouse at CARE in Norwich. Stenhouse established CARE in 1972 following his and colleagues' work on the Humanities Curriculum Project. The original staff of CARE – Lawrence Stenhouse, Barry MacDonald, Jean Rudduck and John Elliott – were all originally members of the Humanities Project team. Between them this group undertook a series of high-profile evaluation projects which led to a number of influential papers which, by the end of the 1970s, in conjunction with the other influences already mentioned, provided a secure foundation for an alternative approach to traditional curriculum evaluation.

By the end of the 1970s, the influence of the CARE tradition was at its zenith. What had appeared dangerously radical 10 years earlier was now common-place and the casual observer could be excused for wondering what all the fuss had been about. But the tide of change was on the turn – the Callaghan Ruskin Speech, the advent of the Thatcher government in 1979, and the demise of the Schools Council marked a dramatic shift in attitudes towards the account-ability and control of education. The tragically premature death of Lawrence Stenhouse in 1982 marked the end of an era, in more ways than one.

Educational evaluation in the 1980s

Without the benefit of hindsight, two phases in the evolution of educational evaluation in the 1980s can be discerned. The first is the broadening of the base of understanding about evaluation within a growing climate of accountability. The second is the practice of curriculum evaluation within the context of categoric funding and all that entails. Chronologically these phases split the decade.

There are two main themes within the first phase, both characterized by an increasing emphasis on accountability. The first reflects a concern with school-level evaluation as seen in the proliferation of school self-evaluation schemes during the late 1970s and early to mid-1980s. Many of these schemes were accountability oriented but some, such as the Schools Council–initiated GRIDS project on whole-school review, had an explicit developmental focus (see Chapter 8). The second theme reflects an interest in the evaluation of the school curriculum. This interest was stimulated through the HMI reports on the curriculum and the work of the Assessment and Performance Unit (APU) that was established in the mid-1970s to develop methods of assessing the performance of children within particular subject areas. The *modus operandi* of the APU is close to the Tylerian or objectives model and bears comparison in many commentators' minds to the testing movement in the USA. It was also initiated at a time when the educational system was under political attack and the school curriculum was coming under public scrutiny. Evaluation within this context was assuming a more political but still quite general role.

The second phase is much more recent and, consequently, far less easy to define. Its major characteristic is a collective response to the mandated evaluation of the increasing number of categorically funded curriculum development projects that have burst upon the educational landscape in recent years. Until recently 'categorical funding' was an unfamiliar concept to those working in the UK. Janet Harland (1987: 39–40) describes the approach:

> Categorical funding is, I suggest, a strategy which can be used to facilitate a policy where the policy makers or their initiating agency, under existing conditions, have neither the *statutory right* nor the *means* to implement desired changes without the cooperation of those who have both. They do however have the *resources* and proceed to use the normal processes of contract to implement their policies. As refined and practised by MSC, policy implementation via categorical funding has several distinct stages:
>
> 1 A policy is developed.
> 2 Funds, generous enough to attract those who can and may deliver, are made available. (This is particularly potent, of course, when local providers have recently felt themselves starved of resources.)
> 3 Voluntary cooperation is invited in exchange for a share of the resources.
> 4 Acceptance of the resources is equated with the acceptance of policy – and also with the ability to deliver.
>
> Within the mechanisms of categorical funding there seem to be certain integral themes which I shall suggest are criteria, bid, contract, monitoring, evaluation and replication.

The advent of categorical funding has led to a burgeoning of evaluative activity and this has had many consequences, a number of which are discussed later, but three need mentioning here. The first is that this activity represents an increased politicization of evaluation; the second that the tight time lines, restricted budgets and an over-emphasis on cost-effectiveness are often distorting currently accepted evaluation methods; and third, that there is enormous diversity in backgrounds of those who assume the evaluator role. Taken together these consequences are creating a tension between the values fought for by those responsible for creating an alternative tradition of evaluation during the 1970s, and the requirements of those currently funding the majority of evaluation activity in the UK. At present the lines of the debate are still unclear but the tension is very real and provides another continuing theme for this book.

Evaluation for school development: an overview

This book is intended to present a fairly practical and comprehensive overview of educational evaluation for those coming new to the field. The sub-plot of the book, however, is equally important. It is the exploration of ways in which evaluation, in times of change, can help teachers and others take more control over their educational practice and future, and move towards improving it. This is what I mean by development.

The book is divided into four sections. The first considers the question 'What is Evaluation?', and provides a general introduction to the content and literature of evaluation. This chapter defines evaluation as it is used in the book and briefly traces the evolution of evaluation as an educational activity in this country, but it focuses on ideas rather than methods. The following chapter critically describes the methods, models and practical applications of contemporary evaluation approaches with an emphasis on evaluation for school improvement.

Section II is concerned with 'Methods of Working' and is about the basic skills, techniques and the 'nuts' and 'bolts' of doing evaluation. Chapter 3 overviews the issues surrounding the setting up and design of evaluations and some of the inherent problems. Chapter 4 reviews the main ways of gathering evaluative data, particularly that of qualitative data, i.e. word rather than number data. Chapter 5 is particularly important as it discusses the often neglected topic of methods for analysing and ensuring validity in evaluation. Chapter 6 describes the various roles that evaluators play in the evaluation process.

Section III, 'Developmental Approaches', is about the evaluation of various activities that often require a different approach. Chapter 7 is concerned with the evaluation of curriculum, classrooms and specific educational activities. Chapter 8 is about whole-school evaluation or school-based review, particularly those strategies that have a developmental focus. Chapter 9 is concerned with the currently fashionable area of the evaluation of INSET. Finally, in this section, Chapter 10 discusses the evaluation of particular educational projects, which is of current interest given the contemporary emphasis on categoric funding.

The final section of the book, 'Making an Impact', is perhaps the most important. It considers the issues involved in ensuring that development flows from evaluation. Chapter 11 is concerned with specific advice about how to present evaluation data in ways that create meaning and encourages those involved to act upon it. Chapter 12 attempts to summarize the main themes of the book and stands back a little from the practical detail of previous chapters in making the argument for linking evaluation to strategies for school improvement.

A list of abbreviations and a note on further reading are included at the beginning and end of the book. I have done this in order to avoid cluttering the text with too many references and countless explanations of the blight of acronyms that currently plague education and evaluation. Each chapter begins with an overview and ends with a summary, which together with the contents page, chapter sub-headings and index should help the reader find his or her way around the book. In this and other ways I hope that the reader will find the style of the book accessible, particularly as it is written for those who are perhaps unwittingly caught up in the current wave of evaluation activity and need some guidance as how to proceed.

2
Approaches to evaluation

In Chapter 1, I began to give some indication of the approach to evaluation taken in this book, i.e. evaluation needs to be linked in some fundamental way to development. I also gave a brief sketch of the evolution of evaluative activity in the UK over the past two decades and of the main contours of evaluation thought. In this chapter I take some of those ideas a little further and expand the range of definitions of evaluation, discuss some of the jargon associated with it, and review briefly some of the major models or approaches which abound in the field of evaluation. The chapter closes by returning to the theme of development by discussing the relationship between evaluation and school improvement.

The complexity of evaluation

Evaluation is a complex activity. Questions such as 'What are its purposes?', 'What are the criteria for judgement?' and 'Who is actually being evaluated?' are illustrative of this complexity. So too is David Jenkins' (1976: 7) evaluative reflection on rock climbers in action (see Fig. 2.1):

> There are a number of 'evaluative' questions I could ask. I could, for example, confine myself to a careful description of what happens, interview all the participants to build in their perspectives and present an account. But let us suppose that my interest is more specific; suppose I ask the question how good are the climbers? I may note the range of techniques that they employ and the speed of their progress up the rock. I should also recognize that the task of the leader is different from that of anyone else, and that direct comparisons would be difficult, although his instrumental role may be premissed on assumptions of superiority. But if I were to ask how good is the equipment, I would need not only to assess its

Figure 2.1   The author climbing 'Heart of the Sun', Baggy Point, North Devon.

reliability in situations where it was used, but also to identify gaps where a need arose which the available technology could not meet. I may also feel that a full-scale climb may not be the ideal way of testing equipment which could be more severely tested in unexposed boulder work. Finally my thoughts may turn to another question: how good is the rock face – or at least the chosen route up it? Now this last question cannot be answered without reference to climbers, equipment, levels of difficulty and standards of achievement. Nevertheless it is a question different in kind from the others. It could be tentatively argued that 'curriculum' evaluation is most clearly illuminated through questions analogous to 'rock' questions rather than 'climber' questions or 'equipment' questions.

Jenkins goes on to relate his evaluative analysis of rock climbing to Cronbach's (1963) important paper on 'Evaluation for course improvement'. Cronbach (1963: 232) identifies:

> three types of decisions for which evaluation is used:
> 1 Course improvement: deciding what instructional materials and methods are satisfactory and where change is needed.
> 2 Decisions about individuals: identifying the needs of the pupil for the sake of planning his instruction, judging pupil merit for purposes of selection and grouping, acquainting the pupil with his own progress and deficiencies.
> 3 Administrative regulation: judging how good the school system is, how good individual teachers are, etc.

He then argues for course improvement as the major focus for evaluative activity. A cursory reflection on current national policy suggests that all three purposes are alive and well in the UK today. The view of evaluation adopted in this book encompasses course improvement, and to an extent administrative regulation, in so far as the term implies a focus on the school system or organization. The explicit assessment of individual student performance, for the purpose of making judgements about that person, lies outside the purview of this book.

David Nevo (1986) has recently attempted to clarify the meaning of evaluation by identifying 10 questions that represent the 'major issues addressed by the most prominent evaluation approaches in education' (1986: 15). A summary of his review is as follows:

> Risking oversimplification, one could summarize the review of the literature with the following most common answers to our ten questions. This could be one way to describe briefly the state of the art in the conceptualization of educational evaluation.

> 1   *How is evaluation defined?*

> Educational evaluation is a systematic description of educational objects and/or an assessment of their merit or worth.

> 2   *What are the functions of evaluation?*

> Educational evaluation can serve four different functions: (a) formative (for improvement); (b) summative (for selection and accountability); (c)

sociopolitical (to motivate and gain public support); and (d) administrative (to exercise authority).

3 *What are the objects of evaluation?*

Any entity can be an evaluation object. Typical evaluation objects in education are students, educational and administrative personnel, curricula, instructional materials, programs, projects, and institutions.

4 *What kinds of information should be collected regarding each object?*

Four groups of variables should be considered regarding each object. They focus on (a) the goals of the object; (b) its strategies and plans; (c) its process of implementation; and (d) its outcomes and impacts.

5 *What criteria should be used to judge the merit of an object?*

The following criteria should be considered in judging the merit or worth of an educational object: (a) responding to identified needs of actual and potential clients; (b) achieving national goals, ideals, or social values; (c) meeting agreed-upon standards and norms; (d) outdoing alternative objects; and (e) achieving important stated goals of the objects. Multiple criteria should be used for any object.

6 *Who should be served by an evaluation?*

Evaluation should serve the information needs of all actual and potential parties interested in the evaluation object ('stakeholders'). It is the responsibility of the evaluator(s) to delineate the stakeholders of an evaluation and to identify or project their information needs.

7 *What is the process of doing an evaluation?*

Regardless of its method of enquiry, an evaluation process should include the following three activities: (a) focusing the evaluation problem; (b) collecting and analyzing empirical data; and (c) communicating findings to evaluation audiences. There is more than one appropriate sequence for implementing these activities, and any such sequence can (and sometimes should) be repeated several times during the life span of an evaluation study.

8 *What methods of enquiry should be used in evaluation?*

Being a complex task, evaluation needs to mobilize many alternative methods of enquiry from the behavioural sciences and related fields of study and utilize them according to the nature of a specific evaluation problem. At the present state of the art, an *a priori* preference for any specific method of enquiry is not warranted.

9 *Who should do evaluation?*

Evaluation should be conducted by individuals or teams possessing (a) extensive competencies in research methodology and other data analysis techniques; (b) understanding of the social context and the unique substance of the evaluation object; (c) the ability to maintain correct human relations and to develop rapport with individuals and groups

involved in the evaluation; and (d) a conceptual framework to integrate the above-mentioned capabilities.

10   *By what standards should evaluation be judged?*

Evaluation should strike for an optimal balance in meeting standards of (a) utility (to be useful and practical); (b) accuracy (to be technically adequate); (c) feasibility (to be realistic and prudent); and (d) propriety (to be conducted legally and ethically). (Nevo, 1986: 24–6)

Although Nevo suggests that the summary represents a consensus on the major issues, there remains considerable disagreement about the purposes of evaluation, its audience, and the criteria to be used. In particular, I have some concerns about his definition of evaluation (Q. 1) and regard his 'job description' of an evaluator (Q. 9) as being ideal rather than realistic. These comments notwithstanding, the summary provides a useful introduction to the vast and often esoteric literature on evaluation.

These paragraphs have done little more than to raise a few questions about the range and complexity of evaluation, but it has pointed to some key areas of focus. Unfortunately, this inherent complexity has not been made any easier to comprehend by evaluators' use of jargon and their creation of a multiplicity of models. It is to a brief description and, hopefully, simplification of these issues that we now turn.

The language of evaluation

It is inevitable that any discipline or area of enquiry develops its own shorthand or jargon, and evaluation is no exception. It is important, therefore, in a book such as this, to provide a glossary of key terms. While preparing this section, I turned for assistance to a book I edited a few years ago. Although the book was on INSET, it includes a chapter on evaluation where, among a series of extracts, Bob Stake describes the 'most common dimensions for clarifying evaluation designs' (Stake, 1986a: 245–8). His descriptions are characteristically lucid, and so I decided, with his permission, to reproduce them here.

Formative–summative. The most pervading distinction is the one between evaluation studies done during the development of a programme and those done after the programme has been completed. It is difficult to distinguish between the summative evaluation of a completed component and the formative evaluation of a part of the programme. The distinction is not clear-cut. The most useful distinction here may be between the users of the evaluation findings. Elsewhere, I have noted that when the cook tastes the soup it is formative evaluation and when the guest tastes the soup it is summative. The key is not so much when as why. What is the information for, for further preparation and correction or for savouring and consumption? Both lead to decision making, but toward different decisions.

Formal–Informal. Informal evaluation is a universal and abiding human act, scarcely separable from thinking and feeling. Formal evaluation is more operationalized and open to view, and less personal. It is needed when the results are to be communicated elsewhere. Of the two, the formal evaluation study is under an obligation to pass tests of accuracy, validity, credibility and utility.

Case particular–generalization. A most important distinction is between the study of a programme as a fixed and ultimate target, or the study of a programme as a representative of others. Most research is expected to be generalized in some ways: over time, over settings or over subject matters, for example. Evaluation research may be done essentially to discover the worth of the particular programme, or the worth of the general approach. Studies are perceived very differently in this regard, both by investigators and their audiences; and a large misperception is possible. The more the study is expected to be a basis for generalization, the more the need for controls, controlled variation, or careful description of uncontrolled variation.

Product–process. Another dimension on which evaluation studies vary is as to whether they give primary attention to the outcomes of the programme or to its transactions. A study of the 'product' is expected to indicate the pay-off value; a study of the 'process' is expected to indicate the intrinsic values of the programme. Both are needed in any effort to get at a full indication of the worth of the programme, but in any actual study only a small portion of either can be examined.

Descriptive–judgemental. many evaluators coming from a social science background define the evaluation task largely as one of providing information, with an emphasis on objective data and a de-emphasis on subjective data. Those coming from the humanities are likely to reverse the emphases. One will find some studies highly descriptive of students and settings, providing careful reports of differences and correlations, but with little direct reference to criteria of worth and value standards. And elsewhere one will find evaluation studies probing into the pluralism of values to be found in any educational setting. As with any of these dimensions, any particular study is not likely to be at one pole or the other, but to make some combination the compromise.

Preordinate–responsive. Studies differ considerably as to how much the issues of evaluation are determined by observation of activities and by the realization of concerns of participants in the programme. Preordinate studies are more oriented to objectives, hypotheses and prior expectations, mediated by the abstractions of language. Preordinate evaluators know what they are looking for and design the study so as to find it. Responsive studies are organized around phenomena encountered – often unexpectedly – as the programme goes along.

Wholistic–analytic. Studies differ also as to how much they treat the programme as a totality, recognizing conceptual boundaries common to non-technical audiences. The more common social science research approach is to concentrate on a small number of key characteristics. A case study is often used to preserve the complexity of the programme as a whole, whereas a multivariate analysis is more likely to indicate the relationship among descriptive variables.

Internal–external. An obviously important difference in evaluation studies is whether they will be conducted by personnel of the institution responsible for the programme or by outsiders. They differ as to how formal the agreement to evaluate, as to how free the evaluators are to raise issues and interpret findings, and as to how changes in plans will be negotiated.

The eight dimensions above do not result in 256 different evaluation designs. Many of the dimensions are correlated, both conceptually and in frequency-of-use. For example, an 'internal' evaluation study is more likely to be formative than summative, more likely to be descriptive than judgemental. These characteristics and correlations might be particular to the places where evaluation has been most common. In new evaluation situations, the key dimensions and combinations might be quite different.

Models of evaluation

Although I mentioned some of the background to contemporary evaluation in the previous chapter it was by no means historically complete. Nor is this book the place for such an analysis. Those interested in such detail should consult David Hamilton's (1976) book *Curriculum Evaluation* and his (1977) scholarly article on the origins and development of curriculum evaluation. Suffice it to say here that educational evaluation has a long history – witness for example the 'payment by results' movement in England and Wales in the late nineteenth century, the development of IQ testing following the work of Binet in the early twentieth century, and the adoption by educational researchers of Fisher's agricultural research designs in the 1930s.

Evaluation designs have tended to be formulated as 'models' which reflect a particular or discrete evaluation method, or an approach to a specific evaluation problem. These models have tended to be named after their originators (e.g. Stake's countenance model), the problem they are committed to (e.g. adversary evaluation), or both (e.g. Stufflebeam's CIPP – Content, Input, Process and Product – model). I personally do not find the proliferation of such models very helpful. They tend towards inflexibility, reduce evaluator autonomy and inhibit eclectism. But as they constitute an important thread in the theory and practice of evaluation, I need briefly to review them here.

The Stake monograph quoted from earlier also contained a list of evaluation models which is summarized in Table 2.1. Stake's comments on each of these models are cogent, but the European reader must remember that he was writing in the American context. These nine prototypes are oversimplifications of the approaches evaluators actually use. Most actual studies draw upon several styles, varying as the programme, the issues and the audiences change.

To complete this overview of models it is instructive to look at a more characteristically British taxonomy. This is provided by Denis Lawton (1980, 1983) who outlines six 'overlapping' curriculum evaluation models:

1 The classical (or agricultural–botany) research model.
2 The research and development (R and D) (or industrial/factory) model.
3 The illuminative (or anthropological) model.
4 The briefing decision-makers (or political) model.
5 The teacher as researcher (or professional) model.
6 The case study (or portrayal) model.

The classical, and research and development models are examples of the traditional pre-/post-test, control group, experimental approach to educational research. The illuminative and briefing decision-makers models are, as we have already noted and will describe later, based on the work of Parlett and Hamilton (1972) and MacDonald (1976), respectively. The teacher as researcher model is associated with the work of Stenhouse (1975) and the case study model represents the position of the so called 'new wave' evaluators.

Lawton's analysis fits well into the semi-historical review of Chapter 1, and the six approaches he describes, in almost chronological order, mark the main developments in evaluation in the post-war period, except for the most recent. I would also agree with his description 'overlapping', as his models represent two or perhaps three trends rather than six discrete approaches. But once again this list helps us to get a grip on the field.

Despite my somewhat deprecatory remarks about models earlier in this section, I want in the rest of this chapter to provide some more information on four approaches. I will first make some comments about the limitations of the classical or agricultural–botany approach and then briefly discuss three other approaches that I have personally found helpful.

The classical or agricultural–botany approach

According to Lawton (1983: 100–102) an evaluator working within this model would:

1 Test two groups of pupils on a specific part of the curriculum.
2 Apply the new teaching technique in one of those groups.
3 Test again.
4 Compare the learning in the experimental group with the results of the pupils in the control group.

Table 2.1 Stake's nine approaches to educational evaluation (from Stake, 1986a: 252–3)

Approach	Purpose	Key elements	Purview emphasized	Protagonists	Risks	Pay-offs
Student gain by testing	To measure student performance and progress	Goal statements; test score analysis; discrepancy between goal and actuality	Educational psychologists	Ralph Tyler Ben Bloom Jim Popham Mal Provus	Oversimplify educational aims; ignore processes	Emphasize, ascertain student progress
Institutional self-study by staff	To review and increase staff effectiveness	Committee work; standards set by staff; discussion; professionalism	Professors, teachers	National Study of School Evaluation	Alienate some staff; ignore values of outsiders	Increase staff awareness, sense of responsibility
Blue-ribbon panel	To resolve crises and preserve the institution	Prestigious panel; the visit; review of existing data and documents	Leading citizens	James Conant Clark Kerr David Henry	Postpone action; over-rely on intuition	Gather best insights, judgement
Transaction-observation	To provide understanding of activities	Educational issues; classroom observation; case studies; pluralism	Client audience	Lou Smith Parlett and Hamilton Bob Stake	Over-rely on subjective perceptions; ignore causes	Produce broad picture of programme; see conflict in values

Approach	Purpose	Key elements	Users	Proponents	Weaknesses	Strengths
Management analysis	To increase rationality in day-to-day decisions	Lists of options; estimates; feedback loops; costs; efficiency	Managers, economists	Leon Lessinger Dan Stufflebeam Marvin Alkin Alan Thomas	Over-value efficiency; undervalue implicits	Feedback for decision making
Instructional research	To generate explanations and tactics of instruction	Controlled conditions, multivariate analysis; bases for generalization	Research methodologists	Don Campbell Julian Stanley Mike Scriven	Artificial conditions; ignore the humanistic	New principles of teaching and materials development
Social policy analysis	To aid development of institutional policies	Measures of social conditions and administrative implementation	Sociologists	James Coleman David Cohen Carol Weiss	Neglect of educational issues, details	Social choices, constraints clarified
Goal-free evaluation	To assess effects of programme	Ignore proponent claims; follow checklist	Consumers, accountants	Mike Scriven	Over-value documents and record keeping	Data on effect with little co-option
Adversary evaluation	To resolve a two-option choice	Opposing advocates; cross-examination; the jury	Expert, juristic	Tom Owens Murray Levine Bob Wolf	Personalistic, superficial, time-bound	Info. impact good; claims put to test

Of course these descriptive tags are a great over-simplification. The approaches overlap. Different proponents and different users have different styles. Each protagonist recognizes one approach is not ideal for all purposes. Any one study may include several approaches. The grid is an over-simplification. It is intended to show some typical gross differences between contemporary evaluation activities.

Similarly, the task of 'R and D' evaluation is five-fold:

1 Translate agreed aims into specific, measurable behavioural objectives.
2 Devise appropriate learning experiences.
3 Devise tests to assess student performances.
4 Administer tests with a sample of classes using the new programme.
5 Process results to yield useful information to the team which is producing the new programme, or to the sponsors and potential users of the project.

Although these approaches are very popular, they have some major disadvantages for the educational evaluator who is committed to development. The reason for their popularity is probably due to the fact that it is apparently simple to use and appeals to the ends–means, cause–effect, linear and bureaucratic view of the world commonly held by policy makers. Its plausibility on further reflection, however, is suspect. The approach 'ignores the fundamental difference between human beings and plants, namely, that human beings perform differently when under observation whereas cabbages do not' (Lawton, 1983: 100). In a similar vein, Parlett and Hamilton (1977: 22) describe the agricultural–botany evaluator as 'rather like a critic who reviews a production on the basis of the script and applause meter readings having missed the performance'.

In the 1930s, educationalists, desiring to link research to action, began to utilize the very successful 'agricultural–botany' designs of R.A. Fisher (1935). The basic idea underlying Fisher's designs is that experiments are conducted on samples, usually divided into a control and an experimental group, with the results generalized to the target population. The point is that samples are randomly drawn and are consequently representative of that target population.

Stenhouse (in Rudduck and Hopkins, 1985: 20–21) describes Fisher's approach like this:

> The strength of Fisher's paradigm is the recognition of random sampling, in which a sample is drawn such that each member of the target population has an equal chance of being included in the sample because it is a device of chance. . . .
>
> The result of an experiment of this kind is an estimate of the probability that – other things being equal – a particular seed strain or fertilizer or amount of watering will result in a higher gross yield than an alternative against which it has been tested. . . . It is in applying experimental methods to teaching and curriculum evaluation in the schools that researchers have used the Fisherian model. The assumption is that one teaching procedure or curriculum can be tested against alternatives as a seed strain or fertilizer can in agriculture, i.e. procedures can be tested against yield without a real theoretical framework.

This approach to educational research is problematic, particularly if its results

results are to be applied to classrooms. First of all, it is extraordinarily difficult to draw random samples in educational settings (e.g. a random sample of schools, pupils and teachers would have to be drawn separately). Secondly, there are a myriad of contextual variables operating on schools and classrooms (e.g. community culture, teacher personality, school ethos, socioeconomic background, etc.) that would affect the results. Thirdly, it is difficult to establish criteria for effective classroom or school performance. Even if one could resolve these difficulties there are two deeper problems that relate to the nature of educational activity.

First, the 'agricultural–botany' approach is based on measures of gross yield (i.e. how much produce can be gathered in total from a section of land). That is an inappropriate measure for education. As teachers, we are concerned with the individual progress of students rather than with aggregated scores from the class or the school. Our emphasis is on varying teaching methods to suit individual pupils in order to help them achieve to the limit of their potential. Stenhouse (in Rudduck and Hopkins, 1985: 85) puts the paradox like this:

> The teacher is like a gardener who treats different plants differently, and not like a large scale farmer who administers standardised treatments to as near as possible standardised plants.

The second deeper problem relates to meaningful action. The teacher–pupil or pupil–pupil interactions that result in effective learning are not so much the consequence of a standardized teaching method but the result of both teachers and pupils engaging in meaningful action. And meaningful action cannot be standardized by control or sample.

Lawton (1983: 101) points to still more problems. He argues quite rightly that exaggerated importance is often given to test results. He also points out that this kind of experiment is often based on a fallacy, because the tests being used make various assumptions about teaching and the kind of context involved so that one is not in reality comparing like with like. Finally, the classical or objectives approach conceives of reality in a narrow and linear way and this can trap the evaluator within the designs of aspirations of the curriculum developer.

Illuminative evaluation

Despite claiming to be eclectic in my approach to evaluation I must admit to finding illuminative evaluation a more satisfactory approach to evaluation than the traditional experimental models. In their paper, Parlett and Hamilton (1972, 1977) describe it as an alternative to traditional forms of evaluation that takes account of the wider contexts in which educational programmes function. Its primary concern is with description and interpretation rather than measurement and prediction.

Central to an understanding of the paradigm shift involved in embracing illuminative evaluation are the concepts of the 'instructional system' and the 'learning milieu'. The 'instructional system' is a catalogue description of a particular teaching arrangement which includes a set of pedagogic assumptions, a new syllabus and details of techniques and equipment. Although this has been the traditional arena for evaluation, it has ignored the details of implementation and the social psychological environment in which students and teachers work. This 'learning milieu' is a nexus of cultural, social, institutional and psychological variables, which interact in complicated ways to produce a unique pattern of circumstances which suffuse the teaching and learning of the instructional system. Illuminative evaluation is committed to an understanding of both of these concepts and their interaction.

Illuminative evaluation is a general research strategy aiming to be both adaptable and eclectic, with its method being defined by the problem in hand. As a strategy it has three characteristic stages: (1) observation, (2) inquiring further and (3) seeking to explain. At the outset the researcher is concerned to familiarize him/herself thoroughly with the day-to-day reality of the setting(s) being studied. Having become knowledgeable in the first stage, in the second, the researcher selects hypotheses and becomes more focused, directed, systematic and selective. In the third stage, having established hypotheses, one seeks general principles, spotting patterns of cause and effect and placing individual findings within a broader explanatory context. Beginning with an extensive database there is progressive focusing on the emerging issues which allows unique and unpredicted phenomena to be given due weight.

Within this three-stage framework, an information profile is assembled using data collected from four areas:

1 *Observation.* The observation phase occupies a central place in illuminative evaluation.
2 *Interviews.* Discovering the views of participants is crucial to assessing the impact of an innovation.
3 *Questionnaire and test data.* While concentrating on observation and interview, the illuminative evaluator does not eschew paper and pencil techniques.
4 *Documentary and background information.* There is often a complex and detailed array of paperwork that accompanies educational changes that can shed light on the purpose and context of the innovation.

The principal purpose of evaluation studies in Parlett and Hamilton's opinion is to contribute to decision making. Given the diversity of audience (programme participants, programme sponsors, interested outsiders, etc.), the evaluator cannot deliver a simple judgement on the innovation's future. So illuminative evaluation concentrates on the information-gathering rather than the decision-making component of evaluation. The task is to provide a comprehensive understanding of the complex reality (or realities) surrounding the programme – in short to 'illuminate'. In the report, therefore, the evaluator aims to sharpen discussion, disentangle complexities, isolate the significant from the trivial and raise the level of sophistication of debate.

This precis of illuminative evaluation is faithful to Parlett and Hamilton's text, but it does not take account of the drawbacks to the method. In his critique of the approach, Lawton (1980: 117–18) suggests that illuminative evaluation suffers from a controversial and non-specific methodology, a tendency towards subjectivity, role conflict and esoteric language. A more damning and sophisticated critique is made by Atkinson and Delamont (1986). The flavour of their critique can be gauged from their concluding paragraph:

> Paradoxically, the relative shortcomings of the 'illuminative' approach mean that its proponents are, in the last analysis, as limited as the practitioners of the denigrated 'agricultural–botany' approach. Without an adequately formulated body of theory or methods, the illuminators have been, and will be, unable to progress and generate a coherent, cumulative research tradition. They cannot transcend the short-term practicalities of any given programme of curriculum innovation. They merely substitute one variety of atheoretical 'findings' – based mainly on observation and interview – for another – based mainly on test scores (Atkinson and Delamont, 1986: 252).

Although I am in sympathy with the critiques of illuminative evaluation – indeed much of the thinking represented in this book is in response to my concerns about the limitations of their original proposition – Parlett and Hamilton's approach provides a much more professional and educationally relevant set of parameters within which evaluators can work. Particularly if, as I hope to show in subsequent chapters, evaluators become increasingly strategic, self-conscious and rigorous about their methodology.

Stake's matrix (N-U)

I have also found Stake's (1967) 'Countenance of educational evaluation' model (see Fig. 2.2) helpful in thinking about and in organizing an evaluation. It also provides a means for applying criteria and making judgements. Dissatisfied with 'objective' (standardized tests) approaches to evaluation, Stake proposed a countenance approach more in keeping with the complex and dynamic nature of education. He distinguishes between *antecedents*, which are any prior condition that may relate to outcomes, *transactions*, which are what actually occurred – 'the succession of engagements which comprise the process of education' – and *outcomes*, which are the impact of the innovation on those involved. In the model, he then contrasts the intentions at each phase with observations of what actually occurred. He assumed quite rightly that there is (or should be) a relationship between intentions and observations at each phase, and a logical flow through phases related to intentions, and an empirical flow through phases related to observations. The descriptive data so gathered and analysed illuminates the situation under review. What results from this methodological approach is a descriptive analysis of an educational programme that should be relatively uncontentious

Figure 2.2   A layout of the statements and data to be collected by the evaluator of an educational programme (Stake, 1967).

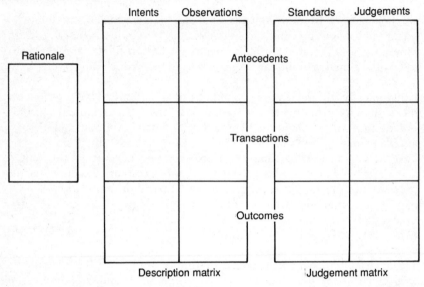

(given that it attempts to be objective) and illuminative (given that it relates intentions to observations or other forms of data gathering analysed in the conventional way).

Stake also proposes a judgement matrix in his model which allows the application of various criteria to the description of the educational programme. The evaluator, having completed the description matrix and possibly negotiated it with the 'client', then proceeds to the more contentious area of the judgement matrix. The standards or criteria column may already have been agreed in advance and will obviously vary from case to case. National and/or local policy, educational theory or research, and commonly agreed good practice, can all provide standards against which to assess curricula in action. Once these standards have been articulated and set against the description matrix, the judgements become almost self-evident. At least the grounds for making judgements are clearly defined and open to scrutiny and debate.

A major advantage of Stake's matrix is that it clearly distinguishes between evidence and judgements. Because evaluation is a highly politicized business (in both the small p and large P sense), such an approach tends to reduce acrimony and defensiveness, particularly if the description and judgement matrices are completed independently and the description is negotiated before the standards are applied. From a developmental point of view it is also helpful if the standards or criteria applied in the judgement matrix are agreed with the 'client' and if the judgements based on the application of the matrices are arrived at collaboratively.

Evaluation and school improvement

The last few comments about the developmental aspects of Stake's model lead well into this short discussion on evaluation and school improvement. Although this is a continuing theme of the book and is taken up in more detail in Chapter 12, some preliminary points need to be made here. Recently, Peter Holly and myself have been exploring the links between evaluation and school improvement (Holly and Hopkins, 1988). We have distinguished between three approaches to evaluation and school improvement, viz. evaluation *of* school improvement, evaluation *for* school improvement and evaluation *as* school improvement (see Fig. 2.3). Each approach carries its own methodo-logical implications and such an analysis helps sharpen our ability to work effectively in each of these areas as well as providing for a deeper understand-ing of the role of evaluation in the school improvement process.

Evaluations *of* school improvement have frequently taken the form of the measurement of the attainment of objectives. In the so-called Tylerian tradition, such 'product' evaluations have tended towards the quantitative and the statistical. Even when this product mentality was somewhat eroded in the 1970s, the new orthodoxy of 'process' evaluation, often based on more qualitative and naturalistic research methods, retained the search for 'process outcomes'. There has been a continuing emphasis, therefore, on the result of any initiative, whether referred to as intended or unintended, mainstream or 'side' effects.

The sense of what is meant by evaluation *for* school improvement is perhaps best captured in the commonly understood phrase 'formative evaluation'. It is evaluation conducted for the purpose of bringing about improvements in practice. The critical feature of this evaluation approach is that its prime focus is on facilitating change. It is not, however, a change process in itself, e.g. evaluation 'as' school improvement, nor is it evaluation 'of' because the

Figure 2.3   Evaluation and school improvement.

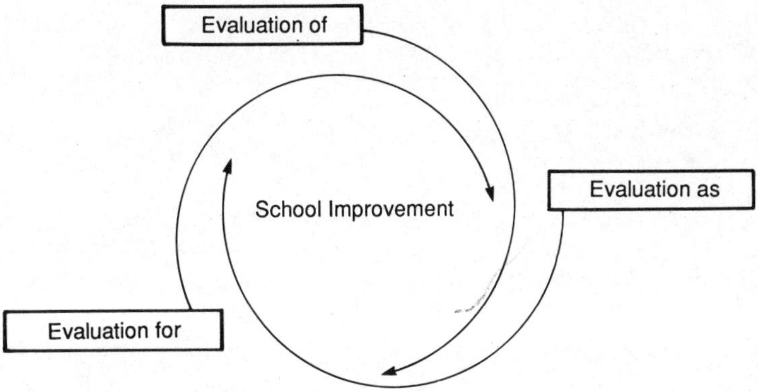

explicit orientation of the evaluation is change and its purpose is improvement, and consequently the evaluation and the change remain distinct.

Evaluation *as* school improvement occurs best when the evaluation has an explicit school improvement purpose and the role of the evaluator and user are clearly linked. Here the evaluation and the school improvement is to all intents and purposes the same process as in some of the more developmental approaches to school self-evaluation, such as the GRIDS project.

The point of distinguishing between evaluation *of*, *for* and *as* is to emphasize that different purposes necessitate different methodologies and have different outcomes. We need to be clear about these aspects of our work if it is to have the maximum practical impact. This is not to imply that one approach is better than another because in practice they build on each other. If evaluation 'of' school improvement is done well, this leads inevitably to evaluation 'for' school improvement, which in turn provides the substance for evaluation 'as' school improvement. Being alert to these distinctions enables the 'change evaluator' to become more effective, but this awareness also needs to be built into the design phase of the evaluation. But design and the more technical aspects of evaluation is properly the concern of Section II of the book.

Summary

I hope that this rapid survey of the field of evaluation literature has provided at least a glimpse of the landscape and has not left the reader too disorientated. The purpose of the discussion has been to outline the repertoire of approaches or the 'tool kit' available to evaluators that they can use in specific evaluation activities. We should not elevate the importance of models unduly. Stenhouse's warning about over-dependence on the objectives model applies here too. Such approaches are like 'a site-plan simplified so that people know exactly where to dig their trenches without having to know why' (Rudduck and Hopkins, 1985: 85). This reaffirms my belief in the need to integrate evaluation and development and to empower evaluators through the acquisition of skills rather than inducting them into models.

Section II
Methods of working

3
Designing and doing evaluation

Good evaluations rarely occur by chance. In the same way as genius is often said to be composed of 99% perspiration and 1% inspiration, so it is that effective evaluations are based on a foundation of seemingly mundane, everyday and commonsense activities. Yet often these apparently common-sense activities are neglected to the detriment of the success of the evaluation. Therefore, this chapter is concerned with design issues and the planning stage of an evaluation.

As I sketched out the various sub-sections of this chapter, I became concerned that I might unwittingly give the impression that this phase of an evaluation is composed of a series of discrete and sequential steps. This is, of course, not the case, because each of the activities intermingle and build on each other. Although the various activities involved in the design of an evaluation – for example, establishing the contract, developing evaluation questions, preparing evaluation designs and worksheets, and establishing ethical guidelines – are, for ease of exposition, described here individually, that caveat needs to be kept in mind. Following the discussion of these issues, the chapter concludes with some amusing and 'highly specific and prescriptive advice' on doing 'Practical Evaluation' from Ian Stronach (1986).

The evaluation contract

The evaluation process is commonly divided into four phases:

- Initiation;
- Data collection or fieldwork;
- Data analysis; and
- Reporting or feedback.

It seems to me that most evaluators spend far too much time on fieldwork to the detriment of the other three phases. I will argue later for the importance of analysis and feedback, but the concern here is for an adequate amount of time to be spent on initiation, on establishing the evaluation contract.

The evaluation contract is critical in setting the parameters, direction and appropriate climate for the evaluation process. Of course, the word contract is a misnomer. It is much more likely to be a letter of agreement than an actual contract, though what is important is that a contractual process is engaged in. That usually means asking pertinent questions, negotiating the responses and setting out the agreed position. Time invested at this stage often saves an enormous amount of hassle later on.

Some of the questions that need to be asked at the contract stage are:

- What are you evaluating?
- Why are you evaluating?
- When are you evaluating?
- Who wants the evaluation?
- How will the evaluation be carried out?
- How will the evaluation report be used?

These types of questions need to be asked not only by the intending evaluator, but also by those who are commissioning the evaluation. Although the questions may vary, it is important to become clear about who the stakeholders are, what their interests are, whether there is a hidden agenda or not, what the concerns of those involved are, and what they see as the issues. It is important, therefore, for anyone undertaking or commissioning an evaluation to compile an agenda of questions to be discussed at the initiation stage. Besides this agenda of fairly general questions, three other issues need to be discussed and resolved: the evaluator's role, the specification of criteria, and the resources available.

The Evaluator's Role

What I mean by the evaluator's role is his/her position *vis-à-vis* decision making. I mentioned earlier Cronbach's (1963) point that evaluation was about informing decisions. Although it is not the evaluator's task to make decisions, they do have to provide the information from which decisions are made, and this has political as well as role implications, as MacDonald (1976) has argued. His point is that an evaluator needs to be clear about the political orientation of the evaluation and negotiate the contract accordingly. Mac-Donald (1976: 133–4) identifies three 'ideal types' in his political classification of evaluation:

1 *Bureaucratic evaluation* is where an evaluator provides an unconditional service to those government agencies controlling education. The evaluator accepts the values of the policy maker and provides information to help

achieve their policy objectives. His/her role is that of consultant; client satisfaction is paramount and the report is owned by the bureaucrats. The evaluator receives a fee for his/her report and has no responsibility over ultimate decisions.

2 *Autocratic evaluation* involves a conditional service where the evaluator is 'autocrat' in so far as he or she provides external validation of policy in return for bureaucratic compliance with its recommendations. The focus of the evaluation is on educational merit and the role of the evaluator is that of expert. The evaluator's methods must be valid and reliable because his/her power base is the academic research community. The contract guarantees complete non-interference and the evaluator retains ownership of his/her report.

3 *Democratic evaluation* provides a service to the community. Sponsorship by one group does not give them a special claim to advice or secret information. The democratic evaluator recognizes the value of pluralism and seeks to represent a range of interests in his/her report. The basic value is an informed citizenry, and the evaluator acts as broker in exchanges of information. Their techniques of data gathering and presentation must be accessible to non-specialist audiences. Confidentiality must be offered to informants and control given to them over use of the information they provide. The report is non-recommendatory and the criterion of success is the range of audiences served. The report aspires to 'best-seller' status. The key concepts of democratic evaluation are 'confidentiality', 'negotiation' and 'accessibility'. The key justificatory concept is 'the right to know'.

These typologies are ideal and obviously never occur in their pure form. They are helpful, however, in assisting the evaluator to assess the power relationships and purposes of an evaluation when forging the contract and to act accordingly.

Specification of criteria

The second issue is linked to the political nature of evaluation and concerns the specification of criteria. I, in common with many other evaluators, have often been accused, to put it mildly, of applying inappropriate criteria to an evaluation. This is usually a reaction to the recipients not liking what I have said or written. In order to avoid these problems (although one must realize that evaluations are inevitably contentious), I either apply criteria to a descriptive analysis (see pp. 25–6) or agree the criteria to be applied at the contract stage. In some evaluations this procedure may not be possible or desirable because the criteria need to evolve during the evaluation. In these cases, one must make the point at the contract stage that criteria will evolve, and clearly articulate them and the generative process in the report. Neither of these strategies will prevent criticism or negative reactions to an evaluation report, but it will at least make such comments less justifiable!

Table 3.1　A bureaucratic evaluation brief.

An evaluation of the role of TVEI in non-advanced further education in relation to the following:

1　The three areas identified for development under TVEI funding, namely the induction of students, the provision of a core curriculum and profiling.
2　The planning, execution and evaluation of these three facets of the TVEI proposals in College A.
3　The planning for TVEI involvement in College B.
4　The extent to which the colleges have learned from each other and the way in which the plans at College B are based on the lessons learned in other colleges.
5　To establish whether TVEI is perceived by the senior management and other staff in the colleges as an initiative to inform future developments or as a 'bolt on extra'.

Figure 3.1　An autocratic evaluation brief.

Dear Dr Hopkins,

Re: TRIST Supplementary Schools Library & Resources Project

I am pleased to be able to inform you that TRIST Central have passed our application for funds to evaluate the above project.

I have attached copies of my preliminary costings and the letter of confirmation. We require now a more detailed costing and evaluation plan from you to support the allocation of funds, as a consultant we will obviously take your advice on the appropriateness of these preliminary costings.

The first training course has already taken place but I will get the Project Tutor to inform you of the dates of subsequent events.

I look forward to receiving your reply as soon as you are able.

Best Wishes,

Resources

The third issue that needs to be confronted at the contract stage is that of resources. Contemporary evaluations of categorically funded projects are notoriously underfunded and this inevitably distorts the evaluation process. The client needs to know what she/he is getting for their money and the evaluator needs to be confident that the enterprise is viable. Such cost–benefit discussions greatly assist in bringing the evaluation 'down to earth' at the contract stage.

Examples

Examples of contractual letters that fall into MacDonald's typology and which illustrate some of the points made in this section are shown in Table 3.1 and Figs 3.1 and 3.2. Table 3.1 gives an example of an evaluation contract where

Figure 3.2 A democratic evaluation brief. A letter from a local TVEI evaluator to a project co-ordinator.

This letter is an attempt to summarize our discussion on 24 September with the school/college co-ordinators about (i) the current evaluation and (ii) a possible consortia-wide effort to counter the problem of low aspiration and under-achievement.

TVEI Local Evaluation

There was broad agreement that a similar pattern should be adopted in this as in previous years, viz.

- standardized survey;
- pupil interviews;
- teacher interviews;
- classroom observation;
- follow-up/feedback in schools.

It was also proposed that:

1 The standardized survey be administered to all the members of the current 5th year.
2 The teacher interviews focus on a different group of staff associated with TVEI.
3 The pupil interviews will again be based at the college and concentrate on those who have continued with the scheme at 16+ (this point was not discussed at the meeting).
4 Follow-up/feedback in schools be more extensive than previously and involve two sessions in each school [the first being a feedback session, the second being devoted to discussion (action planning) with written material being sent in advance].
5 In the FE college further discussion to take place about the substance of last year's evaluation and that this year's evaluation assess the impact of the current staff development programme on teaching styles.
6 The focus of the current evaluation should not only include commentary on previous issues – pupil learning style/sex-role stereotyping/teaching styles – but also investigate the dissemination of the project within the consortia and the problem of under-achievement/low aspirations.

It should be possible to cover all the above in the current academic year, except that doubling the number of feedback/follow-up sessions may have some financial implications.

During the meeting some other issues were raised but not resolved:

- The learning styles questionnaire.
- A suggestion that the ability/aspiration of the current cohort be measured.
- Relevance of curriculum to perceived needs of parents, industry, *etc.*
- Developmental initiative on sex-role stereotyping.

These points need to be further discussed at our next meeting.

the brief was given to me. As can be seen, it is very prescriptive and negotiation was fairly limited. The brief has bureaucratic overtures to use MacDonald's typology and was far less democratic than the contract outlined in Fig. 3.2. In reality, the evaluation turned out to be a mixture of all three types.

The example of a contractual letter (Fig. 3.1) is interesting because the contract was awarded before I drew up the evaluation brief. It was intended to be autocratic, but as we progressed through the evaluation there was increasing tension between the LEA adviser whose project we were evaluating, and who wanted a much more bureaucratic style of evaluation, and ourselves who felt that a democratic approach was more appropriate. We never really did resolve that one!

Figure 3.2 is an extract from a contractual letter I wrote to a TVEI pilot project co-ordinator summarizing plans for an annual evaluation exercise. I do not suggest that this is an ideal example of a democratic evaluation; discussion of criteria, for example, are fudged, and its democratic status *vis-à-vis* MacDonald's typology is implicit and it does have autocratic overtones! These examples do, however, give some indication of what this section is about and underlines the importance of a contract stage in any evaluation.

A comprehensive set of guidelines for planning an evaluation that will also help in establishing the contract has been developed by Harlen and Elliott (1982). A summary of their checklist is contained in Table 3.2 and provides a useful guide for this stage of the evaluation process.

Establishing evaluation questions

Establishing a question is a great help in focusing an evaluation. However, it is not mandatory, because although in some evaluations the questions are obvious and immediate, in others they emerge as part of the evaluation. In the first case one is in a position to proceed with a series of specific evaluation activities almost from the word go; in the latter case more preliminary work needs to be done. There are of course differing views on this. Evaluators such as Patton (1982) suggest that asking questions and pre-specifying criteria help to focus the evaluation, help an evaluator avoid collecting the wrong data and permit discussion of what constitutes improvement. Others such as Guba and Lincoln (1981) argue that as data are collected, new criteria and questions will emerge; and that checking these emerging issues with the 'client' or evaluation audience makes the evaluation more responsive and pertinent.

I do not believe that this is an 'either–or' situation. Although I do believe that questions help the evaluator to focus, it is the particular evaluation problem that defines the situation. In 'closed' evaluations the questions are given, in 'open' evaluations they evolve. A 'closed' evaluation is where the evaluator is given a set of questions upon which to focus. An example of a 'closed' evaluation contract is shown in Table 3.1, where I was presented with a list of questions. Given that starting point it was relatively easy to work out a plan for the evaluation. Figures 3.1 and 3.2 are examples of 'open' evaluation briefs requiring extensive preliminary work before the evaluation plan can effectively be formed.

This process of determining evaluation questions is complex – one way of establishing such questions is through asking even more questions. Some tough

Table 3.2   Checklist for planning an evaluation (Harlen and Elliott, 1982: 296–8)

1   Reasons, purposes and motivations
- Who wants the evaluation to be carried out?
- What reasons do they have for wanting the evaluation to be done?
- Who wants the information it will provide?
- What reasons do they have for wanting the information?
- Who else should have the information?

2   Worthwhileness
- What possible actions or decisions can be taken as a result of the evaluation?
- What possible actions or decisions have been pre-empted?
- What constraints are there on the planning and execution of the evaluation?

3   Interpretation of the evaluation task
- What views do those involved hold about the nature of the evaluation?
- What is the existing decision-making system and how does the evaluation relate to it?

4   Subjects of the evaluation
- What will be evaluated?
- What kinds of information are required?

5   The evaluators
- Who will gather the information?
- Who will co-ordinate the process?
- Who will produce the report(s)?

6   Evaluation methods
- Are the methods to be used appropriate to the information required?
- Can the methods be devised, if necessary, and applied in the time available?
- What resources, equipment, back-up facilities are required for the methods to be used?
- Will the methods for data collection be acceptable to those who will be involved in supplying information?

7   Time schedule
- What time is available for the evaluation?
- Can the information required be gathered and processed in that time?

8   Control of information
- What procedures, if any, will govern the collection and release of information?
- How will ownership of the information be decided?

9   Criteria for making judgements or decisions
- Who will decide the criteria to be applied in using the information?
- Will there be the need or possibility for applying alternative criteria?

10   Reporting
- In what form will the evaluation be reported?
- Will those involved be shown the report before it is made final?
- Who will be the designated audience of the report?
- What steps will be taken to see that the report reaches the designated audience?

but realistic bottom line questions for educational programmes include (Loucks-Horsley *et al.*, 1987: 160):

- What changes have occurred in participants' knowledge base?
- What changes have occurred in participants' skill level and use?
- What changes have occurred in participants' opinions and feelings?
- What changes have occurred in the LEA/College/Schools' organizational capacity?
- What changes have occurred in student performance?

Designing the evaluation

The approach to evaluation design that I intuitively use has recently been described by Susan Loucks-Horsley and her colleagues (Loucks-Horsley *et al.*, 1987: ch. 6) in some detail. This approach, of course, is not the only way to plan an evaluation but is a useful starting point, especially for the less experienced evaluator. Chapters 7 and 12 contain further examples and adaptations of the approach for particular evaluation tasks. There are five major activities to this design process:

1 *Agree on evaluation questions.* The importance of generating questions to help focus the evaluation has already been discussed. It is also important not to be too ambitious about the number and scope of the questions asked.
2 *Determine information needs and collection methods.* Once the questions are generated, clarified and prioritized, some way of answering them has to be devised. Potential information sources and collection methods should be generated for each evaluation question. The more sources and methods used, the greater the likelihood that the information will be valid. One way of structuring this important stage in the design of the evaluation is to use a simple worksheet as outlined in Table 3.3.
3 *Collect and analyse information.* This activity should co-exist with data collection. Early checks allow evaluators to seek new information sources if necessary and to identify emerging and unanticipated outcomes.
4 *Reports.* Feedback should normally occur as soon as possible, and be tailored to their audience and include follow-up activities if required. This difficult yet crucially important aspect of evaluation is discussed more fully in Chapter 11.
5 *Loop back.* It is important to reflect on what one is doing and make 'mid-course' corrections as one goes along. Also, a more thorough evaluation of the evaluation needs to occur at the end of each cycle.

Obviously, this evaluation process is overly linear and rational. In reality, a number of these steps co-exist and time-lines tend to merge. It may also be that questions have to be refined and unanticipated logistical problems often occur during the evaluation. This is inevitable and some misfortune should be expected. An obvious precaution is to ensure that time-lines are realistic, that

Table 3.3 Example of entries on a worksheet for information collection on a consortia/college/school INSET programme (adapted from Loucks-Horsley *et al.*, 1987: 168)

Evaluation question	Information sources	Collection method	Responsibility	Time-line
How do the training and follow-up affect participants' classroom behaviour?	Teachers; advisory teachers; students	Peer observation using checklist; interviews; group discussion	Consortia; teacher-as-evaluator group	Oct.–Nov. (before training) April–May (after training)
Has this year's INSET been relevant to teachers' needs? What changes are desired for next year?	Teachers	Written questionnaire	Staff development co-ordinator	May
What is the impact of the creation of school-based staff development teams?	Teachers; heads; LEA inspectors, advisers and co-ordinators; community members	Case study	Post graduate students on applied research in education course at local Higher Education Institution supervised by LEA Evaluation Co-ordinator and university lecturer	Sept.–Aug.

one is not expecting too much too soon, and that as many problems as possible are anticipated.

Two further points need to be made about this process. The first is that there needs to be a logic or flow between the evaluation question, the data collected, analysis, feedback and the resulting action. In that way the evaluation develops a power of its own because each stage builds on the other. The second is to make certain that the evaluation questions are important to the school or audience involved. Evaluation is so time-consuming that its results should not be gratuitous, but feed a real need and be able to provide useful and pertinent information. Although this section on the evaluation process has taken a school-based theme, the basic principles apply to a range of developmentally oriented evaluations.

Ethical issues

Evaluation is inevitably a personal and potentially threatening activity. The types of activities described in this chapter and the sensitivities involved, make it paramount that evaluators are fastidious in establishing and observing ethical procedures in their work; not in a legalistic sense, but in a humane and caring way. Evaluators are privileged to be allowed to share people's professional lives and this confidentiality needs to be respected.

Table 3.4 lists a set of ethical guidelines that I have used frequently. A number of these guidelines are not solely to do with ethics but also have planning implications. At a practical and profound level, ethics guide behaviour and become part of it.

Practical evaluation

In this chapter I have tried out outline the major steps involved in planning an evaluation. I hope it has been sensible and made sense, but it does lack an image of how it all fits together. To try and overcome this I am grateful to Ian Stronach (1986) for allowing me to reprint his article on 'Practical evaluation'. It provides an amusing antidote to the conventional wisdom on evaluation. I had asked Ian to summarize a day conference we had a few years ago on the local evaluation of TVEI. This was his response to my request:

> I was asked to write up my summary of the day's session. This isn't it.
> Instead, I wanted to help the majority of local evaluators who feel they
> have little training or experience relevant to the task. They are in the same
> position as I was a few years ago – an experienced teacher, ignorant of
> evaluation and vocational education, and unable to be honest about it to
> the project and the schools (it pays to be modest about your incom-
> petence). So what would be helpful? I thought I would offer highly specific
> and prescriptive advice. This would be opinionated, and often inappro-
> priate, wrong, or nonsensical. But it might clarify evaluation design and
> practice issues as evaluators tested their own ideas against it, and it might

Table 3.4 Ethical guidelines (reprinted with permission from Kemmis and McTaggart, 1981: 43–4)

Observe protocol: Take care to ensure that the relevant persons, committees and authorities have been consulted, informed and that the necessary permission and approval has been obtained

Involve participants: Encourage others who have a stake in the improvement you envisage to shape the form of the work

Negotiate with those affected: Not everyone will want to be directly involved; your work should take account of the responsibilities and wishes of others

Report progress: Keep the work visible and remain open to suggestions so that unforeseen and unseen ramifications can be taken account of; colleagues must have the opportunity to lodge a protest to you

Obtain explicit authorization before you observe: For the purposes of recording the activities of professional colleagues or others (the observation of your own students falls outside this imperative provided that your aim is the improvement of teaching and learning)

Obtain explicit authorization before you examine files, correspondence or other documentation: Take copies only if specific authority to do this is obtained

Negotiate descriptions of people's work: Always allow those described to challenge your accounts on the grounds of fairness, relevance and accuracy

Negotiate accounts of others' points of view (e.g. in accounts of communication): Always allow those involved in interviews, meetings and written exchanges to require amendments which enhance fairness, relevance and accuracy

Obtain explicit authorization before using quotations: Verbatim transcripts, attributed observations, excerpts of audio and video recordings, judgements, conclusions or recommendations in reports (written or to meetings)

Negotiate reports for various levels of release: Remember that different audiences demand different kinds of reports; what is appropriate for an informal verbal report to a faculty meeting may not be appropriate for a staff meeting, a report to council, a journal article, a newspaper, a newsletter to parents; be conservative if you cannot control distribution

Accept responsibility for maintaining confidentiality
Retain the right to report your work: Provided that those involved are satisfied with the fairness, accuracy and relevance of accounts which pertain to them; and that the accounts do not unnecessarily expose or embarrass those involved; then accounts should not be subject to veto or be sheltered by prohibitions of confidentiality

Make your principles of procedure binding and known: All of the people involved in your action research project must agree to the principles before the work begins; others must be aware of their rights in the process

---

create more reflection by being controversial and specific than an abstract waffle about methodological or ethical issues. At any rate, that's the intention.

STARTING UP

1 Ignore the literature on research and evaluation. You haven't time to shop around for methods or 'models'. Anyway, most articles are too abstract to be useful – and will leave you with style rather than substance. They're holiday reading.

2 Plan your evaluation on a common-sense appraisal of your own resources (time, skills, personal strengths), the most pressing demands on you from the project (if any, sometimes projects need to be helped to ask questions), and the emerging issues from your fieldwork. Go for penetration rather than coverage. Don't underestimate the relevance of your teaching experience or local knowledge – the ability to talk to students, staff, project workers, to understand subject, department and timetable issues is central.

3 Get to know the project as an educational rather than an administrative event – don't get too distracted by the bureaucratic scenery, bizarre though it may be. That means: ask educational questions – what does student-centred learning mean in school or subject X? What acts of negotiation take place in profiling and what kinds of knowledge are created and exchanged? How do students 'integrate' work experience into their formal and personal curriculum? What classroom interactions represent an equal opportunities policy in action? How is 'relevance' defined in TVEI curricula? (A non-educational example of a question – what percentage of students find 'work experience' worthwhile?)

4 Get to know the substantive areas, like hi-tech and profiling. That also includes project activities and their origins and sponsorship as ideas, other TVEI projects' activities in relevant areas, and parallel projects like Records of Achievement. Some innovations are second or third time round – look for old evaluation reports. Develop a comparative knowledge in key areas so that you can locate your project's practices against that background and generate new issues for further research (e.g. CGLI 365 profiles have been evaluated several times before: work experience schemes have been sorted into various types). Let these other projects be your library. Learn economically – attend workshops, use the phone, tap other evaluations and projects. Read as little as you can get away with.

5 Generate key questions and foci about your project, based on all of the above. Be creative – take chances with ideas, look for meanings as well as opinions (what is TVEI like – modernisation in the Third World, the obelisk in AD 2001, a monetarist attempt at educational theory, a new currency?).

6 Be a source of researched information and judgement about project activities. Let that source be independent of project political influence, but collaborative in terms of enquiry and interpretation.

7 The intellectual 'start-up' problems are easy compared with the diplomatic ones. Rule one: be seen – visit schools, talk to teachers informally, attend residentials, ask everybody what the issues are, what the evaluation ought to be doing.

8 Be tactful. Break the ice before asking to observe classrooms. Explain offers of anonymising or negotiating data. Negotiate your way into the project from the top down (Head, Heads of Department, TVEI Coordinator, TVEI teachers). Negotiate and clear your data in the reverse order to protect informants. Remember that although your job seems a nightmare of uncertainty, incompetence and vulnerability to you, it looks like paid leave to them.

9 Staff will tacitly accord you an equivalence in the hierarchy (=Scale 2, Scale 4, Deputy Head, Advisor, UFO). What they tell you will be influenced by that equivalence. Erode it – try to become acceptable in Steering Groups and Staffrooms.

10 Accept your vulnerability and refuse to become paranoid about it (but bear in mind that just because you're not paranoid doesn't mean that they aren't out to get you . . .). Evaluation may threaten project 'image', LEA accountability to MSC, the Coordinator's career, the Head's autonomy, the teacher's privacy, and so on. Everyone has more power than you, but not necessarily more influence. Expect unfair criticism, and listen to it – understand its political undercurrents as well as its ostensible meanings, without assuming that the former subsume the latter. So for example:

(i) Work for an acceptance of the evaluation's independent role. Set up an evaluation steering group to advise you and protect your integrity. Try to widen membership beyond LEA and MSC. An outsider may assist your independence.

(ii) Spend much longer than you think you need explaining who you are, who you work for, in what way you're independent, where the data goes, what rights informants have over it, and what your specific intentions are. Never assume that written introductions will have filtered through, been read or understood.

(iii) Persuade the project that you need to learn to evaluate just as much as they need to learn to innovate. 'Trial and error' is a mutual condition.

(iv) Accept that projects and especially Coordinators are often under intense pressure to 'deliver'. Image and PR are a necessary part of that. Resist the feeling that you are 'Truth's Representative On Earth' – don't work against their PR so much as on their private ability to distinguish image from real development. And don't be cynical about the Coordinator – s/he has more sleepless nights than you.

(v) Be honest. The dangers are without limit. Three common ones – pretending to understand when you don't (loss of face); exaggerating the reliability and significance of your data (loss of 'Science'); tempering judgements to suit political winds in or out of the project (loss of nerve). Allow research questions to include a testing of your own initial assumptions and values, not simply build on them.

(vi) Watch your time. After the initial bliss of 'no bells' comes the anxiety of a job that doesn't seem to have an end. This kind of self-disciplined work is as hard for ex-teachers as ex-pupils. Two rules of thumb: make fieldwork plans and divide them by two: and double the time for analysis and writing-up. Getting the data is often quick and relatively easy (*e.g.* three days on tape-recorded small-group interviews on work experience); but transcribing, analysing and writing-up is slow and difficult (say three weeks on that task, including some teacher/Coordinator/employer follow-up).

(vii) Keep sane by talking to other evaluators. Your greatest error will be commonplace. Avoid experts: look for the evaluator who 'cocked up' something last term that you're going to look at next term.

DESIGNING AND DOING

1 Abandon the idea that other evaluators may be expert. People often do better evaluation first time around than fifth time because they're more creative, better at talking to kids, more industrious – whatever. There are experts *about* evaluation, but not expert evaluators.

2 Evaluators play their own version of 'Tinker, tailor . . .' in order to decide what to be when they grow up. Most ambitions centre on Anthropologist or Scientist as Role Model, and on Beggarman and Thief (respectively) as Ethical Model. The Scientist appropriates data without negotiation, is 'objective', does surveys, determines correlations and norms, and tries not to contaminate the data. The Anthropologist asks permission to use data, negotiates about interpretation, is inter-subjective (well, subjective), does case studies, draws out understanding, and tries not to go native.

3 Avoid these Role Models. Help evaluation break its academic chains. Both styles are unhelpful to project development (too little, too detached, too late).

4 Acknowledge two of the central myths of evaluation – the myth of audience, and the myth of decision-maker. Accept the need to create debate within projects (often project workers and teachers have no time to think ahead, no mechanism for meeting, no incentive to contribute, no desire to rock the boat etc.). Also promote broader debates about project issues (like student-centred learning, vocationally relevant curricula, management of innovation). There is a

need to act *inside* the project, analysing and reporting, influencing change, 'contaminating' data; and a need to stand *outside* the project, placing its activities in comparative and critical perspectives. So do both: be a double agent, and be open about that duality. Defend the duality – change is a research strategy. Reject claims that you have betrayed neutrality or objectivity; both are imposters.

5 Be a double agent in another sense: not just 'inside and outside' the project, but also formative and summative in your strategy. That means working out a short term evaluation strategy that will also contribute to a long-term summative goal.

For example:

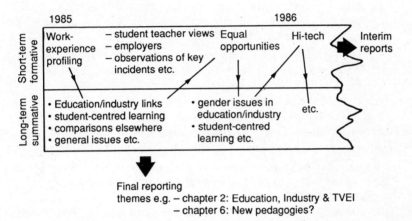

Final reporting
themes e.g. – chapter 2: Education, Industry & TVEI
– chapter 6: New pedagogies?

6 Here's another example, linking an inside approach to an outside goal, taking a developmental process to an eventual summative account:

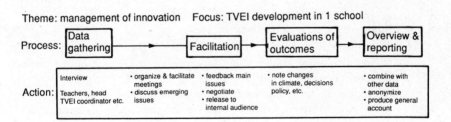

The dilemma, of course, is to include the evaluation's role in the summative account. The potential bonus is richer data, some natural 'experimental' knowledge (what happens if . . .?), and an impact on the project.

7 Finally, a highly condensed version of a comparative approach:

THEME: PROFILING

1. PROJECT→	←LOCAL CONTEXTS→	←COMPARISONS→	←GENERATED ISSUES
• examine blank/ completed forms	• employer/FE/ parent views	• other profiles, assessments, recordings	• is it practical?
• analyse/speculate	• issues re 1. like utility, validity etc.	• develop typology	• is it effective?
• interview teachers, students etc.		• locate own profile	• is it valid?
• observe profiling in action		• interpret, raise issues, research etc.	• is it educational?
			• is it measurement or motivation?
			• is it surveillance or social control etc.?

Forced into boxes like that, the process is mechanical – but no sequence is necessarily implied. Much 'to-ing and fro-ing' between 1, 2, 3 and 4 is likely in working out new questions and testing their signficance against old and new data.

An example of the above strategy would be to take [the] idea of TVEI as 'enclave' within a school, and to identify other types of 'host' relationship. Impressionistically, there's the 'exile' model, with TVEI banished to the periphery. And there's the 'Mutiny-on-the-Bounty' model where the school took the money and ran. What else? Surely there's a 'Marie Celeste', a project floating aimlessly and empty around somewhere? How could these types be better characterised?

8 There is nothing comprehensive or prescriptive in the above illustrations. Work out your own strategy for promoting development while retaining a critical overview of process, outcome and context. The tension between 'inside' and 'outside' role can also be productive in limiting some forms of bias – not least the bias of the spectator who thinks he really understands – and in giving new insights. The evaluation role will also always be problematic, difficult to take for granted, and exposed to reflexive questioning.

9 Developmental evaluation should be a set of practices, not a 'method-in-action': case study, history, dialogue, natural experiment, survey, comparative analysis and social critique may be components but should not be determinants.

Those practices should go beyond information and opinion. Evaluation must conceptualise the project, pick out the ideas and examine the concepts and intentions behind it. At the workshop it was the tea-lady who asked the best question – 'what does TVEI stand for?' Other questions might include: 'what kind of economic theory underlies TVEI rationales?' 'how are educational principles and vocational practices reconciled?' 'If there's a Bad Thing called vocationalism, is there a Bad Thing called educationalism?' If we never ask questions like these, we may end up knowing everything about TVEI except what it means. The project must not become the silent centre round which debate revolves:

If evaluation uncritically accepts Project definitions, and follows the assumptions and boundaries of the Project, then it begins to discuss the meaning of the Project from inside the Project's understandings. (Stronach, 1981)

As a workshop participant playfully suggested, evaluators should 'subvert the project by taking it seriously.'

Developmental evaluation, therefore, should aim to create a critical dialogue both within and about the project. Evaluation should be both a mirror and a window. It should aim for action as well as reflection, and see action as a form of research. Nor should evaluation privilege groups like decision-makers or teachers. When Peter Holly (1986) lumps teachers and students together in arguing for a 'professional' model for evaluation, he is making a powerful ideological move on behalf of teachers, but not necessarily on behalf of students. Evaluation should not privilege such groups by making them into a tacit 'bottom line' but should be informed by a radical scepticism about all values, including its own. Above all, it should not take detachment to be a virtue:

> But to look in order to know, to show in order to teach, is not this a tacit form of violence, all the more abusive for its silence, upon a sick body that demands to be comforted, not displayed. (Foucault, 1976: 84)

10 That's getting a bit grandiose. Some practical tips to conclude this section:

— draw up evaluation plans in conjunction with the project; expect to change them
— keep a record of everything, dated, filed, accessible
— keep a diary of emerging issues, impressions, feelings, embryonic interpretations – very useful at all reporting stages
— allocate enough time for each piece of evaluation work so that you have a reasonable chance of knowing more about it than the participants (or, more usefully, knowing differently about it)
— commission outsiders, if you lack specialist expertise in an area and really need it
— leave plenty of time for the report-writing stage, it's the worst one: a common failing – too much data, no time to process it
— don't forget how ill-informed and over-prescriptive this is, especially in relation to the particular context of your evaluation.

REPORTING

1 Writing reports feels like sitting an exam without being quite sure what the question is, but in the knowledge that the world will read and mark your paper according to an unpredictable whim. The mental blocks, the mad desire to postpone writing for more research, or for

another cup of coffee, is normal. In fact, there's a consolation if you're a beginner – it gets worse later on.

2 People who read evaluations either say they are too long to read, or they are too short to believe. The best bet is a report as short and condensed as you can make it (with detailed justification tucked away in appendices). The biggest temptation is to display your productivity in the number of pages. Resist it.

3 Decide in advance what debate you're trying to influence, or who you are writing for, and what would be the most effective format and style (but this of course may not be exclusively the evaluator's decision). Where length is unavoidable, as in a case study (e.g. student/tutor interactions in profiling or work experience debriefings), provide a summary of the main issues.

4 Follow negotiating procedures to the letter. Try to get full clearance of reports so that other TVEI projects and evaluations may benefit from them.

5 Look for a general theme, or metaphor, that will carry your main point without distorting it too much, for example, if the report were about the management of innovation you might find that the project had moved from the role of researcher (let's make up our own profile), to that of guinea pig (let's test the CGLI 365 profile), or vice versa.

6 Follow up reactions to your reports (you may have to create reactions by begging teachers to read and criticise them for you). Try to get a cross-sectional view – there may be a lot to learn from the distribution of criticism, as well as from its content. Ask what the report ought to have been like. What questions were ignored or inadequately addressed, what the assumptions and values of the writer appeared to have been, and so on. And remember that there's (almost) always a next time.

7 Local evaluation in TVEI runs at over £350,000 pa. It is the largest component in the evaluation budget. There is no reason why it should not also be the most productive.

8 Good luck.

Summary

This chapter has been concerned with issues of purpose and design in evaluation. The importance of the contract or initiation stage which is often treated cursorily was emphasized, as was the necessity of focusing an evaluation through developing appropriate evaluation questions. The advantages of a strategic approach to evaluation were discussed, as was the importance of linking planning to ethical issues. Much of this was contradicted by Ian Stronach's 'highly specific and prescriptive advice', which emphasized the need for evaluators to be pragmatic, eclectic and to treat much of the evaluation literature with appropriate scepticism. In the next chapter we traverse more familiar and less contentious territory by discussing some of the main data collection techniques that fit into our evaluation designs.

4
Evaluation methods

Collecting data is the most visible aspect of doing an evaluation, and for many evaluators it is the most important. Although I have already argued that data collection should be put in its place, i.e. that it should not take an inordinate amount of time compared with other phases in the evaluation process, that is not to underestimate or devalue its importance. Without data collection there would be no evaluation. There is a vast literature devoted to data collection techniques and a wealth of experience to complement it. It is impossible in a single chapter of an introductory text to do justice to such an accumulation of wisdom and experience. The compromise that I have adopted is to outline a framework for data collection and describe some of the methods that I have found particularly useful in doing evaluation; in particular, surveys, question- naires, observation, interviews, documents and case studies. At the end of the book I suggest some sources for further reading which give a more complete overview of data collection techniques.

Frameworks for data collection

Three important points about collecting data for evaluation need to be made at the outset. The first is that the data collected should be systematically related not only to the questions identified in the evaluation design but also to subsequent implications for action and follow-up. Secondly, the data collec- tion technique should be appropriate to the specific evaluation question being addressed, e.g. one would rarely attempt to assess a student's IQ using observational techniques. The third is that as far as possible multiple sources of data should be used as a check on the trustworthiness of the data and consequent hypotheses.

These three issues are of course interrelated and are best addressed early on in the evaluation, usually at the planning stage. The evaluation worksheets

Table 4.1   Taxonomy of classroom research techniques (from Hopkins, 1985a: 82–3)

Technique	Advantage(s)	Disadvantage(s)	Use(s)
Field notes	Simple; on going; personal; *aide-mémoire*	Subjective; needs practice	● Specific issue ● Case study ● General impression
Audio-tape recording	Versatile; accurate; provides ample data	Transcription difficult; time-consuming; often inhibiting	● Detailed evidence ● Diagnostic
Pupil diaries	Provides pupils' perspective	Subjective	● Diagnostic ● Triangulation
Interviews and discussions	Can be teacher–pupil, observer–pupil, pupil–pupil	Time-consuming	● Specific in-depth information
Video-tape recorder	Visual and comprehensive	Awkward and expensive; can be distracting	● Visual material ● Diagnostic
Questionnaires	Highly specific; easy to administer; comparative	Time-consuming to analyse; problem of 'right' answers	● Specific information and feedback
Sociometry	Easy to administer; provides guide to action	Can threaten isolated pupils	● Analyses social relationships
Documentary evidence	Illuminative	Difficult to obtain; time-consuming	● Provides context and information
Slide/tape photography	Illuminative; promotes discussion	Difficult to obtain; superficial	● Illustrates critical incidents
Case study	Accurate; representative; uses range of techniques	Time-consuming	● Comprehensive overview of an issue ● Publishable format

illustrated in Tables 3.3 and 7.2–7.5 are examples of ways in which the evaluation questions can be linked to data collection and action to ensure a logical flow of enquiry. In a similar way, various taxonomies of data collection methods contained in research textbooks help in linking appropriate data collection techniques to specific evaluation questions. An example of such a taxonomy or list of data collection approaches is found in *A Teachers' Guide to Classroom Research* (Hopkins, 1985a) and is reproduced here as Table 4.1.

Table 4.2   Establishing questions and identifying data collection methods (adapted from Loucks-Horsley *et al.*, 1987: 160)

	Surveys and pre-post measures	Question-naires	Observation	Interview	Document analysis
Changes in participants' knowledge base	x	x		x	
Changes in participants' skill level and use		x	x	x	
Changes in participants' opinions and feelings		x		x	
Changes in organizational capacity		x		x	x
Changes in student performance	x	x	x	x	x

Note: the 'x' entries are only illustrative.

Another way of identifying data or information sources is by constructing a matrix that links data to questions, or data to analysis. Table 4.2 contains a matrix that links the 'bottom line' questions already mentioned to five different sources of information. Depending on the circumstances a different question can imply a different information source and such a configuration may allow the evaluator to become a little more strategic in his/her choice of data. For example, changes in a participant's knowledge can easily be assessed through a questionnaire, whereas changes in skill are better observed, and attitude is often best illuminated through an interview. Similarly, Table 5.2 (p. 70) shows a matrix that sets the various stages of analysis against the data sources described in this chapter. In practice, I find that a different level of analysis requires different data and such a matrix assists in planning data-gathering activities.

Each evaluation has its own unique information sources, but these frameworks may help the evaluator become more systematic and targeted in the way she or he collects information. In the rest of the chapter some of the information sources identified in the matrix in Table 4.2 are described in a little more detail.

Surveys and pre–post measures

Surveys, pre–post and other standardized measures can yield an enormous amount of information in a very economic way. Although there is a resistance to quantitative measures (in the same way as there is a resistance to qualitative approaches) among some of the evaluation community they have a very important role in the armoury available to the eclectic evaluator. Surveys can be of great value, particularly when used in conjunction with other data collection techniques. They enable the evaluator to reach a wide range of respondents and are particularly useful at tracing attitude shifts over time. Even if I was competent to do so, this is not the place to discuss statistical techniques or the construction of standardized questionnaires. Instead I will describe three different approaches to the use of surveys that I have used in various evaluations.

The first example is taken from an ongoing evaluation of a local TVEI pilot scheme where we administered an IQ test to all the pupils in the fourth year of a consortia of TVEI schools. We did this as one of a battery of paper and pencil tests which were designed to provide some baseline data and to compare the relative abilities of TVEI and non-TVEI pupils. We found that the intake of TVEI pupils was 'negatively skewed' and this enabled us to argue for a more balanced intake in future years. We were also able to match IQ to pupil learning style, which was one of our current interests. This collection of data also allowed us to make the following observations (Hopkins, 1986b: 21):

1 More boys than girls are attracted to the scheme.
2 There is evident sex-role stereotyping in option choice.
3 The local evaluation TVEI girls have very high IQs.
4 The cohort enjoys relatively low socio-economic status.
5 The cohort has relatively low expectations and aspirations of jobs and qualifications.
6 Heads and teachers perceive TVEI pupils as being of average or low ability.
7 Pupils perceive themselves as being of mid- to low ability.

My interpretation of this data is that not only was there evident sex-role stereotyping (which to be fair is not restricted to this authority or TVEI in general and is, given our social and educational milieu, unfortunately to be expected), but that despite high levels of measured ability among the girls, their teachers' perceptions of their ability was low, their own perception of their ability was low and their expectations were also low. This suggests to me some deeply embedded cultural determinates at work within the school and local community which TVEI is going to have some difficulty in overcoming.

These findings obviously provided a great deal of heart searching and material for feedback and follow-up within that particular pilot. This is also a good example of the benefits of using multiple data sources. In this case, the conclusions were based on two surveys with different foci, i.e. IQ, attitude to TVEI, complemented by teacher and headteacher interviews.

A second example is provided by our evaluation of the School Teacher Appraisal Pilot Project in England and Wales. Part of the evaluation strategy was the administration of a survey to gauge teacher attitude to appraisal. Although the construction of the survey was too complex to describe in detail, one section is particularly illustrative of our approach. The agreed (ACAS) document on which the pilot was based listed a number of outcomes of the

Table 4.3　Technology across the curriculum questionnaire

1　What do you understand by 'Technology Across the Curriculum'?
2　What is your curriculum area?
　Is the technological process applicable to it?
　If yes, please give some brief examples.
3　Have you received any INSET or curriculum development for 'Technology Across the Curriculum'?
　If so, what? If not, what support do you feel you need to teach the technological process?
4　What benefit will 'Technology Across the Curriculum' have for pupils in your curriculum area?

---

appraisal process. We wanted an indication of the importance attached by teachers to each of these outcomes, yet did not want to make the analysis too complicated. Consequently, we listed the outcomes as neutrally as we could and asked respondents to rank their three most desirable and three least desirable outcomes. On the follow-up survey we asked respondents to state for each outcome whether it was very important/important/unimportant. This allows for comparison of what teachers thought desirable before being appraised with what actually happened to them. This approach is one way of assessing reaction to a policy decision without leading questions.

The third example is asking the Guide to Institutional Learning (GIL) instrument which is part of the IMTEC/NFER Institutional Development Programme described in detail in Chapter 8. Suffice it to say here that the GIL is a standardized measure of a range of variables associated with school organization and climate. The instrument, therefore, provides an accurate measure of a range of critical variables, allows for comparison with other schools and, because of its real/ideal scale, provides a basis for target identification in a whole-school review process.

Questionnaires

I am making an arbitrary distinction in this chapter between surveys and questionnaires. I have already defined a survey as a standardized instrument that has a relatively high degree of reliability, i.e. it is consistent when used across a range of settings. In this chapter I define a questionnaire as a more informal instrument that may not be reliable in the technical sense but has a high degree of validity, i.e. it measures what it intends to measure. Many evaluators do not require reliability in their instuments because they are 'one-offs' designed for a particular discrete situation. However, these instruments do need to be valid in so far as they measure what they are supposed to measure, and that what is interpreted as cause produces the effect (internal validity). When data from a questionnaire is to be collated and fed back to respondents, then it is also important that the instrument has face validity (i.e.

Table 4.4   A matrix for classifying observation in evaluation

Role	Method			
	Open (exploratory)	Clinical supervision (developmental)	Focused (valid)	Systematic (reliable)
Peer observation				
External observation				

it looks as if it measures what it purports to measure), that it has content validity (i.e. it covers all the relevant subject matter), and that it has respondent validity (i.e. those who complete it agree that it is valid).

A valid if not reliable questionnaire has a number of advantages for the evaluator. They are relatively easy to construct and elicit a range of views. I would typically use such a questionnaire when wanting to solicit the views of staff in a school or consortia about a particular issue. After preliminary observation and interview to identify the key issues (content validity), I would construct a questionnaire normally on one side of A4 paper with a series of four to six open-ended questions. These questionnaires are relatively quick to complete, phrased to be 'user-friendly' (respondent validity) and also contain a description of the evaluation (face validity). These questionnaires are distributed through staff mail boxes and the results are tabulated and fed back promptly, thus engaging staff interest and the building of a positive attitude for possible developmental activity. Table 4.3 lists the questions for such a questionnaire on 'Technology Across the Curriculum' used during a recent evaluation.

Observation

One can think about the range of approaches to observation in evaluation in the form of a matrix (see Table 4.4). Although the matrix is not comprehensive it does cover the usual range of roles and methods which are now discussed individually.

Peer observation

Peer observation refers to a collegial form of observation where teachers observe each other's teaching for developmental purposes. Such collaborative activities can also have a formative evaluative purpose when linked to school self-evaluation and teacher appraisal. Insufficient attention has been paid to the role of peer or paired observation as a link between evaluation and such professional development activities. The use of coaching as an INSET strategy as described in Chapter 9 is another form of peer observation.

External observation

External observation, for want of a better phrase, is the typical situation where the observation reflects an implicit power imbalance between the observer and the observed. Although this power imbalance may not be very pronounced in most observations, it is still its characteristic feature, i.e. someone is doing something to someone else.

Open observation

Open observation is the term I have given to the exploratory form of participant observation that is associated with ethnographic research. The observation is unstructured and relies entirely on the evaluators' skills of interpretation and intuition. Parlett and Hamilton (1977: 15) describe this particular approach to observation in this way:

> ... the observation phase occupies a central place in illuminative evaluation. The investigator builds up a continuous record of on-going events, transactions and informal remarks. At the same time he seeks to organise this data at source, adding interpretative comments on both manifest and latent features of the situation. In addition to observing and documenting day-to-day activities of the programme, the investigator may also be present at a wide variety of other events (e.g. faculty and student meetings, open days, examiners' meetings, etc.).

Clinical supervision

Clinical supervision is a technique that was developed as a method of supervising student teachers, but is well suited for use in evaluations and other activities (e.g. teacher appraisal) that have a developmental purpose (Acheson and Gall, 1980). It is a structured form of observation that focuses on a teacher's instructional performance utilizing a three-phase approach to the observation of teaching events. It is a particularly appropriate format for peer observation.

The three essential phases of the clinical supervision process are a planning conference, classroom observation, and a feedback conference. The planning conference provides the observer and teacher with an opportunity to reflect on the proposed lesson, and this leads to a mutual decision to collect observational data on an aspect of the teacher's teaching. At this stage, observer and observed often establish a form of 'contract' in so far as they agree how to collect data, how it is to be used, who sees it, and how the observation is to be carried out. During the classroom observation phase, the observer observes the teacher teach and collects objective data on that aspect of teaching they agreed upon

Figure 4.1   The clinical supervision cycle.

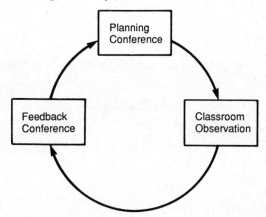

earlier. It is in the feedback conference that the observer and teacher share the information, decide on remedial action (if necessary), and often plan to collect further observational data. Variations on this process (see Fig. 4.1) are suggested by different writers on the topic, but all follow the same basic pattern. It is important, however, to realize that to be effective all three phases of the process need to be gone through systematically, and sufficient time given to planning and feedback in particular.

There are a number of principles that are important to consider in clinical supervision. First, the climate of interaction between teacher and observer needs to be non-threatening, supportive and one of mutual trust. Secondly, the focus of the activity should be on improving instruction and the reinforcing of successful patterns, rather than on criticism of unsuccessful patterns, or changing the teacher's personality. Thirdly, the process depends on the collection and use of objective observational data, not unsubstantiated value judgements. Fourthly, teachers are encouraged to make inferences about their own teaching from the data, and to use the data to construct hypotheses that can be tested out in the future. Fifthly, each cycle of supervision is part of an ongoing process that builds on the other. Sixthly, both observer and teacher are engaged in mutual interaction that can lead to an improvement in teaching and observational skills for both, and to formative evaluation within the school. It is very much a two-way process.

Focused observation

Focused observation is the term I have given to the approach that utilizes checklists or observation schedules drawn up by the observer or observed to suit a particular situation. This approach could also be used within a clinical supervision framework. When evaluators are observing teaching, all they often require are simple ways of gathering information on basic topics, such as

Figure 4.2   TVEI observation schedule.

Comment and Provide Evidence on these Items

Date:_____School:_____Teacher:_____Class:_____

Observer: | Boys___ | Girls___ |

Change in teaching style

Vocationalism

Active learning/problem solving

Pupil negotiation of learning process

Perceived ability of pupils: (i) Teachers and (ii) students

Do the teachers/students recognize their involvement in TVEI?

Work experience or visits?

General comments

---

questioning techniques, on-task and off-task behaviours and classroom management. It is usually preferable for evaluators to devise their own observation schedule, to 'invent' them for a particular purpose. By doing this, more ownership is implied over the investigation and there is probably a better 'fit' between the object of the observation and the data-gathering method. Consequently, these instruments have high validity, in the sense that the term was used earlier, in so far as they pertain to specific situations.

Before devising the observation checklist, it is useful to ask some organizing questions in order to ascertain the purpose of the observation:

1 What is the purpose of the observation?
2 What teacher behaviours are to be observed?
3 What is the focus of the observation?
4 What data-gathering methods will best serve the purpose?
5 How will the data be used?

There are a number of examples of observation schedules developed by teachers concerned with gathering data on questioning techniques and on-/off-task behaviours in my classroom research book (Hopkins 1985a). An approach to formal observation that I have found particularly useful in evaluation work has been the use of a 'grounded observation framework'. Many recent curriculum initiatives have highlighted the importance of changes

Table 4.5 Flanders' interaction analysis categories

		Indirect influence
Teacher talk	1	Accepts feelings: accepts and clarifies the feeling tone of the student in a non-threatening manner. Feelings may be positive or negative. Predicting and recalling feelings are included
	2	Praises or encourages: praises or encourages student action or behaviour. Jokes that release tension, not at the expense of another individual, nodding head or saying 'uh huh?' or 'go on' are included
	3	Accepts or uses ideas of student: clarifying, building, or developing ideas or suggestions by a student. As teacher brings more of his own ideas into play, shift to category five
	4	Asks questions: asking a question about content or procedure with the intent that a student answer
		Direct influence
	5	Lectures: giving facts or opinions about content or procedures, expressing his own idea; asking rhetorical questions
	6	Gives directions: directions, commands, or orders with which a student is expected to comply
	7	Criticizes or justifies authority: statements, intended to change student behaviour from non-acceptable pattern; bawling someone out; stating why the teacher is doing what he is doing, extreme self-reference
Student talk	8	Student talk-response: talk by students in response to teacher. Teacher initiates the contact or solicits student statement
	9	Student talk-initiation: talk by students, which they initiate. If 'calling on' student is only to indicate who may talk next, observer must decide whether student wanted to talk. If he did, use this category
	10	Silence or confusion: pauses, short periods of silence, and periods of confusion in which communication cannot be understood by the observer.

in teaching method. These teaching methods will obviously vary and be moderated through the teacher's own style. In these situations, after an initial period of observation and interviews, an *aide-mémoire* or framework of characteristics of this teaching method is developed that is 'grounded' in that particular curriculum or teaching situation. The framework allows observation of a number of classrooms quite rapidly and seemingly informally, because the prior analysis helps to identify key features or characteristics of the method. Such an observation scale has high face validity and can consequently be used as the basis for feedback. An example of one of these 'grounded observation frameworks' is shown in Fig. 4.2. Any other 'purpose-built' framework that is grounded, i.e. emerges out of the context to which it applies, falls into this category.

Systematic observation

Systematic observation uses standardized coding scales to analyse classroom interactions. The statistical rigour and analytic detail of the approach seems to me to lead to abstraction rather than reflection on (or in) action. To misquote T. S. Eliot, systematic observers may well have the experience but in so doing are in danger of losing the meaning.

One of the best known coding systems is the Flanders Interaction Analysis Categories (FIAC). It is widely used and has influenced the design of many other category systems. FIAC is based on 10 analytic categories that reflects Flander's conceptualization of teacher–pupil verbal interaction (see Table 4.5). Each of the categories has a number, but no scale is implied (Flanders, 1970).

Two main advantages of the Flanders system are that it is fairly easy to learn and apply, and that the 10 categories describe a number of behaviours which many would agree are important. On the other hand, much information is lost, especially non-verbal aspects of communication. In particular, some categories are too broad, and others discriminate insufficiently. Also, there are too few pupil categories, and it is difficult to use in informal classrooms. Other examples of systematic classroom observation scales can be found in Galton (1978) and Croll (1986).

One of the problems in this approach is that each scale represents the author's concept of a situation. One is looking at classrooms through someone else's eyes, and their purposes and perceptions could be very different from one's own. It is easy, therefore, to get trapped within the intentions of the researcher who designed the scale. Consequently, it is important for the evaluator to match his/her needs closely to the intent and focus of the scale. In that way they can maintain control over the situation. The second problem is that most scales were not designed for formative evaluators. Their original intent was mainly as research tools for analysing classrooms. Consequently, they are not always the most appropriate observation method, particularly for the evaluator concerned with relatively small-scale situations.

Interviews

Interviews allow for depth of response and provide a chance to discover and explore subjective meanings. They are generally more time-consuming than questionnaires but allow for more 'in-depth' data to be generated. There are a number of excellent texts on interviewing (e.g. Powney and Watts, 1987) and the interview is also covered in most introductory texts on research methods. We can distinguish three different types of interview: structured, unstructured and focused.

Structured interviews are very much like oral questionnaires, where the content, procedures and schedules are fixed in advance. There is very little room in this approach for initiative by the interviewer, because the power of this type of interview lies in its standardized nature and hence its generalizability.

Unstructured interviews, on the other hand, are open to change by the interviewer as he or she follows the nuances of meaning and reality proposed by the interviewee. An extreme form of this approach would be the non-directive interview which grew out of therapeutic experience where there is minimal direction by the interviewer.

Although both of these approaches, particularly the unstructured interview, have their uses in evaluation, neither are entirely appropriate for the types of time-limited evaluations that are the main focus of this book.

More useful perhaps is the focused interview, whose distinctive quality is the prior analysis of the subject matter of the interview by the evaluator. Merton and Kendall (1946: 541) describe the characteristics of the focused interview as follows:

1 Persons interviewed are known to have been involved in a particular concrete situation.
2 The hypothetically significant elements, patterns and total structure of this situation have been previously analysed by the investigator.
3 On the basis of this analysis, the investigator has fashioned an interview guide, setting forth the major areas of inquiry and the hypotheses which locate the pertinence of data to be obtained in the interview.
4 The interview itself is focused on the subjective experiences of persons exposed to the pre-analysed situation. The array of their reported responses to this situation enables the evaluator to:
  (a) to test the validity of hypotheses derived from content analysis;
  (b) to ascertain unanticipated responses to the situation, thus giving rise to fresh hypotheses.

A particularly useful distinction they make is between unstructured, semi-structured and structured questions. Unstructured questions are those free of stimulus and response (e.g. 'What impressed you most in this video?'); semi-structured questions are those where either the stimulus or the response is structured, but not both ['What did you learn from this lesson that you didn't know before?' (response structured), or 'What did you feel about seeing that classroom?' (stimulus structured)]; and structured questions are those where both stimulus and response are structured ('As you listened to the lecture did you feel it was more entertaining than informative?').

Unstructured questions possess their greatest utility during the opening stages of the interview where the interviewee is constructing his/her own definition of reality. Usually, it is necessary for the interviewer to assume more control at later stages of the interview where it may be necessary to become quite specific (i.e. specify stimulus and response towards the end of the interview), particularly if the interviewer was unable to follow cues on specific aspects of the situation during the interview.

The interview schedule we use with TVEI students (Table 4.6) follow these principles. It was constructed to allow the interviewee as free a range of responses as possible to the initial question. This allowed their perception of

Table 4.6   TVEI student-focused interview

1 How would you describe TVEI to a new student in your school?
2 What would you like to do after 16?
3 What are your two most important subjects in school?
    (Prompt: Why do you think that?)
4 Please describe a lesson or part of a lesson that you enjoyed.
    (Prompt: Why?)
5 Please describe a lesson or part of a lesson that you did not enjoy.
    (Prompt: Why?)
6 What ways do you work best in lessons?
    (Prompt for: group, alone, teacher directing, etc.)
7 How do you find your work in school most of the time?
    (Prompt: very interesting, quite interesting, not very interesting, uninteresting)
8 Do you think your fourth-year options will help you in the future?
    (Prompt for: a great deal, a little, not at all, not sure)
9 Has the TVEI programme attracted any particular groups of students?
    (Prompt for: Are there more girls than boys, equal, more boys, practical people,
    academic people, a mixture)
10 Would you advise third years to take up TVEI?
    (Prompt for: strongly advise them, up to them but worth doing, doesn't matter
    whether they do it or not, not to do it, some to do it but others not, not give them
    any advice. Why do you say that?)

TVEI and construction of reality to emerge unhindered by the interviewer's prompts, cues or perceptions. As the interview progressed the questions increasingly focused on specific aspects of the innovation of interest to the researcher. At the end of the schedule there were some specific questions which would only be asked if a response to them had not emerged naturally during the interview. I should also note that the interview schedule in Table 4.6 is often used with groups of three or four students in order to elicit responses from a large number of students in a short space of time. As long as the appropriate climate is set and individual and possibly contrary responses encouraged, the schedule proves to be very reliable.

By describing the focused interview in such detail is not to belittle the importance of the unstructured interview. The unstructured interview has received so much attention in the literature (e.g. MacDonald and Sanger, 1982; Simons, 1980) that I wanted to make the case here for a complementary approach.

Documents and background information

Innovations, as Parlett and Hamilton (1977: 17) comment, do not arise unheralded. They are preceded by committee minutes, funding proposals, architectural plans and consultants' reports. Also, other primary sources are obtainable, e.g. non-confidential data from registrars' offices; autobiographical and eye-witness accounts of the innovation; tape-recordings of meetings; and examples of students' assignments. The assembly of such information can serve a useful function. It can provide an historical perspective of how the innovation was regarded by different people before the evaluation began. The data may also indicate areas for inquiry (e.g. how representative were the students taking part?); may point to topics for intensive discussion (e.g. why were certain major features of the original proposal later abandoned?); or may expose aspects of the innovation that would otherwise be missed (e.g. why were subject requirements not fulfilled?).

The consequent question of course is how does one analyse documentary evidence? Useful accounts can be found in Guba and Lincoln (1981: ch. 8) and Bell (1987: ch. 6). The following questions are suggested by Bell (1987: 56) as the basis of subjecting a document to rigorous analysis:

1 What kind of document is it? A statute? A policy paper? A set of minutes? A letter from a long correspondence? How many copies are there?
2 What does it actually say? Are the terms used employed in the same way as you would use them?
3 Who produced it? What was its purpose? Did the author aim to inform, command, remind (as in a memorandum) or to have some other effect on the reader?
4 When and in what circumstances was it produced? How did it come into existence?
5 Is it typical or exceptional of its type?
6 Is it complete? Has it been altered or edited?

Other very helpful frameworks for analysing curriculum materials are found in the Open University (1981) course on 'Curriculum Evaluation'. In a number of our recent evaluation projects, documentary evidence has proven very helpful in establishing a framework for the evaluation, in helping us to identify initial issues and in providing criteria for judgement. However, such documentation is often politically initiated, unsophisticated or represents a compromise situation. All documents therefore need to be treated with scepticism, just as any other form of data.

Case study

Case studies are not, despite a common confusion, a method of collecting data. They are a means of presenting data about a specific case; a systematic investigation of a specific instance. Much has now been written about the utility of case studies in evaluation research (Simons, 1980). There are also a number of useful guides to the methodology of analytic case studies (Yin, 1984). Case studies have also become increasingly 'respectable'.

Case studies aim to give a portrayal of a specific situation in such a way as to illuminate some more general principle. The definition adopted in the 1976 Cambridge conference on the topic is that 'case study is an umbrella term for a family of research methods having in common the decision to focus an inquiry round an instance'. The method attempts to give a fair and accurate account of a specific case in such a way as to allow the reader to penetrate the superficial record, and also to check the author's interpretations by examining appropriate selection of the objective evidence from which the case study has been built (Nisbet and Watt, 1984).

Case studies are appealing to many evaluators as a means of conveying the findings of an evaluation (this issue is discussed in Chapter 11). What is of more interest here is how does one begin to collect data for a case study? In our evaluation of the teacher appraisal project we collected 'case study specific' data in a number of ways. For example, we encouraged teachers to keep a diary of their experience of appraisal during the life of the pilot project and enlisted the help of some schools in describing their experience with appraisal. Following, is some of our advice on collecting data in these areas.

Diaries

Here are some extracts from our 'Keeping an Appraisal Diary' booklet:

Why am I being asked to keep a diary?

ESTAPS (Evaluation of the School Teacher Appraisal Pilot Study) is conducting an independent evaluation across the six Local Authorities in the teacher appraisal pilot. As part of this study, the ESTAPS team would like to gain some understanding of the process of appraisal as it is experienced by teachers and their appraisers. Records kept in continuous diary form will help us to do this.

What sort of things would I put in the diary?

One major purpose of the diaries is to gain a reasonably accurate recording of the sequence of the more formal parts of the appraisal process, e.g. self-appraisal, observation, feedback discussion, appraisal interviews – when they happen, where they happen, how they are conducted. A diary entry of this kind might read:

May 11th
Started jotting down responses to self-appraisal questions at home last Friday night. Very tired and couldn't think clearly but didn't have time at lunch-time. Decided to leave it until today (Sunday). Much better. The questions have focused my mind on the things I was worried about (see notes). Raymond is looking after the children so I've the peace and quiet I need to do it properly. Told R. I felt rather apprehensive about the whole thing but he said he thought I might find it v. useful. They have a scheme at the bank which he says helps him a lot.

How often should I make diary entries?

Whenever anything occurs that you think is of significance. This will vary for different people, but try to capture as much as you can, even if it means writing it up in brief note form. If you have not made an entry in any one week, please record the fact that nothing of significance has occurred, e.g.

July 15th
Nothing happening on appraisal front. Hasn't entered my head all week. Been v. busy with final plans for school concert.

School descriptions

Here are some extracts from our 'What It Means to be a Case Study School' notes:

Why is the evaluation team conducting case studies?

In order to gain a deeper understanding of appraisal as it happens in normal school life. Case studies will help us to see how the various aspects of appraisal link together. They should give us a deeper understanding of people's experience of appraisal.

How will the case study be done?

Depending on the particular study and agreement with those involved, data may be collected by:

- talking to teachers and headteachers;
- asking teachers and headteachers to record their experiences;
- examining the appraisal documentation produced and used by the school;
- observing some aspects of the appraisal process.

Although not all of these aspects will be appropriate to the particular case study, it is important to use a variety of sources of evidence.

All data gathering will be negotiated in advance between the evaluators and the schools. None of these techniques will be used without the willingness and permission of the head and teachers involved.

Summary

Although I have had to be selective in writing this chapter, I hope that some of the examples of approaches to data collection that have proven helpful to me will be useful to others. The references cited in the section on Further Reading at the end of the book give a more complete description of the various data collection methods. I will close by reiterating one of the most important points in this chapter, namely the need to be strategic about linking the most expedient information source to a particular evaluation question, thus establishing a causal chain between question, information source, feedback and action. In Chapter 5, the next step in the evaluation process is discussed, i.e. how to analyse the data so laboriously collected.

5
Analysing data and enhancing validity

The information sources described in the previous chapter tend to be qualitative rather than quantitative in nature. Put another way, data for the type of evaluations described in this book are more often expressed in words rather than numbers. Qualitative methods are especially suited to educational evaluation, particularly where the *raison d'être* of the enquiry is understanding rather than proof. However, this is not to imply that qualitative methods are unable to provide proof, but rather to emphasize that evaluation is often more concerned to generate hypotheses about complex social situations rather than test them. Many evaluators stress the value and appropriateness of qualitative methods when 'the phenomena to be studied are complex human and organisational interactions and therefore not easily translatable into numbers' (Skrtic, 1985).

Unfortunately, as Miles and Huberman (1984a) note, there is an Achilles heel here: there are few agreed on the procedures for the analysis of qualitative data, and therefore the truth claims and validity underlying such work are uncertain. They illustrate this concern graphically in the following extracts (Miles and Huberman, 1984a):

Despite a growing interest in qualitative studies, we lack a body of clearly defined methods for drawing valid meaning from qualitative data. We need methods that are practical, communicable, and not self deluding: scientific in the positivist's sense of the word, and aimed toward interpretive understanding in the best sense of that term.

The problem is that there is an insufficient corpus of reliable, valid, or even minimally agreed on working analysis procedures of qualitative data. Worse still, there appears to be little sharing of experience, even at the rudimentary level of recipe exchange. We don't know much about what other qualitative researchers are actually doing when they reduce, analyse, and interpret data.

It seems that we are in a double bind: the status of conclusions from qualitative studies is uncertain because researchers don't report on their methodology, and researchers don't report on their methodology because there are no established conventions for doing that.

Consequently, the analysis of qualitative evaluation often tends to be done badly if done at all. Yet unless the data we use is trustworthy then it is immoral as well as foolhardy to engage in development work on data that has been inadequately analysed. This chapter is therefore concerned with the analysis of qualitative evaluation data; the analysis of quantitative data is adequately covered elsewhere (e.g. FitzGibbon and Morris, 1987). I shall first outline a general approach to analysis that builds on the discussion in previous chapters, then look at some specific techniques, and discuss the particular problem of validity in qualitative evaluation.

The analysis of qualitative data

I have previously outlined (Hopkins, 1985a) an approach to the analysis of qualitative data based on two classic statements on sociological fieldwork made by Becker, and Glaser and Strauss. Becker (1958) described four stages in the analysis of fieldwork data and Glaser and Strauss (1967) described the concept of the constant comparative method as a means of analysing qualitative data. There are basic similarities in their approaches to the analysis of field data. Each envisages the analytic process as having four distinct generic phases (i) immersion in the data and the initial generation of categories, (ii) validation of categories, (iii) organization and interpretation of categories, and (iv) action, i.e. presentation of theory or conclusions. These various stages are summarized in Table 5.1. To these four stages I would add a preliminary phase, that of anticipation, where the evaluator delineates his or her area of study and formulates a tentative evaluation design; which like the evaluation question becomes more clearly defined as the process proceeds.

In the first stage the researcher begins by collecting 'broad spectrum' data relevant to the evaluation question. By doing this the evaluator can be said to be immersing him or herself in the data. The data can be collected from observation, discussion, interview, written recordings or from perusal of any pertinent document. This stage of the process is usually characterized by the evaluator's constant association with the data (immersion) and by procedures which enable the data to be analysed and stored according to the various categories arising within it. 'Coding' the data according to the categories to which they relate is perhaps a sub-stage of data collection, but is, in practice, more likely to co-exist with it.

Of critical importance is the way in which these interpretations of hypotheses or categories are handled and validated, and this comprises the second stage in the process. It is here, unfortunately, that qualitative evaluators have traditionally not done well. How is the validity of a category established? Both Becker, and Glaser and Strauss point to a similar technique: Becker refers

Table 5.1   The analysis of qualitative data (adapted from Hopkins, 1985a: 108)

Qualitative analysis	Becker	Glaser and Strauss
Anticipation		
Immersion	Selection and definition of concepts	Compare incidents applicable to each category
Validation	Frequency and distribution of concepts	Integrate categories and their phenomena
Interpretation	Incoporation of findings into model	Delimit theory
Action	Presentation of evidence and proof	Write theory

to 'the check on the frequency and distribution of phenomena' (1958: 653) and Glaser and Strauss to 'saturation', a situation where 'no additional data are being found . . . [to] develop properties of the category' (1967: 67). When applied to the evaluation situation this implies that the hypothesis or category generated from observations is tested repeatedly against data in an attempt to modify or falsify it. It is difficult and perhaps reckless to suggest a frequency that ensures the validity of a category, for that will vary from case to case, but during this process a number of predictable events can occur. The first is that if, on repeated testing, the category is found wanting, it is then discarded. Secondly, the category may have been conceptualized crudely, and through testing the concept is modified, refined and amplified. Thirdly, although the process of falsification is never complete, there comes a time when repeated observation leads neither to refutation nor amplification and only serves to support the hypothesis. At this point, when the utility of observation decreases, saturation can be said to have occurred and the hypothesis has been validated.

Another important technique for the validation of categories is triangulation. This concept was popularized by John Elliott and Clem Adelman during their work with the Ford Teaching Project. It involves contrasting the perceptions of one actor in a specific situation against those of other actors in the same situation. By doing this, an initial subjective observation or perception is fleshed out and given a degree of authenticity. Elliott and Adelman (1976: 76) describe the technique thus:

Triangulation involves gathering accounts of a teaching situation from three quite different points of view; namely, those of the teacher, the pupils, and a participant observer. . . . Each point of the triangle stands in a unique epistemological position with respect to access to relevant data about a teaching situation. The teacher is in the best position to gain access via introspection to his/her own intentions and aims in the situation. The students are in the best position to explain how the teacher's actions influence the way they respond in the situation. The participant-observer is in the best position to collect data about the observable features of the interaction between teachers and pupils. By comparing his/her own account with accounts from the two other standpoints, a person at one point of the triangle has an opportunity to test and perhaps revise it on the basis of more sufficient data.

Let me now restate the important methodological point. I am arguing that by employing analytic techniques such as saturation and triangulation, evaluators can produce hypotheses and concepts from qualitative data that are valid, methodologically sound and to an extent generalizable. By engaging in this process of concept or hypothesis generation, qualitative researchers are producing what Glaser and Strauss have called 'grounded theory'. This is theory grounded in data gathered from and applicable to a specific social situation.

The third stage in Becker's typology is the incorporation of findings into a model, and for Glaser and Strauss this is 'delimiting' the theory. In other words, it involves taking a valid construct and fitting it into a frame of reference which gives it meaning. What this means in practice, of course, depends on the particular questions originally asked by the evaluator. The hypothesis and contents should at this stage fit together to provide an account of the area of enquiry undertaken by the evaluation and defined by the evaluation questions.

This process should not be regarded as unproblematic and should also include a validation process. The two most common techniques used at this stage in the analysis are rival explanations and the search for negative cases. Michael Patton (1980: 327–8) describes these techniques like this:

> Once the evaluator has described the patterns, linkages, and accompanying explanations that have emerged from the analysis, it is important to look for rival or competing themes and explanations. . . . When considering rival hypotheses and competing explanations the strategy to be employed is not one of attempting to disprove the alternatives; rather, the analyst looks for data that *support* alternative explanations. Failure to find strong supporting evidence for alternative explanations helps increase confidence in the original, principal explanation generated by the evaluator. . . . It is important to write down what alternative classification systems, themes, and explanations are considered and 'tested' during data analysis. Reporting on what alternative explanations were considered and how those alternatives were considered in the formal evaluation report lends considerable credibility to the final set of findings offered by the evaluator.

Closely related to the testing of alternative explanations is the search for negative cases. Where patterns and trends have been identified, our understanding of those patterns and trends is increased by considering the instances and cases that do not fit within the pattern.

Table 5.2 An evaluation matrix

Analysis	Information source				
	Surveys	Questionnaires	Observations	Interviews	Documents
1 Immersion and generation of hypotheses					
2 Validation of hypotheses					
3 Interpretation by reference to evaluation questions and criteria					
4 Plan action for development					

At the end of this stage the evaluator is to give meaning to a particular observation or series of observations that can then lead to action. Here, both the sociologist and the evaluator are involved in the creation of meaning out of hitherto discrete observations and constructs.

The fourth stage identified by both Becker, and Glaser and Strauss is the culmination of their work – the presentation of theory. This stage implies action, because the new theory leads to new ways of understanding and appreciating social phenomena. In a similar way this stage implies action for the evaluator who, having related observation to theory, is now in a position to plan or suggest future action on the basis of this knowledge.

In summary, the four stages for the analysis of qualitative research data, preceded by a preliminary anticipatory stage, are as follows:

1 Immersion in the data and the generation of hypotheses.
2 Validation of hypotheses using, for example, techniques of saturation and triangulation.
3 Interpretation by reference to evaluation questions, established criteria, rival explanations and negative cases.
4 Action for development (and a further cycle of evaluation).

These steps are very similar to the stages of analysis identified by Parlett and Hamilton (1977). These steps can also be represented as a matrix (see Table 5.2). This discussion has tended towards the abstract. Let me make amends by providing an example from the evaluation of the School Teacher Appraisal Project. In the design of the evaluation we followed the analytical procedures described in this chapter. An overview of the methodology of the project is found in Fig. 5.1 and a more detailed description in Chapter 10.

Figure 5.1 Evaluation of the School Teacher Appraisal Project: data analysis framework.

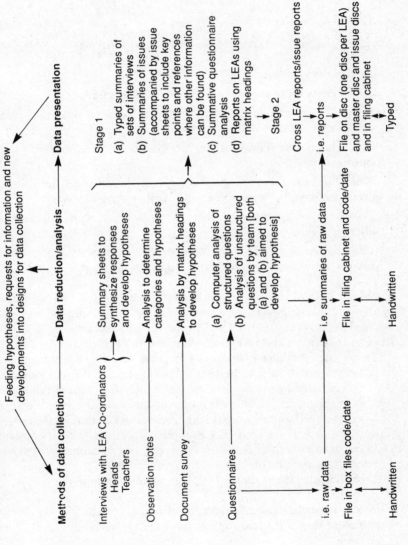

Some specific techniques

A few years ago I wrote a paper which gave some advice to action researchers about how to enhance the validity of their data (Hopkins, 1987b). In that paper I described eight strategies, four of which – plus one other that I have recently discovered – are described here.

Call things by their right name

My point is nicely illustrated by this well-known exchange:

> 'There's glory for you.'
>
> 'I don't know what you mean by "glory",' Alice said.
>
> Humpty Dumpty smiled contemptuously, 'Of course you don't – till I tell you. I meant, "there's a nice knock-down argument".'
>
> 'But "glory" doesn't mean "a nice knock-down argument",' Alice objected.
>
> 'When I use a word', Humpty Dumpty said, in rather a scornful tone, 'it means just what I choose it to mean – neither more or less.'
>
> 'The question is', said Alice, 'whether you can make words mean so many different things.'
>
> 'The question is', said Humpty Dumpty, 'which is to be master, that's all' (Lewis Carroll, quoted in Kirk and Miller, 1986: 23–4).

The point is an obvious one – we need to know what we intend to evaluate before we evaluate it so that we know what we are looking for. As evaluators we need to do our conceptual work properly. We need, for example, to beware of suggesting that a child who is looking intently at a teacher is in fact paying attention; or of dictionary definitions that define intelligence as mental ability; or of operational definitions that regard paying attention as not looking out of the window. None of these help us very much. Conceptualization involves articulating a full clear and coherent account of what constitutes being an instance of something; that is to say it necessitates elaborating the criteria that have to be met if, for example, a pupil is legitimately to be described as engaging in enquiry/discovery learning. It requires an explicit statement of the defining characteristics of the concept (Barrow, 1986).

Robin Barrow (1985) summarizes the argument in four points:

1 Researchers must understand what true conceptual analysis involves; in particular they must not confuse it with mere synonyms or the giving of examples.
2 Whatever their personal area of interest, they must all show concern for conceptualising the context – the nature of the educational enterprise – adequately.
3 Empirical researchers must, in addition, conceptualise what they intend to

look at properly. If there are compelling reasons to operationalise a concept, then it must be clearly pointed out that the research is actually not into X, but into something else that has a bearing on X. The nature of the bearing on X needs to be explained, by articulating the relationship between the operational definition and a fully articulated account of the concept.

4 The methodology adopted must be chosen in the light of the concepts being researched, rather than by some ideological commitment to a style of research.

A good example of this lack of conceptual clarity is the way in which the phrases 'pupil-centred learning' or 'changes in teaching style' are used in TVEI. Although most people have an intuitive grasp of what is meant, few are able to articulate their implications in a way that enhances practice. Consequently, evaluators that investigate these issues without adequate operational definitions may risk evaluating a non-event.

Know what you are looking for

This is a similar injunction to 'calling things by their right name', but comes somewhat later in the research process, having more to do with the observation phase of fieldwork. In 1980, Rob Walker wrote a paper on 'The conduct of educational case study'. In it he refers to a data-gathering approach called condensed fieldwork:

> In developing ways of using case study methods within a democratic mode of research we have to think in terms of condensed fieldwork; we have to find ways of collecting and presenting our data with some speed. Inevitably this takes us even closer to the endemic problems of case study research, especially the problems of reliability and validity, confidentiality, consultation, publication and control over data. It is one thing to publish a study five years after the period of fieldwork, but quite another to spend a week in a school and to produce the case study a week later.

Since Walker wrote this paper the necessity for more rapid forms of data gathering has increased. Smaller budgets, categorical funding, and an increased emphasis on responsive evaluation all require forms of condensed fieldwork. But as Walker notes, this places a great strain on validity.

One response to this pressure is to generate 'grounded observational frameworks' for condensed fieldwork. On the basis of initial observations and analysis, a series of categories are developed which seem to comprise the reality of the situation under review. These are not *a priori* categories but the result of observation and analysis, and emerge from the data. These categories form the basis of the observation schedule. Because I know what I am looking for, having been intimately involved in the evolution and validation of the categories from the data, fieldwork and observations can be drastically reduced. I have recently used this technique in observations of teaching style in TVEI classrooms as described in Chapter 4 (see Fig. 4.2). The observation schedule was constructed on the basis of prior experience, observation and analysis. Because of this, it allowed rapid observation of many classes while still producing valid results.

Be catholic in the use of data sources

In the same way as one triangulates the perception of various actors, so too must we triangulate our sources of data. As we have seen, there are five main data sources open to the evaluator: surveys, questionnaires, observation, interviews and documents. There is, however, a wide range of activity within these broad groupings. The evaluation matrix shown in Fig. 5.1 helps illustrate the range of data sources available at different levels of analysis. Although not every cell should be completed, a wide scatter should usually be employed and the most appropriate source used for each evaluation question and stage of analysis.

A recent experience has highlighted the importance of this suggestion. At a meeting of TVEI evaluators organized a couple of years ago, one local evaluator remarked that she was about to examine change in teaching style in her evaluation. In order to do this she was going to interview teachers. Interestingly, I had just completed an evaluation of this aspect of TVEI and had found (apart from little change in teaching style) that teacher interviews on teaching style did not correlate well with the observational data on the same topic; yet, responses from the student questionnaires correlated far more closely with the classroom observations. This is a strong argument for being catholic in the use of data sources.

Set audit trails

An audit trail is a fairly recent technique that borrows from the concept of a financial audit to increase the reliability of one's data and to contribute to meta-evaluation. In their recent book, Schwandt and Halpern (1988: 73) describe the usefulness of an audit trail to the evaluator in this way:

> Preparing an audit trail is important for two reasons. First, it documents the inquiry in a fashion that facilitates a third-party examination. The audit trail contains information that describes the methods used to control error and to reach justifiable conclusions. Second, an audit trail is also important for the evaluator. We have found that when evaluators systematically document their enquiries in anticipation of an audit, it helps them manage their record keeping. They find an organized trail useful when they need to retrieve information easily and when they prepare their final reports. Some evaluators have suggested that when they document each inquiry decision, they become more thoughtful, critical, and reflective.

Figure 5.2 Preparing an audit trail (from Schwandt and Halpern, 1988: 74).

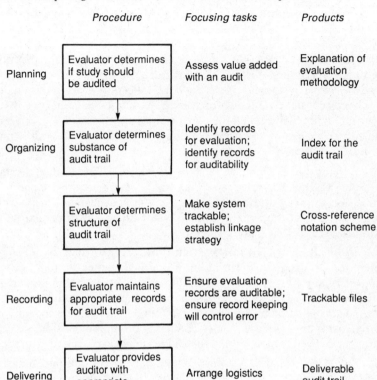

A systematically kept documentation system will serve a quality control function during an evaluation and will help guide the evaluation process in accord with generally accepted evaluation principles.

Figure 5.2 illustrates a simple four-stage model for planning, organizing, recording and delivering an audit trail. Although an audit trail may appear an unduly mechanistic process, such systematic data collection and analysis always enhances rigour and may be particularly useful in situations where one's conclusions and the data they are based on are open to question and scrutiny.

Reduce and display data

In their effort to make explicit the procedures and thought processes that qualitative researchers actually use in their work, Matthew Miles and Michael Huberman suggest the flow and interactive models seen in Fig. 5.3. They describe the main components of these models in the introduction to their source book on *Qualitative Data Analysis* (Miles and Huberman, 1984b: 21–2) like this:

> *Data Reduction:* Data reduction refers to the process of selecting, focusing, simplifying, abstracting, and transforming the 'raw' data that appear in written up field notes. As data collection proceeds, there are further episodes of data reduction (doing summaries, coding, teasing out themes, making clusters, making partitions, writing memos). And the data reduction/transforming process continues after fieldwork, until a final report is complete.
>
> *Data Display:* The second major flow of analysis activity is data display. We define a 'display' as an organised assembly of information that permits conclusion drawing and action taking. Looking at displays helps us to understand what is happening and to do something – further analysis or action – based on that understanding.
>
> *Conclusion Drawing/Verification:* The third stream of analysis activity is conclusion drawing and verification. From the beginning of data collection, the qualitative analyst is beginning to decide what things mean, is noting regularities, patterns, explanations, possible configurations, causal flows and propositions. The competent researcher holds these conclusions lightly, maintaining openness and scepticism, but the conclusions are still there, inchoate and vague at first, then increasingly explicit and grounded.
>
> In this sense, qualitative data analysis is a continuous, iterative enterprise. Issues of data reduction of display, and of conclusion drawing/verification come into figure successfully as analysis episodes follow each other.

Although space precludes a detailed discussion of the range of techniques Miles and Huberman describe, there are two sections in their chapter on 'Drawing and verifying conclusions' that are so pertinent to the discussion in this chapter that they need to be briefly reported here. They comment that a general analysis strategy is a necessary but not sufficient condition and that there is also a flow of specific analysis tactics, ways of drawing and verifying conclusions that the evaluator needs to employ during the analytic process. They distinguish between 'tactics for generating meaning' (Miles and Huberman, 1984b: 215) and 'tactics for testing or confirming findings' (pp. 231–2) as follows:

Tactics for generating meaning

People are meaning-finders; they can make sense of the most chaotic events very quickly. Our equilibrium depends on such skills: we keep the world consistent and predictable by cognitively organizing and interpreting it. The critical question is whether the meanings found in qualitative data through the tactics outlined here are valid, repeatable,

Figure 5.3 Components of data analysis: Miles and Huberman's flow and interactive models

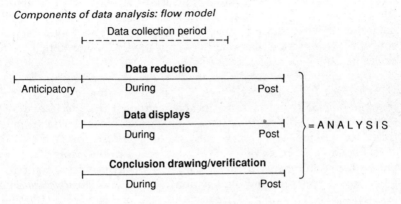

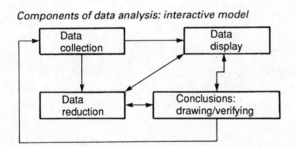

right. The following section discusses tactics for testing or confirming meanings, avoiding bias, and assuring the quality of conclusions.

Here is a quick overview of the tactics for generating meaning, numbered from 1 to 12. They are roughly arranged from the descriptive to the explanatory, and from the concrete to the more conceptual and abstract. *Counting* (tactic 1) is a familiar way to see 'what's there'. *Noting patterns, themes* (2), *seeing plausibility* (3), and *clustering* (4) helps the analyst see 'what goes with what'. *Making metaphors* (5), like the preceding four tactics, is a way to achieve more integration among diverse pieces of data. Differentiation is sometimes needed, too, as in *splitting variables* (6). We also need tactics for seeing things and their relationships more abstractly. These include *subsuming particulars into the general* (7); *factoring* (8), an analogue of a familiar quantitative technique; *noting relations between variables* (9); and *finding intervening variables* (10). Finally, how can we assemble coherent understanding of data? The tactics discussed are *building a logical chain of evidence* (11) and *making conceptual/theoretical coherence* (12).

Tactics for testing or confirming findings

The twelve tactics for confirming conclusions are numbered as before. They begin with tactics that are aimed at assuring the basic quality of the data, then move to those that check findings by various contrasts, then conclude with tactics that take a sceptical, demanding approach to emerging explanations.

Data quality can be assessed through *checking for representativeness* (1); *checking for researcher effects* (2) on the site, and vice versa; and *triangulating* (3) across data sources and methods. These checks may also involve *weighting the evidence* (4), deciding which kinds of data are most trustable. Looking at differences tells us a lot. *Contrasts/comparisons* (5), *checking the meaning of outliers* (6), and *using extreme cases* (7) are all tactics that test a conclusion about a 'pattern' by saying what it's not like. How can we really test our explanations? *Ruling out spurious relations* (8), *replicating a finding* (9), *check-out rival explanations* (10), and *looking for negative evidence* (11) are all ways of submitting our beautiful theories to the assault of brute facts, or to a race with someone else's beautiful theory. Finally, a good explanation deserves attention from the very people whose behaviour it is about – informants who supplied the original data. The tactic of *getting feedback from informants* (12) concludes our list.

Many of these tactics have been described earlier, but this economical list of tactics provides a useful overview of the techniques available to the qualitative evaluator in linking broad analytical strategies to more specific activities.

Enhancing validity in qualitative evaluation

In this final section of the chapter, I wish to bring the discussion together by looking at the analytical process in a different way, using the concept of validity as the advanced organizer. Concepts of validity and reliability are of great importance to quantitative researchers who have elaborate statistical techniques at their disposal to ensure the trustworthiness of their data. Although validity is also an important concept to the qualitative evaluator, the techniques for ensuring it are very different, not well understood and still being developed. In this discussion I want to summarize the current state of play on this topic.

Validity is usually regarded as the degree to which the evaluator has measured what he or she has set out to measure. I take a catholic view of the word 'valid'. My dictionary defines it as 'sound, defensible, well grounded . . . executed with proper formalities', and these are the general senses in which I use the term. McCormick and James (1988: 188–9) give us a more traditional definition of validity:

Researchers are expected to demonstrate that the observations they actually record and analyse, match what they purport to be recording and analysing. This is the concept of validity. . . . Validity is concerned with errors that may occur in the research process . . . the validity of a method is basically the extent to which the observations recorded are those that the researcher set out to record.

They identify six different types of validity:

1 *Face validity:* requires that a measure looks as if it measures what it purports to measure.
2 *Content validity:* requires that data produced covers all relevant subject matter.
3 *Criterion related validity:* refers to agreement between, for example, scores on a test and some other criterion such as teachers' estimates of ability.
4 *Construct validity:* measurement must reflect the construct in which researchers are interested.
5 *Internal validity:* the soundness of an explanation; whether what is interpreted as cause produces the effect.
6 *External validity:* the generalizability of results to the whole population.

This book is mainly concerned with the general notion of validity and with the threats to internal validity. Internal validity is the basic minimum without which any evaluation is uninterpretable: did the new educational programme make a difference in this specific instance? If the various threats to validity are not taken into account, then one cannot claim that one's interpretation is correct. The existence of possible sources of invalidity potentially offer plausible, rival interpretations to our findings when we do not account for them in our evaluation designs.

Campbell and Stanley (1963) carefully documented the major threats to validity. Although their monograph was written for those concerned with experimental and quasi-experimental research rather than qualitative evaluation, some of their threats to validity still apply. Although it is probably impossible to take account of each of the variables, they do serve as a useful checklist and guide to good practice. Those that cannot be accounted for should at least be recognized and, if necessary, a rival explanation discussed. A discussion of each of their variables would be redundant, but some examples may be of interest.

1 *History.* Over the time span of data collection many events occur in addition to the study's independent variable. The history factor refers to the possibility that any one of these events rather than the hypothesized independent variable might have caused observed changes in the dependent variable. For example, in the 'TVEI and Information Skills' project (Howard and Hopkins, 1988), any increase in information skills teaching may well be due to the impetus given by the introduction of GCSE rather than TVEI.
2 *Instrumentation.* Changes in the measurement process may be spuriously attributed to the dependent variable. For instance, where interviewers or

Table 5.3   Enhancing validity in qualitative evaluation (adapted from Yin, 1984: 36)

Test	Analytic technique
Construct validity (i.e. the evaluation must focus on the operational issues it purports to reflect)	<ul><li>use multiple sources of evidence</li><li>call things by their right name</li><li>establish a chain of evidence</li><li>know what you are looking for</li><li>have key informants review evaluation drafts</li><li>use tactics for verifying conclusions</li></ul>
Internal validity (i.e. the integrity of the evaluation; that what is interpreted as cause produces the effect)	<ul><li>collect data at different points in time (time series design)</li><li>seek for alternative or rival explanations</li><li>be clear and rigorous over the four stages of analysis</li><li>triangulation</li><li>use tactics for generating meaning</li></ul>
External validity (i.e. the generalizability of findings from one case to others)	<ul><li>try and collect data from more than one site</li><li>replicate the focus of evaluation during the period of the evaluation</li></ul>
Reliability (i.e. minimizing the errors and biases in a study so that another researcher could conduct the same evaluation study and arrive at the same conclusions)	<ul><li>case study protocol (see Chapter 10)</li><li>construct an audit trail</li><li>Huberman and Miles' Interactive Model of Data Analysis</li></ul>

observers become increasingly sloppy, fatigued, or more competent and experienced, results may be subtly changed. For example, the LASS project (Rudduck and Hopkins, 1984) used a large number of interviewers: did this affect the internal validity of the case records?

3 *Differential mortality.* On any occasion that non-random subsets of subjects drop out of a study, comparison of the dependent variable across groups might be accounted for by these differential 'mortality' rates rather than by actual effects of the independent variable. For example, in a series of recent TVEI pupil interviews the majority of the cohort previously interviewed were absent from school/college when we returned to interview them a year later.

Although the style of evaluation implied in this book is inevitably mainly concerned with validity, concerns about reliability should not be ignored. As we have already noted, reliability is concerned with consistency and generalizability and the use of standardized instruments. McCormick and James (1988: 188) describe it thus:

Basically reliability is concerned with *consistency* in the production of results and refers to the requirement that, at least in principle, another researcher, or the same researcher on another occasion, should be able to *replicate* the original piece of research and achieve comparable evidence or results.

In concluding this discussion, I have attempted to draw together the various analytical techniques described in this chapter and link them to particular tests of validity and reliability (see Table 5.3). This is inevitably a somewhat arbitrary exercise as the various techniques inevitably overlap from category to category. The exercise does, however, demonstrate that just because one's data is qualitative does not mean that one's results need be based on any less rigorous analysis than the more traditional quantitative approaches.

Summary

This chapter began by emphasizing the usefulness of qualitative data in the types of evaluation described in this book. A general four-stage analytical strategy based on the conventions of sociological fieldwork was then outlined. Within this broad strategy a number of specific techniques such as saturation and triangulation were described. These were complemented in the following section by a discussion of some other specific conceptual and analytic techniques. The chapter concludes with a discussion on the criteria of validity and reliability and the linking of these *desiderata* to particular analytic strategies. Although this chapter has made an excursion into some complex methodological and technical terrain, it has been a very necessary journey. As evaluators committed to development, using mainly qualitative methods, there is a double obligation to ensure that our conclusions are 'sound, defensible and well grounded'. I hope that this discussion has outlined some ways of doing that for those who are concerned with evaluating for development.

6
Evaluation roles

The contemporary role of the evaluator is not as clear cut as it used to be. The external 'evaluator as expert' role envisaged in MacDonald's autocratic, bureaucratic, democratic distinction, although still prevalent, is complemented by a wide diversity of evaluation roles that have emerged in the wake of the pressures for increased accountability over the past decade. As the question of who carries out the evaluation is crucial, this chapter is devoted to exploring some of the tensions and possibilities in that role.

In the following section I discuss some of the influences and responses to this democratization of the role of evaluator. Subsequent sections of the chapter comprise extracts from colleagues who have written and researched on this topic. Marvin Wideen presents an overview of the roles open to an evaluator. Carol FitzGibbon discusses the role of the 'local' evaluator in categorically funded curriculum projects such as TVEI; and Colin McCabe provides some advice to bureaucrats on how to choose their local evaluator. The final extract from Marilyn Leask reports on the research she has done on the emerging role of the teacher evaluator.

Perspectives on the internal/external evaluation role

When Lawrence Stenhouse (1975: 121) argued 'against the separation of developer and evaluator and in favour of integrated curriculum research', he was living in a different educational culture from our own. His world was of the large curriculum development projects, it was decentralized, and the role of the evaluator *qua* evaluator was just emerging. Now we live in a world of categoric funding, that is increasingly centralized and which contains diversity of evaluation roles. Yet, ironically, part of Stenhouse's argument, the integration of development and evaluation, is implicit in much of the current government's educational policy. Through categoric funding, curriculum development has been devolved to the school/consortia level, albeit within the framework of a national curriculum. And, similarly, the evaluation function is being devolved 'downwards' to the consortia and school because the emphasis on monitoring and evaluation is so great that it cannot be handled at the LEA or HMI level. So, largely by default the development and evaluation functions are coming together at the school level but under different circumstances than Stenhouse originally envisaged.

Despite this trend, and the increasing pressure on schools and consortia to evaluate curriculum initiatives, most of those involved in evaluating TVEI, ESG initiatives and other categorically funded projects at the local (LEA) level are often, initially at least, external to the project. Although these are usually academics from the local college or university, evaluators are increasingly being drawn from those closer to the scheme (e.g. seconded teachers). However, this statement represents more of an ideal that local evaluations can work towards, rather than typifying, a cross-initiative trend. While some local evaluations have been organized to allow for increasing responsibility from within the project, others seem to have established a fairly static framework, often involving from the outset delimited areas of responsibility for internal and external evaluators. External and internal evaluators are equally impor-tant: the former provide expertise and objectivity, the latter familiarity and understanding. These two roles are distinct yet complementary and both are necessary for effective evaluation.

Local evaluations are a very important part of the overall evaluation strategy for categorically funded and other similar initiatives. Because local evaluation is essentially formative (i.e. feeding back information to participants for the purpose of improving practice) and as each evaluation is tailored to its own scheme, it is one of the most fruitful ways of improving the quality of projects.

This argument for the importance of local evaluations needs to be considered alongside a number of problems inherent in the local evaluation approach. There are four fairly obvious problems. The first is the lack of co-ordination between local evaluators; each local evaluation is established independently and there are no other established structures for substantive communication or collaboration between local evaluators. Secondly, the range of expertise and experience of local evaluators differs widely: on the one hand, there is the seconded teacher with no previous evaluation experience and, on the other, the widely experienced 'executive evaluator' in a university. Thirdly, and as a consequence of the above, some local evaluators because of their relative inexperience in evaluation need support in designing and carrying out their evaluation. Fourthly, the implementation characteristics of many schemes have created a tendency, as in TVEI, to produce innovation 'enclaves' which, in time, have resulted in a micro-climate or culture surrounding the innovation in individual schools. For the evaluator, the predicament is obvious – either join the enclave and thus risk your evaluation being too 'cosy' or risk being ignored by the project you are trying to help. Despite the difficulties, I still remain convinced that local evaluation has a very important part to play in improving the quality of education for pupils in our schools.

Figure 6.1   Evaluation, roles and school improvement.

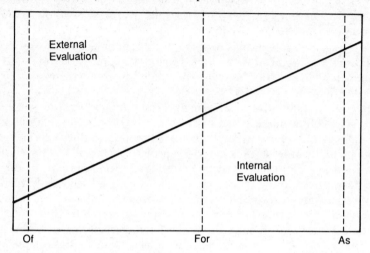

Perhaps part of the problem is a lack of clarity about the nature of the external–internal evaluation role. We have already noted the distinction between evaluation of, for and as school improvement. I have made an attempt to identify the various balances between external and internal evaluation during these different evaluation and school improvement activities in Fig. 6.1. So, for example, in evaluations of school improvement, evaluation is mainly by an external 'expert'. Those evaluations which are 'for' school improvement imply a collaborative approach where the external 'expert' may still carry out the evaluation but where his or her activity is related to formative feedback and action planning at the local level. In the third situation, 'evaluation as', the evaluators are internal to the school organization but still require some technical assistance.

Rob Fiddy and Ian Stronach (1987) talk about the importance of the erosion of internal–external evaluation roles: that over time there is no call for a division of labour, and that the essential prerequisite for participative learning is reflexivity, which makes the external 'partner-in-praxis' more important not less. Within the participative partnership, all members (whether internal or external) are both teachers and learners; all have something important to offer the dialogue. And what the external members have is 'externality' from the culture of the school; what the internal members have is 'knowledge' of internal practice. Both perspectives are vital. This I think is close to Peter Holly's (1986a) 'emerging model' of 'professional evaluation' which is collaborative, formative, illuminative, non-hierarchical and where the evaluator acts as a critical friend.

Although I find these images appealing, I am concerned that when I have seen the approach working it has been as a function of personality rather than infrastructure. What we need is a clearer indication of the conditions necessary to achieve that ideal and the means to do it. If all the groups affected by the evaluation are to be involved in formulating the questions and interpreting the answers, then a number of questions are raised (Loucks-Horsley *et al.*, 1987: 161). Whose goals for the project will be evaluated? Who decides what the data mean? What decisions will be made about using the data? Co-ordinators might want to use the information to improve the programme. DES and LEA officials might want to use the information to make global decisions. At the same time, teachers might want to use the information to help them understand the relationship between their new skills and their students' performance.

From all this a picture of the new evaluation emerges. As Colin McCabe (1987: 7) comments:

> There is still need and scope for independence, initiative, flexibility, conceptual analysis and sensitivity but for the evaluator it is possible to have a code of practice, a set of role prescriptions and even a grounded framework within which to operate, analyse and prescribe. There is more acceptance of evaluation among teachers, pupils and organisations and so more evaluation by those who learn and teach. The place of the evaluator is now more understood, but it has to be more defined now that the place of negotiation and the aims and methods of evaluation are more generally known and appreciated. The objective is no less than self-evaluation throughout education – with key but precise roles for evaluation consultants.

We are obviously still some way from this ideal, but the teacher-evaluator approach described by Marilyn Leask at the end of this chapter coupled to an explicit role for the external evaluator offers a structure that could begin to operationalize these ideas. Before we come to that model, however, we will look at some other ways in which evaluators have discussed the problem of evaluation roles.

Generic roles of the evaluator

There are many roles that evaluators are likely to play assuming they are eclectic and select generic strategies from different models as the situation dictates. Marvin Wideen (1986) identified six such roles which I have summarized as follows:

1 *The descriptive role.* A basic role the evaluator must play in every situation is that of being a describer of situations and events. He or she seeks information about the process as well as the product and about various perceptions of decisions not just those of the administrator.

2 *A communicator.* The evaluator must assume the function of one who relays information at every stage; but this role is affected both by the temporal aspects of a project and by the audience to which reporting is done.

Ultimately, failure to discharge the role of communicator destroys the purpose of developmental evaluation.

3 *The judgement role.* Some models of evaluation require a greater degree of judgement than others. The choice of design and model is in itself a judgement. Selecting data to report also requires judgement as does the way in which such data are presented.

4 *Decision making.* A consistent and significant role of the evaluator is that of decision maker and the facilitating of decision making. This is a particularly important role where the evaluator is working with a group having no clearly defined structure. To avoid the implicit kinds of decisions that lead to courses of action not sanctioned democratically, evaluators may need to probe the explicit goals and expectations of the group with whom they are working.

5 *The facilitator.* At most points in an evaluation the evaluator must play the role of a facilitator. The need for this role becomes particularly important where the 'client' attempts to implement action plans from evaluation data. Evaluation for development is essentially a group process. The evaluator's role is to facilitate that process.

6 *The provocateur.* In some situations the evaluator will be obliged to play the role of 'a devil's advocate'. Here the evaluator probes beneath the surface to reveal motives, or to find information germane to the success of a programme. The role of the provocateur can result in an improved progamme, but it can also create situations in which evaluators can easily overstep the mark and destroy their own credibility.

The main purpose of this section has been to identify the various roles of the developmental evaluator. The most effective role that an evaluator can play is that of an eclectic. From the broad spectrum of designs, the evaluator develops a conceptual framework, tempers it with an eclectic approach, moulds the endeavour to suit the situation, sprinkles it with his or her own life-style, and with luck assists in creating a better way.

The roles of the TVEI 'local' evaluator

In order to strengthen the network of local TVEI evaluators, I among others organized a series of informal conferences where we discussed issues of mutual interest. Some of these conferences resulted in books being published (Hopkins, 1986a, 1989). In one of these Carol FitzGibbon gave the following advice to TVEI local evaluators. Although her remarks were intended for TVEI evaluators, they apply equally well to others engaged in local evaluation activity (FitzGibbon, 1986: 28–30):

The foregoing can be summarised in terms of what the local evaluators should be expected to do and what kind of stance and professional conduct should be expected from them. Local evaluators should:

1 Identify those who speak for the LEA with respect to the evaluation of the TVEI project. In some cases this may be the LEA TVEI coordinator alone. In other cases there may be other officials who are maintaining a close management role, or a steering committee which must be negotiated with directly.

2 In negotiation with the LEA, the local evaluation steering group, or other body identifying issues or areas of interest, identify topics which they and the evaluators agree are important and undertake to produce information on a feasible number of these topics. (Feasibility is a function of personnel and other resources committed to the evaluation. Secondments to fellowships could amplify the resources in some instances and might be available if the LEA sees sufficient work of interest to be done by the evaluation team.) The negotiations about the topics to be examined will powerfully influence the evaluation activities and may well determine the extent to which the local evaluation is useful. These negotiations are the responsibility of both the evaluators and the LEA.

3 Provide research quality information about topics which the LEA and evaluators have agreed are important. Research quality implies that the information collected is open and as correct as possible. The sources of information are identified, documentation is complete, measures are checked for reliability and validity. Portrayals based on impressions may be informal but quantitative data are collected in ways which are systematic, open, and replicable and the raw data are retained for inspection for at least 5 years after the release of reports based on the data.

4 Exercise a guarded tongue and, in particular, scrupulously avoid chatting upwards. Social scientists suffer from a particular problem which does not afflict the physical scientist: their data, their hypotheses, indeed their entire science is a topic of general conversation. Everyone has opinions and impressions about such difficult research topics as how to measure effective teaching, what constitutes a good school, whether TVEI represents an enclave strategy, *etc.* But the social scientist must not treat these problems casually and therefore cannot deal with them in a superficial and chatty manner. Social science exists because impressions, rumours, reputations and gut feeling are not accurate guides to what is happening. Thus the casual passing along of un-considered and un-challengeable opinions is to be scrupulously avoided. The social scientist's responsible approach is to speak only on the basis of carefully considered reports.

5 Provide the LEA with regular written documents in draft form for negotiation prior to release. This negotiation involoves checking for accuracy and guarding confidentiality where desirable. In some cases it might be agreed to limit the audience for some reports, particularly reports identifying problem areas. These negative feedback reports

need to be dealt with carefully. Their purpose is to lead to resolving the problems and sometimes the reports should be held back until that is accomplished. Indeed, such negative feedback might be reported orally and taped, rather than written. The point of the tape-recording is to avoid the loss of these possible valuable reports, to help eventually to create a literature of how institutions and projects can learn from mistakes.

How to choose your evaluator

In the same volume as the previous extract, Colin McCabe looked at the other side of the local evaluator coin. Given that local evaluators cannot remain independent, 'at best they can be described as semi-detached', what risks do administrators take in appointing evaluators and what principles can they apply in their selection. In the following extract, Colin McCabe (1986a) summarizes his advice:

Before trying to pull all this together and drawing up a list of what to consider in choosing your evaluator I should like to summarise what I see as the essential problem of the evaluator's position. All too often evaluators find themselves regarded in much the same way as is a correlation co-efficient in educational measurement or, still more appositely – because expected to bring simple order to a complex set of situations and variables – the factors resulting from a factor analysis. That is, there exists a range of data and measurements of considerable complexity which any interested individual or group can observe and interpret generally or selectively. Human nature hopes and often expects that there will be a symbol – a coefficient, a set of factors, an evaluator – which will simply, significantly and authoritatively subdue, summarise and encapsulate all the available evidence. And no evaluator can do this.

So at one side of the evaluator is the total situation to be reported upon . . . made up of a complex of situations, opinions, attitudes, and changes, some measurable, some immeasurable; some expected, many not, some developing early, some going on beyond the life of the project. And in any real sense the 'total' situation is probably not known to anyone nor does it matter to anyone of the individuals involved.

At his or her other side are the clients who are funding the investigation and for whom the evaluator is working. What they think is important or of interest, the categories in which they think, the form of explanation, reasoning, or causal relationship which they find acceptable must be a major concern. The clients' list may of course not overlap greatly with the evaluator's personal list of cognitive priorities.

In the middle then are the evaluators in the typical human situation – perceiving, conducting, assessing, interpreting, reporting according to their own set of categories and priorities, trying in the interests of proper responsibility to balance the demands, often conflicting, of hard and soft processes, whether presented under the guise of objective v subjective, thinking v feeling, scientific v humanistic. And since the armoury of techniques which can be applied is wide – see any text book on assessment and evaluation – the evaluators will have their own preferred and practised technical preferences among them.

I do not suggest that much sympathy is wasted on evaluators – they know that their work is privileged and worthwhile; they want to do it. But it can be appreciated that they are asked, to change metaphors, to hold a difficult pass, in a position where they can be attacked from both sides, knowing that there are also other routes that can be taken.

So from all the foregoing we try to put together a checklist of what it is wise to expect and decide on before choosing your evaluator. The amount of money available will often be a determining factor since travel especially is expensive but this should have been settled at an earlier stage.

What you expect is that your evaluator will negotiate with you, discussing processes, techniques and principles through the life of the project. The commentary and feed-back so supplied will significantly influence development. The evaluator – or team or organisation – you invite should therefore be one with whom you feel at ease, not necessarily in complete agreement, the evaluators should bring some new perspectives, some new ideas and added ingredients to the project, but they should be people with whom the dialogue and process can be carried on easily. Part of the process may involve the evaluator in inservice work or discussions on your behalf and this may be a consideration in selection.

Before the selection is made the administrator has to decide what the evaluation is wanted or expected to look at, or question and I suggest that the main points raised have been seven in number:

1 What cannot be questioned *eg* can your own hierarchy, organisation, stance, opinion, competence be questioned?
2 Are you primarily interested in changes in teachers, pupils or organisation?
3 Are the real aims and outcomes to be professional development, system changes, or shifts in social policy?
4 Are you only interested in the attainment of predicted goals – or the actual outcomes . . . anticipated or unanticipated consequences?
5 Do you expect evidence to be objective or subjective, cognitive or affective?
6 How far are you prepared to go in applying principles of participation, co-operation, democracy, over and above those necessary to have the project accepted?
7 If politics are not to be involved – which politics do you mean?

Many of these questions may have obvious answers or be irrelevant in any individual case, very often you have to do what you can rather than what you would prefer. There remains a further point – the future development and the value of evaluation depends upon its acceptance, an appreciation of its worth and a readiness to cooperate on the part of teachers in schools as well as a willingness of pupils to be involved. Evaluation is as much an ethos, a state of mind or a set of attitudes as it is the task of an individual. The ethos has to be developed. So the dialogue, preliminary and continuing is not just a matter for administrator and evaluator.

Teacher-evaluators: the missing link?

The teacher-evaluator approach to educational evaluation combines the strengths of external professional evaluations with those of classroom action research. This role has recently been researched by Marilyn Leask (1988), and what follows is a summary of her findings.

The teacher-evaluator approach is based on small teams of teachers evaluating issues of LEA-wide importance. These teams are made up of teachers of varying status who work in different institutions. The express purpose of the work is to provide timely formative evaluation in order to influence curriculum development, but there is a secondary role to inform outside funding bodies of progress made in particular educational programmes. This approach could also be adapted for use at the school level by a supportive Head through the use of strategic timetabling and/or reallocation of resources.

The LEA evaluation framework

Crucial to the success of teacher-evaluations is the construction of a clearly defined and supportive LEA framework which provides accepted ethical guidelines, checks quality and standards of the working papers produced and ensures that findings are considered and acted upon by the appropriate groups. The LEA support structures and the team structure play a vital part in allowing teachers to work independently of LEA or school pressures.

Figure 6.2 sets out a possible framework for developing the teacher-evaluator strategy. There are three stages, each of equal importance. The first stage is the setting up of an initial planning group consisting of LEA staff and a professional evaluator to design the evaluation, and the establishment of an ethical code and procedures to be followed. The second stage involves establishing groups with three differing roles:

● an Evaluation Advisory Group which oversees the evaluation work;
● a reading panel to examine individual reports before publication for methodology/scope/relevance/clarity (the group does not have a censoring function);
● teacher-evaluator teams who plan evaluations, collect data and write the reports.

The third stage is that of discussion and use of findings.

Once the Evaluation Advisory Group accepts that an issue is to be evaluated, a team of staff interested in the area is established and given appropriate training in evaluation skills. When the group has been working for some time, it is usual for a number of members to be quite experienced and new members are drawn in.

Other key elements influencing the successful development of the approach within an LEA include:

● the 'atmosphere' in the LEA and within schools;
● the quality of training provided for teachers;
● the team structure and the personal qualities and status of the teacher-evaluators;
● the appointment of a co-ordinator;
● the role of the professional evaluator.

Benefits and problems

There are benefits on an LEA-wide level, on an institutional level, and on an individual level for both pupils and teachers. The LEA and institution gain with the building up of expertise among teaching staff, the creation of a more reflective profession, the welding of a sense of common purpose across the LEA and a growth in evaluation as teacher-evaluators apply their skills in other areas. Channels of communication within the LEA are improved as the views and experiences of those involved in curriculum change (from pupils to heads to administrators) are reported. Aspects of the day-to-day functioning of schools and classrooms and aspects of administrators' decisions can be communicated with staff at all levels of the LEA. This type of information has hitherto not been easily exchanged.

The evaluations are a tool for improving the curriculum and management structures. The findings provide an extra dimension to decision making and reports depersonalize issues so that discussion is not hampered by personality conflicts. There is a cross-fertilization of ideas between institutions, something that staff find particularly stimulating and enjoyable. Students and staff are given a voice through qualitative evaluation which can be heard at all levels.

Staff gain through the personal and career development afforded by the acquisition and use of new skills. Many staff already have evaluation expertise and experience gained through their initial training or through subsequent courses, which is often not utilized.

As with any evaluation, there are difficulties to be faced. The adherence to an ethical code eliminates the most obvious difficulties relating to confidentiality and use of data. Staff wariness needs to be anticipated and dealt with as does the potential non-use of reports. Discussion of the findings must be built in as part of the original evaluation design if the evaluations are to be effective. The reports should be presented as working documents providing a basis for change rather than as statements of fact. The problem of divided loyalties

Figure 6.2 Teachers as evaluators: LEA evaluation framework.

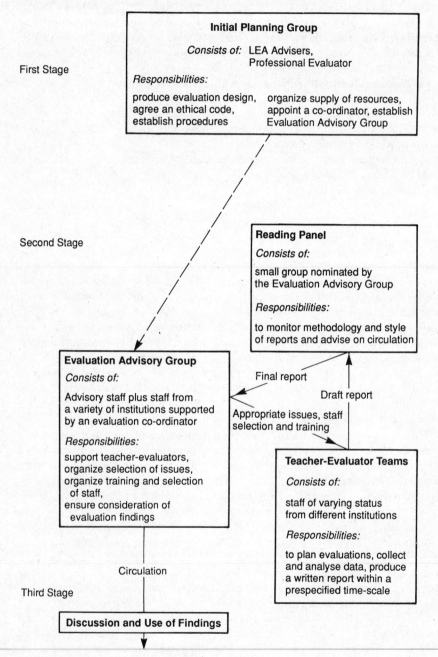

First Stage

Initial Planning Group

Consists of: LEA Advisers,
Professional Evaluator

Responsibilities:

produce evaluation design,
agree an ethical code,
establish procedures

organize supply of resources,
appoint a co-ordinator, establish
Evaluation Advisory Group

Second Stage

Reading Panel

Consists of:

small group nominated by
the Evaluation Advisory Group

Responsibilities:

to monitor methodology and style
of reports and advise on circulation

Evaluation Advisory Group

Consists of:

Advisory staff plus staff from
a variety of institutions supported
by an evaluation co-ordinator

Responsibilities:

support teacher-evaluators,
organize selection of issues,
organize training and selection
of staff,
ensure consideration of
evaluation findings

Final report

Draft report

Appropriate issues, staff
selection and training

Teacher-Evaluator Teams

Consists of:

staff of varying status
from different institutions

Responsibilities:

to plan evaluations, collect
and analyse data, produce
a written report within a
prespecified time-scale

Circulation

Third Stage

Discussion and Use of Findings

arises for staff, and the procedures and training for coping with this needs to be planned at the outset.

Resource provision must be made in the form of tape-recorders, printing facilities and clerical support. The other most important resource is time – evaluation is time-consuming. The time commitment must be realistic and time made available for the work where possible, e.g. non-teaching periods kept free and supply provided.

The possibility that teacher-evaluators may avoid difficult issues needs to be recognized and the expertise and wider perspective of the professional needs to be used together with the inside knowledge of practitioners in making decisions about appropriate issues for investigation. Clearly, the evaluations need to be responsive to audience need and procedures should be established to check the relevance of issues being considered.

In conclusion

The teacher-evaluator approach has the potential for providing timely, effective and relevant evaluation to inform decision making and influence practice. It places the power of evaluation in the hands of the teachers to use as a tool for improving education. The implementation of the National Curriculum, the change to Local Management of Schools and the introduction of appraisal of teachers are all initiatives which require teachers to justify their methods and actions – the teacher-evaluator approach develops the professional skills which teachers must possess if they are to respond to the challenges faced by education in the 1990s.

Summary

There are many aspects to the role of evaluator, as is seen by the various contributions to this chapter. The local (i.e. LEA) evaluator has been the main focus of discussion and most of the debate has been around the internal–external dimension. As I mentioned at the beginning of the chapter, we need more knowledge of the conditions necessary to support the ideal models suggested by a number of commentators. The infrastructure described by Marilyn Leask in the previous section is an example of an LEA which is tackling the problem seriously and doing something about it.

Section III
Developmental approaches

7

Evaluating classrooms, departments and cross-curricular initiatives

It is impossible to present in one short chapter a description of how to evaluate classrooms, departments and cross-curricular initiatives. What I intend to do instead is first to review briefly an approach to the evaluation of both classrooms and departments which reflects the bias of the book. I will then present a more extended discussion of a specific and pragmatic approach to evaluating cross-curricular initiatives that subsumes classrooms and departments and leads towards a multi-level approach to whole-school evaluation. This strategy helps me to do two other things. First, it avoids an extended discussion of curriculum evaluation, which although intellectually interesting, would certainly be counterproductive because such discussions tend towards the abstract and theoretical when not grounded in specific educational contexts. Secondly, because I do want to be practical and to focus on specific educational contexts, such a strategy allows me to describe approaches that I am already using in my work with schools, consortia and LEAs and to relate them to such current issues as performance indicators and school development plans.

Classrooms

I have already discussed some approaches to the evaluation of classrooms, in particular systematic classroom observation. Systematic classroom observation involves the use of standardized coding instruments such as FIAC. This approach lies within a positivistic research tradition that tends to lead away from rather than into the classroom.

If one takes an evaluation for development approach then I am far more enthusiastic about an approach to classroom evaluation that utilizes the methodologies commonly associated with 'action research'. I describe these techniques in some detail elsewhere (Hopkins, 1985a) and will therefore not

Figure 7.1   Action research in action (from Kemmis and McTaggart, 1981: 11).

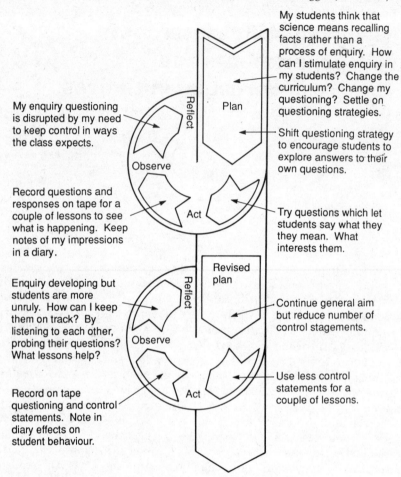

My students think that science means recalling facts rather than a process of enquiry. How can I stimulate enquiry in my students? Change the curriculum? Change my questioning? Settle on questioning strategies.

Shift questioning strategy to encourage students to explore answers to their own questions.

My enquiry questioning is disrupted by my need to keep control in ways the class expects.

Record questions and responses on tape for a couple of lessons to see what is happening. Keep notes of my impressions in a diary.

Try questions which let students say what they they mean. What interests them.

Enquiry developing but students are more unruly. How can I keep them on track? By listening to each other, probing their questions? What lessons help?

Continue general aim but reduce number of control stagements.

Record on tape questioning and control statements. Note in diary effects on student behaviour.

Use less control statements for a couple of lessons.

repeat them here. I define classroom research as an act undertaken by teachers either to improve their own or a colleague's teaching or to test the assumptions of educational theory in practice. Classroom research generates hypotheses about teaching from the experience of teaching, and encourages teachers to use this research to make their teaching more effective. The vision is of teachers who have extended their role to include critical reflection upon their craft with the aim of improving it. I describe the range of skills and techniques that are part of a classroom action research repertoire and argue that they need also to become subject to the teachers' professional judgement (Hopkins, 1985a).

In order to give an idea of the approach, Fig. 7.1 contains an example of 'action research in action' using the action research spiral developed by Stephen Kemmis and discussed in some detail in Kemmis and McTaggart

(1981). Another way of summarizing the action research approach to classroom evaluation is through the example of Jane:

> As part of the requirements for a course I taught on the 'Analysis of Teaching', Jane made a videotape of herself experimenting with various models of teaching. After reviewing the videotape, Jane felt that among other observations she had been rather abrupt in her questioning technique and had given the pupils little time to formulate responses to her questions. I suggested to Jane that she explore this observation a little further and ascertain whether this was a consistent behaviour or an aberration. She did this by taking a further videotape of her teaching, and by asking a colleague to observe her teaching. Jane also developed a short questionnaire on her questioning technique, which she administered to her pupils and subsequently analysed. As a result of this endeavour, Jane realized that she did in fact interject very quickly after asking a question, and quite often answered her own questions. All well and good, Jane thought, but what does this mean? Thinking that recent research on teaching might help, Jane did some reading and came across an article on think-time. The article reviewed a number of studies on the relationship between the amount of time that elapsed after questioning and the quality of pupil response. Jane felt that she was not allowing her pupils enough time to think after she had asked a question to the detriment perhaps of their level of cognitive functioning. So she developed a plan to change and monitor her questioning technique. It took Jane some six months to complete these tasks (teaching is a time consuming job!), but there was no pressure on her to complete the research. In fact, the longer time frame allowed for more valid data, and she was pleased with the results. Not only did she find evidence of higher level repsonses from her pupils, but also, by involving them in the evaluation of her teaching, the climate of her class was enhanced by the mutual and overt commitment of both teacher and pupils to the learning process.

Departments, faculties and other teaching groups

I make mention of departments, faculties and other teaching units because of the importance that the working group has for quality in education. By 'working group', I simply mean a group of teachers collaborating within the same or similar curriculum area. It is through the working group, irrespective of its size, formality or phase of the school, that teaching is most effectively delivered. And it is this group that has the most impact on developing the curriculum and evaluating its effectiveness. Although much of the following section applies to departmental evaluation, I felt it important to stress the important role that the working group plays in curriculum development and evaluation. The principles apply equally therefore to groups of colleagues working together in primary schools.

The importance of this collaborative role has also been recognized by others engaged in developmental evaluation. In the next chapter I discuss whole-school evaluation and describe in some detail the GRIDS approach. The second phase of the GRIDS project (Abbott *et al.*, 1988) has made a particular study of self-evaluation in secondary school departments. The method could also be adopted for use by other groups of teachers, e.g. those concerned with the pastoral system of a school, or with special educational needs. In the GRIDS handbook, *Reviewing School Departments* (Birchenough *et al.*, 1989), the overall approach to departmental review is described in this way:

> A decision to review the work of a department could arise in several ways as a result of: the department's own initiative; a GRIDS whole school initial review; a senior management initiative; or an LEA initiative.
>
> However it arises, the kind of review which is described in this booklet is focused on the work of a single department and is carried out mainly by members of the departmental team. If a review of a department is not undertaken as part of a wider review of a school's work, particular care will be needed to relate the departmental review to the work of other groups in the school.
>
> In effect the approach recommended here is to use the five stages of the GRIDS method for departmental review. The idea, therefore, is to carry out a 'mini-GRIDS' review and development. This means that there will be some changes in the details of the procedures in the handbook. It also means using a new survey sheet, because the original one is suitable for a whole school review and was not designed for departmental review.

Although there are other approaches to departmental evaluation, I consider the GRIDS method to be extremely well suited to the type of developmental evaluation discussed in this book.

A developmental evaluation strategy

In this section I outline a simple but systematic approach to evaluation that can be used by consortia, colleges, schools and their departments or faculties involved in cross-curriculum initiatives such as TVEI Extension. (Although for ease of expression I refer only to schools in what follows, the principles apply equally to colleges.) The *raison d'être* for this evaluation process is again development, to help improve the teaching–learning process in the classroom. In order to do this, the evaluation process needs to be linked to school development plans, assist in identifying priorities and targets, establish criteria for success and provide feedback on progress which then contributes to a further cycle of development work.

The basis for this approach is found in the TVEI local evaluation framework (Hopkins, 1988a). The main components of the framework (described in detail in Chapter 10), are the three cells associated with policy (P), evaluation (E) and the formative process (F). The development process moves from policy formation and implementation, to evaluation, to formative discussion, which

Figure 7.2 Exploding the 'E' cell.

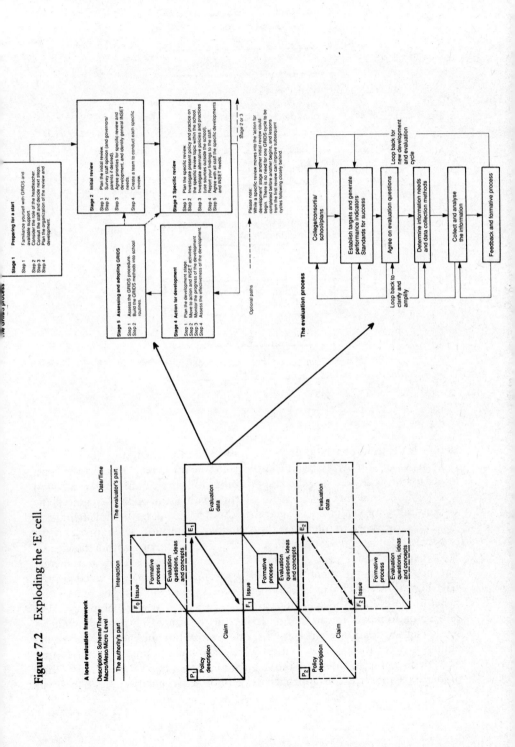

Figure 7.3   The evaluation process.

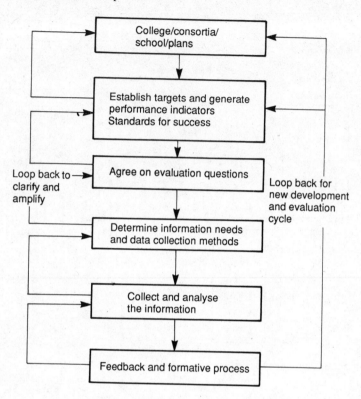

in turn leads to improved policy formation and implementation and another cycle of evaluation. Although the initial policy position may be set by the LEA, in discussion with schools, the responsibility for curriculum implementation lies at the school level. The logic of this evaluation approach places the responsibility for evaluation also at the school level, but both implementation and evaluation need to interact if the formative or developmental process is to be successful. The main concern here is the activity occurring within the 'E' cell. If we 'explode' the 'E' cell as in Fig. 7.2, we discover two major components. The first is a commitment to school development as characterized by the GRIDS problem solving cycle and the second is the evaluation process.

Before describing the specific evaluation process, I need to emphasize the self-evaluation assumption that underlies the approach. This commitment to school self-evaluation contrasts with other more bureaucratic and account-ability-oriented forms of evaluation which, although popular, do not contri-bute much to improvements at the classroom level. In Fig. 7.2, I use the GRIDS model to symbolize the approach to school self-evaluation. As shown in

Chapter 8, GRIDS provides a well-documented and well-known model for problem solving that is adaptable to a range of school development situations.

The evaluation process, as seen in Fig. 7.3, follows a linear sequence that starts with the school development plan, from which priorities and targets are derived with associated criteria or performance indicators. Evaluation questions that follow from these targets and indicators are established and they in turn give rise to certain information needs that have data collection implications. Once this information has been collected and analysed it is fed back into the formative process which leads to further development and another evaluation cycle.

This process has a number of important features. The first is that it assists with implementation and development because the establishment of targets and criteria specifies, at the outset, the development process. Secondly, it establishes a logical chain of action that relates aims to targets to evaluation questions and to particular information sources. In other words, evaluation data are specifically related through the evaluation questions to curriculum aims. Thirdly, the process is formative and cyclical. The evaluation report feeds into the formative process that results in a revision of the development plan and a new cycle of evaluation. Fourthly, although the process is represented in the diagram in a linear and sequential fashion it is in practice a lot messier than that! Once the evaluation process is underway, departmental groups work at different speeds as they intermingle their development and evaluation activities. On a more formal level, development plans are normally reviewed annually, but they represent only the tip of the iceberg.

Let us now look at each of the stages of the process in a little more detail.

The school development plan provides the key to this evaluation process. In Fig. 7.4 I have attempted to sketch out the links between local and national curriculum aims, development plans, performance indicators and school evaluation. The school development plan is derived from national LEA, consortia and school TVEI aims, and contains a series of curriculum objectives at the consortia, school, departmental and individual teacher level. These objectives are then operationalized for year 1 and more loosely defined for the following 2 years. The curriculum objectives for year 1 are translated into a series of performance indicators which become a blueprint for curriculum development and monitoring. This blueprint is then subject to evaluation by the school and the whole process is monitored by the Inspectorate.

A scheme for translating objectives into a curriculum blueprint is shown in Table 7.1. The issue or target is the area of interest and the performance indicators are the key components and subsequent sub-divisions. An example is given of how a target, say pupil-centred learning, is translated into a series of key components or performance indicators which themselves are amenable to further specification in terms of quality (i.e. how well) rather than quantity (i.e. how many). It is also important to give some indication of anticipated pupil outcomes. These four components will most probably remain constant across schools and departments as they are content-specific. What will be different are the staff actions, the time lines, the expectations that a school or department

Figure 7.4   Development plans, targets and performance indicators.

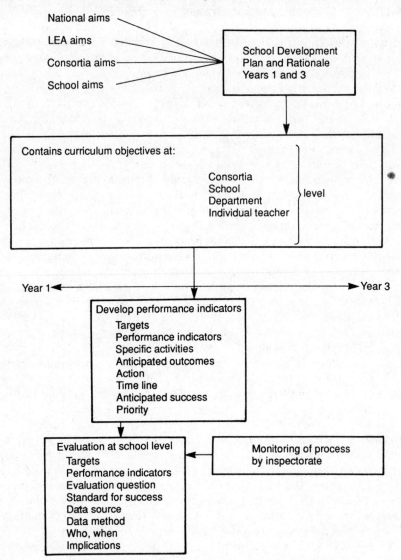

may have of their progress, and the priority that they give to this particular objective. These components of the figure are all context-specific.

Evaluation questions may be of a more general nature and relate to a wide variety of initiatives, for example:

● To what extent have the aims been met?

Table 7.1 Developmental performance indicators

| Issue or theme | Performance indicators | | Anticipated outcomes, i.e. what do you want to see happening? | Action and by whom? | Deadlines | Realistic anticipated success given anticipated starting point | LEA, school/department priority |
	Key components	Sub-division of key components					
Pupil-centred learning	● Group learning ● Research skills ● Problem-solving activities ● Reporting skills ● Responsibility for own learning ● Organization ● Teaching/learning styles, etc.	*For group learning, it could be quality of:* ● pupil–pupil cooperation ● listening skills ● communication ● research skills ● consensus of topics ● negotiation, etc.	● depth of study ● use of different resources ● different ways of displaying learning	Modules $x + y$ in 4th year TVEI(E) to use group learning as main teaching method. Staff involved in programme to take responsibility	Sept./Oct. half-term	No background of pupil-centred learning and, therefore, progress may be slow	Very high

Some teachers may find it helpful to shift this column here

- How effective has the programme been and what was its quality?
- Was it worth the money?
- Who was involved?
- Were the content, methods and balance appropriate?
- How effective was it in meeting training needs?
- Did it fulfil expectations?
- What effects has it had on practice, e.g. teaching and learning?

The development of performance indicators, however, provides a basis for more specific evaluation questions. The evaluation questions are also informed by the standards for success or the criteria used to assess performance. A criteria describes a desired state of affairs and a standard which should be achieved. A criterion:

1 Makes it clear what is desired.
2 Implies the necessary changes.
3 Points to evidence which will be needed to show success.

It is in this sense that 'standards for success' are used in the worksheet. Using this approach to develop performance indicators allows for more systematic curriculum development as well as providing a basis for evaluation.

The evaluation worksheet shown in Table 7.2 gives an indication of how these questions are generated and related to subsequent evaluation activities. I have completed the worksheet using a simplistic and hypothetical example based on the example in Table 7.1. The performance indicators obviously provide the context for the evaluation question and will vary from situation to situation. All of the changes identified in Chapter 3 (i.e. changes in teacher knowledge, skills, attitudes, the schools organizational capacity and student performance) will be important at some stage in the evaluation process. Similarly, the data collection method (see Chapter 4) needs to be matched to the question asked.

It is difficult and time-consuming enough to conduct an evaluation, but all this effort is wasted unless it is used in and assists the development process. The first step is to present or feedback the results of the evaluation in an accessible form. The basic rule is that the information should be presented in a positive rather than a negative way. This knowledge is the vital ingredient in the formative process and therefore needs to be framed as strategically and helpfully as possible.

The formative process can take a number of forms but three may be helpfully distinguished. The first is where a department or group of teachers discovers through doing its evaluation work that their course materials are not sufficiently explicit and almost immediately revise them in the light of the data they are gathering. The evaluation has in this instance a direct influence on the teaching–learning process. This informal process is very common and a good example of how evaluation can be integrated into the normal rhythm of a school's curriculum development.

Table 7.2 Evaluation worksheet

Issue or theme	Performance indicator	Evaluation questions	Standards for success	Information sources	Collection method	Responsibility Who?	Time line When?	Implications for action
Pupil-centred learning	Group learning	e.g. What is the extent and quality of pupil–pupil cooperation	(i) pupils cooperate during X module	Student behaviour	Observation schedule	Teacher		
			(ii) group learning is a more effective means of learning X	Teacher opinion	Interview teacher	School TVEI co-ordinator	End of module	Do results meet standards for success?
				Student opinion	Student questionnaire	School TVEI co-ordinator	End of module	If not, what should be done in curriculum and Staff Development terms?
				Evidence from project work	Teacher's report on projects	School TVEI co-ordinator	End of module	→ Formative process

A second and more formal type of formative process occurs each year when the school development plan is revised in the light of the current evaluation. This discussion and revision sets the pattern for the next school year and will affect timetabling, option choices, staff development plans, teaching assignments, and so on. Through these structures the teaching–learning process will also be affected.

A third form of formative process is where the school management team discuss the evaluation with the local inspectorate or external evaluation consultant. The inspectorate will be concerned to monitor the school's development and to make certain that it is in line with national and local priorities. The evaluation consultant's questions are normally of a different order to practitioners' questions, which tend to be related to the day-to-day activities of the project. These questions, or 'sensitizing concepts', are usually to do with trends or ideas that transcend individual classroom concerns and relate to the wider implications of the scheme. Obviously, these different order questions need to promote dialogue if an effective formative process is to occur.

A further note on performance indicators and school development plans

Performance indicators are currently a vogue concept which are often regarded as a bureaucratic device with a quantitative and accountability bias. This approach contrasts with my own interest in linking performance indicators to strategies for school improvement. In the previous section, I tried to outline an evaluation approach that links performance indicators to school development through a mechanism such as a school development plan. The concept of a school development plan with the school setting its own priorities within the context of national and local aims allows for a great degree of autonomy in professional matters. Such a combination of strategies offers, I believe, a great potential for integrating a variety of school improvement initiatives. If performance indicators can assume a more qualitative nature, are based on targets identified in school development plans and are subject to ongoing evaluation at the school level, monitored by the inspectorate, then we have a blueprint for bringing together a number of previously disparate areas of activity that could have a powerful impact on school development. This is because such a focus operates at a number of different organizational, cultural and curriculum levels within the school at the same time.

Elsewhere, Hopkins and Leask (1989) have defined performance indicators as:

A statement against which achievement in an area or activity can be assessed; they are also useful for setting goals and clarifying objectives. For some performance indicators, a brief statement is sufficient; for others, the statement should be more specific and refer to supplementary processes which would give a measure of depth, quality, and/or commitment in the particular area. In our view there is a place for both quantitative and qualitative indicators. For the purposes of school improvement performance indicators should reflect a synthesis of LEA, National and local aims and be constructed in such a way as to provide signposts for development.

We should also have added that ideally such indicators should be negotiated at the school–LEA interface. This process-oriented approach to performance indicators involves the school and LEA in a complex but eventually very productive developmental relationship.

Despite the national prominence given to quantitative performance indicators, a number of LEAs working with us on the evaluation of TVEI(E) are piloting this change-oriented approach to performance indicators. An example of this is provided by the following summary of recommendations that describes the approaches of one of these LEAs:

1 Performance indicators should be based upon the one-year plans of individual schools and colleges.
2 They should be viewed as an integral part of school and college evaluation procedures.
3 There should be an emphasis on qualitative indicators rather than on numerical measures.
4 Indicators should be established in areas of a cross-curricular nature.
5 A set of common indicators should be used in each cross-curricular issue together with area-specific indicators and appropriate statistical indicators.
6 Performance indicators should focus on:
   (a) those concerned with *enabling or facilitating* developments;
   (b) those concerned with the *process* by which change occurs in practice.

Performance indicators by themselves, however, are not likely to affect school development. A more powerful organizing concept is the school development plan which is discussed in Chapter 12. The concept and potential of school development plans themselves are not at present well developed, but given the impetus of the National Curriculum and TVEI extension, could provide an influential vehicle for school improvement.

The strategy in action: cross-curricular initiatives

It may be helpful to provide a few examples of how this stategy works. These examples are taken from some recent evaluation work and also illustrate the different approaches taken by internal and external evaluators.

The first example is summarized in Table 7.3 and involves profiling. In this case, I was asked as an external evaluator to report on the status of, and progress with, profiling in a TVEI consortia of four schools. The same approach was used for each school and a composite report produced for the LEA TVEI co-ordinator. Informal feedback was also given to the Heads and

Table 7.3 Evaluating profiling

Issue or theme	Performance indicator	Evaluation questions	Evidence of success	Information sources	Collection method	Responsibility Who?	Time line When?	Implications for action
Profiling	(i) Core skill: competency statements	How representative are they of the received curriculum?	Competency statements represent received curriculum	Profiling document and curriculum statements	Document analysis	In this case it was an external evaluator	Two days field-work in autumn term	External evaluator feeds back report to LEA co-ordinator (action slow to materialize)
				Teacher opinion	Interview			
	(ii) Formative process	Does it happen?	Students and staff feel comfortable with process and report positively on it	Teachers	Interview			
				Students	Interview			

TVEI co-ordinators in the schools involved. It was decided to focus on two indicators – core statements and the formative process. One was suggested by the TVEI co-ordinator, the other by myself; both are key aspects of successful profiling. The evaluation questions, criteria, information sources and data collection method are self-explanatory and were similarly negotiated. I tried to be as economical of time as possible and data collection took the equivalent of 2 days for the four schools. In this case all the activities could have been carried out by an internal evaluator. The report to the LEA co-ordinator had little impact on the schools, most probably because it had been commissioned by him not by the heads: a predictable and common problem.

The second example concerns Technology Across the Curriculum (TAC) and is summarized in Table 7.4. In this case I was asked by the LEA to assess the ability of two (representative) schools to deliver 10% technology across the curriculum. I took as the 'performance indicators' the well-developed LEA definition of the TAC process, and as the evaluation question the brief that they gave me. I purposely set no criteria for success and relied solely on the LEA's definition of TAC and the original question. I interviewed the LEA officers and school senior management team, sent a one-page open-ended questionnaire to each of the teachers (see Table 4.3), and conducted classroom observation with half of the teachers involved in TAC. The LEA team also did an audited survey of curriculum delivery. This took a total of 12 days, including write-up and two fairly brief feedback sessions. I concluded that the schools were able to deliver 10% TAC but also pointed to a series of organizational factors that could improve delivery. The first draft of the report was not well received by the schools: some defensiveness on their part, some sloppy phrasing on mine. I negotiated the final draft with the senior management team and LEA quite amicably. I do not know what if anything happened as a result.

Despite the short time line and some problems with feedback this was a fairly thorough if limited example of condensed evaluation. In this case that approach could not be replicated easily or appropriately by an internal evaluator. The bottom half of Table 7.4 describes how I would suggest an internal evaluator should approach the task. There would be three main differences. First, and assuming that the 'school' wanted the evaluation, the question 'are we delivering . . .' is sufficiently relevant and personal for the school to take it seriously and act on the results. Secondly, the school has in-built criteria, i.e. the participating department's expectations. If these are not thought through, then they should be, and the evaluation is best delayed until they are developed. The third difference is the information source and data collection method. Although the teachers remain as a source of information, classroom observation could prove problematic. Peer observation as a professional development activity based on the department's own criteria is a more positive approach that fits the twin goals of evaluation and development. An internal evaluator would also have more access to and time for monitoring student performance.

A final example is shown in Table 7.5. It concerns a whole-school approach to multicultural education and illustrates how evaluation for development can

Table 7.4 Evaluating Technology Across the Curriculum (TAC)

	Issue or theme	Performance indicators	Evaluation question	Evidence of success	Information source	Collection method	Responsibility Who?	Time line When?	Implications for action
External evaluation	TAC	LEA definition of TAC	Are the schools able to deliver 10% TAC across the curriculum?	No criteria established initially except 10% TAC	LEA officers; Senior management team in school; Teacher's opinion behaviour; Curriculum analysis	Interview; Questionnaire Classroom observation Audited survey	External	c. 12 days (including writing the report and feedback)	Yes, but?
Internal evaluation	TAC	LEA definition of TAC	Are we delivering 10% TAC across the curriculum?	Criteria established by subject departments or faculties	Teacher's opinion behaviour; Student's attitude outcomes	Questionnaire Peer observation; Interviews, questionnaire Analysis of project work	Internal	Internal evaluator feeds information back to staff on INSET day which is also used for planning future development	

Table 7.5 Evaluating multicultural education

Issue or theme	Performance indicators	Evaluation question	Evidence of success	Information source	Collection method	Responsibility Who?	Time line When?	Implications for action
Multicultural education (school policy)	School policy	Is it working?	?	Teachers	Questionnaire (1 × A4)	Deputy Head	Over half a term	Feedback followed by INSET day and action plan
Multicultural education (school action plan)	Aspects of INSET action plan (a) (b) (c)	→ → →	Related to individual aspects of plan	Teachers Students Community	Interview Questionnaire	Deputy Head	Following term	Further discussion at staff meeting
Multicultural education (Department or work group)	Humanities curriculum unit X Teaching method Y	How well?	Negotiated in department	Teachers Students	Interview Observation Questionnaire	Work group leader	During implementation of unit	Feed results back to staff
Multicultural education (Teacher)	Principles of multicultural education checklist	Do I do this?	Standards Personal	Teachers	Self-monitoring	Individual teachers	Following and subsequent terms	Action research

assume a different focus at different levels of the school. The first step is for the school to evaluate the effectiveness of its policy. If it does not have one then it should not proceed with evaluation but develop one instead. Once it is in place evaluation can begin. The question is simple – does it work? No criteria other than the policy is implied. The teachers are the source of information and a one-page questionnaire is the data collection method. This should serve to give sufficient diagnostic information for feedback to staff, and on which to base an INSET day. The outcome of this should hopefully be a school-wide commitment (at some level) to multicultural education and an agreed action plan. If it is not possible to provide rapid feedback or have a follow-up INSET day, then the evaluation activity is probably not worth initiating.

Certain activities should follow on from the action plan which can be evaluated on a school-wide basis, e.g. eradicating racist policies and practices, encouraging more multi-ethnic discussion (e.g. posters and displays throughout the school), and holding more community meetings that celebrate cultural diversity. At one level these types of activities are fairly easily monitored if not evaluated. Specific indicators of progress should be part of the action plan and the community should also be involved. Data collection and subsequent action depends on circumstances.

It is more than likely that, as a result of the INSET day, a department or group of teachers would decide to develop a module or unit that had a specific multicultural focus both in terms of content and teaching method. This module would therefore be evaluated at departmental level and the results of the experience fed back to staff. This then may encourage other departments to develop similar units.

Finally, at an individual level, all staff should ideally be involved in multicultural education. It may be that a working group have devised a 'multicultural checklist for teachers' that could form the basis for voluntary self-monitoring at regular intervals. If all staff were encouraged to do this, then it may be that some staff would wish to take it further and form an action research group that focused initially on multicultural education, but could over time look at other cross-curricular initiatives.

Summary

This chapter has hopefully served to illustrate a strategy that combines evaluation and development, and that is *au fait* with current developments and practicable despite all the other demands on time. The strategy itself links monitoring and evaluation to cross-curricular initiatives at a variety of levels within the school. If a school decides to adopt this or a similar approach it should not initially be too ambitious. Evaluation topics should be carefully prioritized according to the principle 'start small, think big'. As far as possible they should also fit into the rhythm of the school's ongoing activities. It is also a good idea to use such a strategic approach to evaluation and development to highlight common factors in the multiple changes currently facing schools (teaching methods that focus on the pupil and are more experiential in approach are a good example). This strategy for evaluating cross-curricular developments is only one aspect of whole-school evaluation. In the following chapter a series of other approaches that are more organizational in character are discussed.

8
Whole-school evaluation

The focus of this chapter is whole-school evaluation, school self-evaluation or school-based review. These are a set of synonyms which refer to a school level evaluation process that focuses on the school's curriculum and organization. These terms are used interchangeably in this chapter. Much of the school self-evaluation activity in the UK in the early 1980s was undertaken for accountability purposes, as is the school accreditation process in the USA. But whole-school review can also have a school development purpose, and three influences on the approaches to school evaluation as a school improvement strategy are discussed here. The first is the work of the OECD-sponsored International School Improvement Project, known by its acronym ISIP (Hopkins, 1987a). The second is the GRIDS project funded by the Schools Council and latterly the SCDC (McMahon *et al.*, 1984; Abbott *et al.*, 1988). The third is the Institutional Development Programme (IDP) developed by IMTEC, the Norwegian-based educational consultants and organized in the UK by the NFER (Dalin and Rust, 1983). The description of these three methods is followed by a brief review of some other popular approaches to whole-school evaluation and the chapter concludes with some advice for practitioners on how to engage in the process.

School-based review

School-based review (SBR) is a diagnostic activity undertaken by a school staff as the first step in a school or departmental improvement process. The concept of SBR has been developed, refined and popularized over the past 4 years by the members of the Area One group of the International School Improvement Project (ISIP). Within the International School Improvement Project, school-based review is regarded as a necessary but not sufficient condition for school improvement. For example, Van Velzen (quoted in Hopkins, 1985b) originally defined SBR as:

> . . . a systematic inspection (description and analysis) by a school, a sub-system or an individual (teacher, school leader) of the actual functioning of the school. . . . In ISIP we consider (frequent) diagnosis as a vital and important activity, if for only one reason: it should always be the first step in a systematic school improvement process to gather diagnostic information in order to improve the functioning of the school.

The implications of the definition are clear: SBR is a school-based diagnostic activity initiated for school development purposes. In summary, SBR can be said to have at least six characteristics:

1 It is a systematic process, not simply reflection.
2 Its short-term goal is to obtain valid information about a school's or department's condition, functions, purposes and products (effectiveness).
3 The review leads to action on an aspect of the school's organization or curriculum.
4 It is a group activity that involves participants in a collegial process.
5 Optimally the process is 'owned' by the school or sub-system.
6 Its purpose is school improvement/development and its aspiration is to progress towards the ideal goal of the 'problem-solving' or 'relatively autonomous' school.

One of the lessons learned from the work on SBR during ISIP is that it is difficult to ensure that development results from review. In an attempt to bridge the gap between review and development, Robert Bollen and I produced a matrix (Fig. 8.1) to assist in the execution of SBR efforts (Bollen and Hopkins, 1987). One of the key elements in the practice of SBR is the successful linking of review to development. To achieve this, a clear perception of process and role is required. The matrix arrangement identifies the major roles involved in SBR, the main components of the SBR process and defines the relationship between them. The matrix is a conceptual framework for thinking about SBR, a planning and evaluation tool for doing SBR, and provides a basis for dialogue with practitioners.

As the idea of the matrix developed, it became apparent that the 'roles and functions' axis, i.e. those involved in the SBR process and performing specific functions, could contain an ever-increasing list of people. It also became apparent that the 'process of SBR' axis was in fact more than that, because it constituted a generic school improvement strategy. When the two were fitted together, a myriad of interactions, encapsulated in cells, were produced.

In the original matrix the horizontal axis represented the significant persons and groups involved in SBR, viz. pupils, teachers, promoted teachers, internal change agents, school leaders, external support, local education authorities, inspectors, central education authorities, and the environment. On revision, it

Figure 8.1　Process and roles in SBR: A matrix.

Process \ Role	Subject to review	Doing the review	Managing the review	Supporting the review	Controlling the review	Influencing the review
START CONDITION – past experience, history						
PREPARATION (READINESS) PHASE: – Initiation						
– Negotiation over –						
• participation						
• control						
• training						
– Decision to proceed						
– Training for SBR						
REVIEW (INITIAL) PHASE: – Planning for review						
– Decision on instrumentation						
– Data gathering and analysis						
– Reporting and discussion of findings						
– Decision to proceed						
REVIEW (SPECIFIC) PHASE: – Setting priorities						
– Planning for review						
– Mobilization of resources/expertise						
– Training for the review process						
– Gathering information						
– Validating conclusions						
– Feedback and evaluation						
– Decision to proceed						
DEVELOPMENT PHASE: – Establishing policy						
– Planning for implementation						
– Training (INSET) for implementation						
– Implementation of policy with particular reference to:–						
• school organization						
• materials						
• teaching style						
• knowledge utilization						
• acceptance of change						
– Monitoring and evaluation						
INSTITUTIONALIZATION PHASE: – Monitoring of action						
– Utilization of SBR process in other areas of curriculum and school organization						
– Development of problem solving capacity as an organizational norm within the school						

was found that the list of actors had expanded so much that it became unwieldy. Consequently, we decided to focus on role (i.e. the part to be played) and the function (i.e. the work involved) rather than on particular individuals and identified the following roles in the SBR process. Those who are:

● subject to review;
● doing the review;
● managing the review;
● supporting the review;
● controlling the review; and
● influencing the review.

The vertical axis represents the SBR process and it is divided into five major phases: Preparation, Review (Initial), Review (Specific), Development and Institutionalization. Preceding the preparation phase, however, are the start conditions. These are the past experiences or history of the school, its organizational climate, its predispositions that determine whether or not it does actually engage in review, and, if so, how much preparation is required to bring it to a state of readiness.

The *preparation* phase refers to those activities that ensure readiness for the review process. These include the initiation of the review, the negotiations over participation, control and training. Then the eventual decision to proceed (or not) with the review is taken. If this decision is positive, it is complemented by some training for the review.

The *review (initial)* phase involves the initial review process that gathers general information about the school's organization and curriculum. This results in the decision to proceed to the more specific review phase.

The *review (specific)* phase involves the setting of priorities for an indepth review of a particular aspect(s) of the school. This results in the feedback of findings amenable to the establishing of policy should the decision to proceed to development be taken.

In the *development* phase decisions on policy are taken in the light of the findings produced during the previous review phase and an implementation plan is put into action. Effective implementation of policy involves change at a number of levels, viz. organization, materials, teaching style, knowledge and beliefs, some of which are more difficult to achieve than others. Evaluation is an important final step in the development phase.

The SBR process can be said to be *institutionalized* when a school's organizational norms, climate or culture involves activities such as periodic monitoring of previous SBR activity and when the SBR process is used in other areas of the school's curriculum and organization. When these activities occur regularly, then one can say that the school has developed a capacity for problem solving and improvement. The distinction between the institutionalization of a problem-solving capacity, which is the ultimate goal of SBR, and the institutionalization of some activity (e.g. a new reading scheme) that was the focus of the development phase of the project, needs to be kept in mind.

Obviously, the SBR process is not as linear as it is represented by the matrix which provides an indication of the chronological sequence of phases and stages in the process. It is important also to remember that movement from one phase of the process to another proceeds on the basis of a conscious decision based on an evaluation of the activities involved in that phase. Evaluation itself is an integral feature of the whole process: it encourages reflection on, and refinement of, the process while it is in progress.

The matrix, therefore, is a planning tool not a specific model or approach. It is specific yes, prescriptive no. It is designed to help those responsible for implementing SBR to understand the process by providing a detailed analysis and also to act as an *aide-mémoire* and basis for comparison. With this general conceptual framework in mind we now turn to a discussion of two well-known approaches to whole-school evaluation: GRIDS and the IMTEC/IDP. These descriptions are based on a much more extended discussion of approaches to school self-evaluation contained in Hopkins (1988b).

Guidelines for review and internal development in schools (GRIDS)

GRIDS began as a Schools Council project based at the University of Bristol. In its second stage, it was sponsored by, and based at, the School Curriculum Development Committee in London. The focus of GRIDS is the internal development of schools. This is in contrast to most LEA-initiated school evaluation efforts in England and Wales where the main purpose is external accountability. The project is designed to help teachers who wish to review and develop the curriculum and organization of their school, and two practical handbooks – one primary, one secondary – were produced for the purpose (McMahon *et al.*, 1984). In its second stage, GRIDS has been modified in order to recognize the need to be externally accountable, widen the roles of those who contribute to a review and to assist with the identification of in-service needs and the management of change. New materials have also been developed to assist teachers in establishing criteria for effectiveness, in using GRIDS in secondary schools at the department level, and for those with an external perspective (Abbott *et al.*, 1988, 1989; Birchenough *et al.*, 1989; Steadman *et al.*, 1989).

Aims

The aims of GRIDS can best be judged from this extract from McMahon *et al.* (1984):

The materials in this handbook are designed to help teachers review and develop their curriculum and organisation. The title 'GRIDS', or 'guidelines for review and internal development in schools' has been carefully chosen. First, the materials are guidelines: they contain structured step-by-step advice about how to conduct a school review and development exercise; schools are not expected to follow these suggestions slavishly but rather to adapt and amend them as required.

Second, the focus is on review leading to development for improvement and not on something that stops short at the review stage. Third, the word internal indicates that the review is not for external accountability purposes. Finally, the word school emphasises that the GRIDS process is directed at the whole school rather than at individual teachers or small groups.

These aims have, however, been modified in the light of experience, as is seen in the following list of principles.

Principles

The change in the educational climate since the original development of GRIDS necessitated a reassessment of its underlying principles. Aware of those developing pressures the second-phase GRIDS team rethought the principles underlying GRIDS. The revised key principles are:

1 The GRIDS process is first and foremost intended to be a whole school process. However, a modified process may be applied to secondary school departments and specialist teams.
2 The main purpose is to move beyond a review stage into development for internal school improvement, and not to produce a report for accountability purposes.
3 The process should be jointly controlled by the school Head and staff, with a realistic appreciation of the necessary relationships with governors and LEAs.

Other principles include:

1 *Control.* Decisions about what happens to any information or reports generated in the GRIDS process should rest with the teachers and others involved. The Head and teachers should decide whether and how to involve the other groups in the school, e.g. pupils, parents, advisers, governors.
2 *Involvement.* The staff of the school should be consulted and involved in the review and development process as much as possible. Genuine consultation and involvement of staff is necessary if teachers are to commit themselves to implementing changes in their schools.
3 *External help.* It is strongly recommended that experienced outsiders should be invited to provide help and advice both on the process of GRIDS itself and as 'experts' to help specific developments when the school has decided its priorities.
4 *Resources.* The demands made on key resources like time, money and skilled personnel should be realistic and feasible for schools and LEAs.
5 *Accountability.* Engagement in the GRIDS process cannot relieve staff of the need to be accountable to pupils and parents, to fellow teachers, or to their employers. However, the GRIDS process requires an initial staff review of all school activities, and aims for developmental changes so that the

school accomplishes its goals more effectively. Therefore, doing GRIDS should help schools answer calls to be accountable in their own terms.

Process

The central practical recommendation in the GRIDS method is that the staff should not attempt to make a detailed review of all aspects of the school at once. Instead, they should take a broad look at what is happening in the school, on the basis of this identify one or two areas that they consider to be priorities for specific review and development, tackle these first, evaluate what they have achieved, and then select another priority. The process has been broken down into a series of key steps and tasks which have a logical structure, and a systematic step-by-step approach is recommended throughout. The five stages in this cyclical problem-solving process are outlined in Fig. 8.2.

Stage 1, *preparing for a start*, is where preliminary decisions have to be made about whether or not the GRIDS method would be appropriate for the school and, if so, how it should be managed. The purpose of Stage 2, the *initial review*, is to identify the topics that the staff consider to be priorities for specific review and development. Stage 3 is a *specific review* of the topic(s) that have been identified as priorities – it entails a careful examination of current practice and an assessment of its effectiveness before making recommendations about development. Stage 4 is *action for development*, when the recommendations are put into practice. Stage 5, *assessing and adopting GRIDS*, is where evaluation of the development work and of the whole process takes place, and a new cycle of review and development begins.

Instruments

The main data-gathering instrument used in GRIDS is the survey sheet that is administered to the whole school staff during the initial review stage. There are two versions of the survey sheet, one for primary schools and one for secondary schools; an extract from an analysed primary school survey sheet is given in Fig. 8.3 (Abbott *et al.*, 1988: 24). The survey sheet gives each teacher the opportunity to state anonymously what she or he feels are the priority areas for improvement. It falls into two parts. In the first, the teachers are asked to say whether an area of the school is a strength or weakness and whether or not it is in need of specific review and development; in the second they are asked to identify three aspects of school life and rank them in order of priority for specific review and development over the next 12 months.

To ensure that teachers have access to information that will enable them to make an informed rather than superficial judgement, it is recommended that basic information about the school's position on the issues raised in the survey are summarized and made available before the teachers complete the sheet. Once the survey sheet has been completed, the school co-ordinator analyses the findings and presents the results to the staff before organizing a meeting to agree on the areas to be selected for specific review. Because GRIDS is not a

Figure 8.2 The stages and steps of GRIDS.

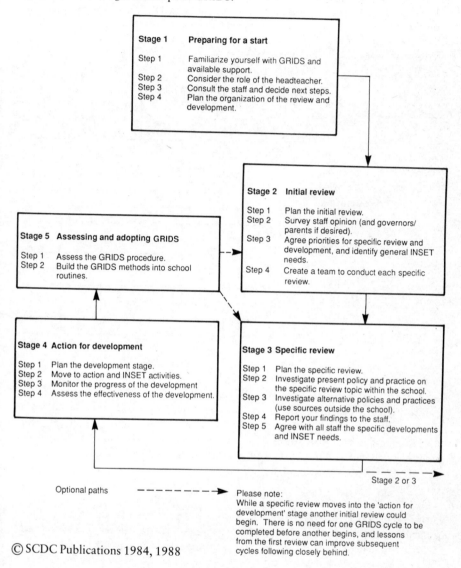

Stage 1   **Preparing for a start**

Step 1   Familiarize yourself with GRIDS and available support.
Step 2   Consider the role of the headteacher.
Step 3   Consult the staff and decide next steps.
Step 4   Plan the organization of the review and development.

Stage 2   **Initial review**

Step 1   Plan the initial review.
Step 2   Survey staff opinion (and governors/parents if desired).
Step 3   Agree priorities for specific review and development, and identify general INSET needs.
Step 4   Create a team to conduct each specific review.

Stage 5   **Assessing and adopting GRIDS**

Step 1   Assess the GRIDS procedure.
Step 2   Build the GRIDS methods into school routines.

Stage 4   **Action for development**

Step 1   Plan the development stage.
Step 2   Move to action and INSET activities.
Step 3   Monitor the progress of the development
Step 4   Assess the effectiveness of the development.

Stage 3   **Specific review**

Step 1   Plan the specific review.
Step 2   Investigate present policy and practice on the specific review topic within the school.
Step 3   Investigate alternative policies and practices (use sources outside the school).
Step 4   Report your findings to the staff.
Step 5   Agree with all staff the specific developments and INSET needs.

Stage 2 or 3

Optional paths   ------->

Please note:
While a specific review moves into the 'action for development' stage another initial review could begin. There is no need for one GRIDS cycle to be completed before another begins, and lessons from the first review can improve subsequent cycles following closely behind.

© SCDC Publications 1984, 1988

standardized instrument, additional or substitute items can be added to the sheet to suit a particular school situation.

Development

The logic of GRIDS is that development follows from review. Once the teachers have identified particular aspects for specific review and development,

Figure 8.3   Extract from Section 1 of a GRIDS primary school survey sheet (Abbott *et al.*, 1988: 25). Note that 10 teachers put ticks in Section 1. Seven thought that the communication skill 'speaking' would benefit from a specific review; three teachers thought it would not. Six teachers thought this aspect of the school's work was satisfactory; four thought it a weakness.

Aspect of the school		(i) Would benefit from specific review			(ii)		
		YES	NO	DON'T KNOW	Strength	Satisfactory	Weakness
Curriculum Communication skills:	1 Speaking	7	3	–	–	6	4
	2 Listening	9	–	–	–	1	8
	3 Reading	8	1	–	1	7	2
	4 Writing	9	–	–	–	4	5
	5 Welsh as a second language	5	2	2	–	3	4
Mathematics:	6 Practical	6	3	–	5	4	–
	7 Number	6	3	–	5	4	–
Creative work:	8 Music	6	2	1	2	4	3
	9 Drama	9	–	–	–	3	6
	10 Art and craft	9	–	–	1	3	5

the co-ordinating team are advised to follow a series of key steps as shown in Fig. 8.2. Having completed the specific review, the co-ordinating team is ready to initiate development work, especially providing support for the implementation of innovations – something that has been all too frequently neglected. The Head and school co-ordinator must be centrally involved in any decisions about how to implement the recommendations from the specific review.

Commentary

The GRIDS experience has provided lessons both for curriculum developers in general and for those interested in SBR in particular. Attention here is confined to the lessons most relevant for the development of SBR.

1 SBR requires an atmosphere of cooperative endeavour, not only within the schools which are expected to take on the process, but also in the educational system which supports the schools.
2 School autonomy cannot be total, and it is important to consider what parents, school governors and different levels of government would present as priority issues. In order to engender commitment for change, however, it is still the GRIDS team's view that the school staff must make the final decisions on priority for review and development.

3 The GRIDS team is still concerned at an apparent lack of rigour and objectivity in many review and development procedures. But to ask schools to produce clear criteria by which to judge their effectiveness is to set a complex task under the guise of apparent simplicity.

4 Schools which have worked through more than one cycle of GRIDS demonstrate a sequence growth. The first cycle serves to generate shared experiences, team-work, ownership of the process and confidence. Realistically, it is in the second and subsequent cycles that one should expect increased rigour in procedures, application of clear criteria to present practices, greater openness with consultants and others, and a readiness to cope with external pressures for accountability.

The IMTEC Institutional Development Programme (IDP)

The Institutional Development Programme (IDP) originated within IMTEC (International Movements Towards Educational Change), the Norwegian Educational Foundation, as a result of international collaboration which began in Scandinavia in 1967. The IDP is based on a survey feedback design with the emphasis being placed on a standardized questionnaire, consultant support and a systematic feedback–development process. The IDP utilizes a series of instruments of which the GIL (Guide to Institutional Learning) questionnaire is the best known. The GIL has been widely used in and adapted to a variety of educational settings and a number of countries.

Aim

Per Dalin, the founder of IMTEC and main developer of the IDP, and his colleague Val Rust describe the central aim of the IDP (Dalin and Rust, 1983: 44) as:

> to help institutions diagnose their present situation, plan, implement, evaluate, and readjust themselves in order to meet internal and external requirements with increasing effectiveness. The focus of the IDP is on the educational institution as an organization.

Principles

The IDP is based on an explicit conceptual framework about the nature of schools. Change occurs on the basis of identifiable real needs that can be conceptualized within a triangular framework of leadership, ownership and staff security (technical and psychological). From this conceptualization are derived a number of assumptions that underpin the IDP method. These assumptions are (Dalin and Rust, 1983: 46–7):

> *Assumption one:* In spite of a much greater segmentation of organizational variables in educational institutions than exists in most industrial

or commercial institutions, there remains a dynamic inter-dependence between most organizational variables.

Assumption two: Because the organizational picture possessed by each member of an institution is both unique and limited, all members have an equal right to provide input data about the real nature of the organization and what it ought to become.

Assumption three: An institutional renewal programme must be a collaborative effort involving as wide a scope of individuals in the institution as possible.

Assumption four: Conflicts are normal organizational events and can be used constructively to facilitate the institutional development process.

Assumption five: Institutional renewal usually requires some form of external support.

Assumption six: Even though the consultation process of the IDP is unavoidably not value free, the consultants attempt to remain goal-free in terms of anticipated outcomes in the institutional renewal.

Assumption seven: Sufficient degrees of freedom in environmental frames exist to tolerate school renewal efforts.

Assumption eight: The effectiveness of the organization can be assessed only within a contextual framework.

Assumption nine: Schools can learn.

Process

The IDP includes a well-developed process of seven distinct phases based on a model that moves from the present to the desired situation, as shown in Fig. 8.4 (Dalin, forthcoming). Dalin cautions that real-life events involving human beings never fall into a neat and orderly sequence and that in reality certain phases – e.g. data collection – often occur out of sequence and at various stages in the process. He claims, however, that despite that discrepancy between reality and the model, the process as outlined above does provide a map of the various activities that occur in the IDP.

Instruments

The GIL is central to the IDP process. It is a standardized questionnaire designed for the review (initial) phase of SBR. There have been a number of versions of the GIL designed for different groups, but all focus on organizational factors, are statistically reliable and quite lengthy. The version called 'The School Development Guide' (SDG; Dalin *et al.*, 1987), currently distributed through the National Foundation for Educational Research (NFER) in England, has 12 scales representing values and goals, school objectives, staff relationships, school climate, leadership and management, decision making, communication, influences, assessment and evaluation, changes in the school,

Figure 8.4 The IDP process.

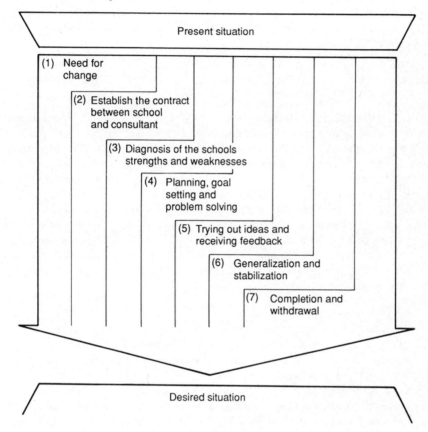

Figure 8.5 Extract from SDG scale relating to school climate.

D.	School Climate	YES	Yes	yes	no	No	NO
D1.	Would you say that the climate (ethos, milieu) of your school . . .						
	(a) is rewarding to pupils?	1	2	3	4	5	6
	(b) supports innovation in teaching and curricula?	1	2	3	4	5	6
	(c) is controlled yet relaxed?	1	2	3	4	5	6
	(d) favours staff development?	1	2	3	4	5	6
	(e) reflects enthusiasm in the staff and pupils?	1	2	3	4	5	6
	(f) promotes punctuality?	1	2	3	4	5	6
	(g) values academic attainment?	1	2	3	4	5	6
	(h) emphasizes hard work?	1	2	3	4	5	6
	(i) is supportive to those in difficulty?	1	2	3	4	5	6

teaching method, teacher activities. The example shown in Fig. 8.5 is taken from the SDG scale relating to school climate. An interesting feature of the questionnaire is its ability to contrast real and ideal responses, as shown in Fig. 8.6 (Dalin and Rust, 1983: 77).

Development

The IDP is, by definition, committed to development. The logic of the IDP process is that feedback of the results of the GIL is followed by a dialogue that leads to goal setting, planning and action. The school development phase is contingent on action planning and, because this linkage is particularly problematic, IMTEC advocates consultancy which can take the form of either external or internal support. Some form of consultancy is integral to IMTEC's view of the IDP process. IMTEC does not, however, see consultants as autonomously running the project. The consultants' role is to provide advice, motivation, expertise and support and, consequently, they report to a steering committee at the school level. School level development therefore is a function of leadership, management and assistance. The assistance is usually provided by a consultant who acts as a catalyst and leaves the school with the ownership of any changes the staff decide to implement.

Commentary

The IDP is a well-developed SBR process that has a standardized questionnaire as its cornerstone. The questionnaire measures a wide spectrum of organizational factors but is dependent on computer analysis and consultancy for data feedback and interpretation. As IMTEC have developed the IDP they have continued to produce a range of additional diagnostic instruments adaptable to individual schools that focus on defining real needs. IMTEC have also expanded their concept of consultancy to include an emphasis on the initial contract negotiations, skill training for participants and developing ownership at the school level. All this activity is based on the realization that although the IDP is generalizable, the actual reality of the process varies from school to school.

Other approaches to whole-school evaluation

GRIDS and the IDP are of course not the only approaches to whole-school evaluation, although in many ways they are the most complete. There are two other developmentally inspired approaches to school review that are currently used in our schools: Helping Schools Change (Focus) and DION/SIGMA. A third approach is represented by the LEA-initiated schemes for school self-evaluation.

The *Helping Schools Change* approach to school review is based on the FOCUS (Framework for Organization Change and Underlying Style) instrument developed by Harold Heller (1985). It is published by the Centre for the

Figure 8.6 GIL profile: instructional goals.

	Not important				Very important
1. To develop an integrated, balanced person	4	3	5	32	56
	11	25	43	18	3
2. To develop problem-solving skills	8	8	9	42	33
	6	17	41	35	11
3. To gain technical–vocational skills	27	13	10	23	20
	2	28	46	23	3
4. To understand ideas, concepts and theories	11	31	43	12	8
	8	30	45	11	6
5. To develop and improve social attitudes and skills	2	2	4	3	89
	2	19	39	16	15
6. To develop a sense of aesthetic qualities	0	20	29	32	19
	30	34	24	0	8
7. To develop an independent, critical, and tolerant person	5	3	3	15	24
	18	38	25	16	3
8. To develop the ability for creative work	3	5	22	43	17
	2	23	36	26	6

Numbers over line = distribution in % of ideal
Numbers under line = distribution in % of real

- - - - = means of ideal
———— = means of real

Study of the Comprehensive School in York, England and has been used in many secondary schools. FOCUS consists of three separate but related scales which set out to measure the individual's response to change and his/her assessment of the way in which the leadership and the school approach change and development. The instrument is usually analysed statistically and the print-out is plotted on the FOCUS grid which graphically illustrates the socio-emotional state of the school and its staff.

The FOCUS instrument and its display grid tends to have a powerful impact on school staff. The graphic interpretation of the instrument arouses a great deal of interest and is potentially very motivating. It also assists a school staff in understanding the complexities of a school's organization and climate and the contribution of individuals to the school culture. It is a pity, therefore, that the handbook does not describe an explicit developmental phase which could extend the usefulness of the instrument. It is, of course, perfectly possible to use FOCUS within GRIDS or at the review (initial or specific) stage of the matrix.

DION is a diagnostic instrument for the articulation of individual and organizational needs for staff development and in-service training in schools. DION is essentially a 66-item inventory that focuses on the organizational climate of schools for the purpose of school-focused in-service. The inventory is easy to administer, is participative, and experience to date suggests that it has high face validity. It has been used in a variety of school situations both in the UK and overseas. John Elliott-Kemp and Graham Williams (1980),

DION's originators, describe the rationale for and aims of the instrument like this:

In-service training for isolated individuals often fails to bring about whole school improvement. The work situation often constrains the individual from bringing about the changes he would like. DION is an approach for identifying in-service training needs at the organisational level rather than the individual level, although the needs identified will of course include individual development needs. This focuses attention onto the problems and possibilities within the whole school. Training and development can then be concentrated on priorities for the organisation rather than exclusively for the individual, including development needs related to interpersonal relationships both within and between groups in the school such as departments, year teams and other task groups.

DION has to an extent been superseded by SIGMA, a boxed package of materials for school-based staff review and development, which was also developed by John Elliot-Kemp and B. West (1987). The SIGMA package includes papers on the background, rationale, terminology and operation of the system, together with a collection of instruments and resource materials for a school staff to initiate the review and development process. The SIGMA materials provide a comprehensive collection of resources for school-based review and development. The system also includes an associated process. As the SIGMA system is relatively new there is little in the way of long-term evaluation data. Initial feedback suggests, however, that it is a powerful system which generates and channels enthusiasm and commitment from participants. As both a complement and successor to the DION instrument, it appears to present a much more comprehensive and well-documented resource package for school-based review and development.

One result of the increased interest in the accountability of the educational system in the UK since the late 1970s has been the emergence of the LEA-initiated schemes for school self-evaluation. The Inner London Education Authority (ILEA) published, in the summer of 1977, a booklet entitled *Keeping the School Under Review* (revised versions, ILEA, 1983). The booklets offer a framework for self-assessment for primary and secondary schools in the form of a checklist of pertinent questions. The ILEA *Keeping the School Under Review* approach to school-based review has been very influential in popularizing a LEA-initiated checklist approach to school reviews. The questions contained in the booklets are comprehensive, open-ended and stimulating; they also contain an implicit agenda for school reform. The lack of an explicit statement of principle and process for development, however, will inevitably inhibit the usefulness and effectiveness of the booklets as a means of school improvement. This lack of an explicit developmental process and the *laissez-faire* attitude to implementation is characteristic of the approach to SBR in England and Wales, and limits its effectiveness. It is unsurprising therefore to find that the research contained in Phil Clift's (1987: 60) ISIP case study of such schemes suggests that:

> . . . school based review in accordance with LEA initiated schemes has not been effective in the ways intended. It does not seem to have generally motivated the teachers involved to make tangible changes in their working practices or to redeploy the resources already available to them to any greater effect. This failure to operate in the way intended seems to be due to teachers' lack of experience and expertise in the process of SBR and perhaps to a lesser extent to their lack of commitment to a scheme originating outside their school. For school based review to be of any real value, therefore, substantial resources need to be devoted to the inservice training of teachers as evaluators. School based review is also time consuming and demanding, requiring teachers to divert substantial amounts of their time and energy to it from their other duties. This has obvious cost, or at any rate, 'opportunity cost' implications.

Conditions for school-based review

In addition to Clift's comments about the need for training and the resource implications noted in the previous paragraph, there are a number of other conditions that are vital for the SBR process. In the first place, there is the need for time. As SBR is based not just on skills and techniques but also on clear concepts and attitudes, SBR needs adequate time to be developed, particularly if it is to be institutionalized. Secondly, SBR needs the active support and participation of the headteacher. If he or she is not convinced of the usefulness of the SBR strategy then it probably will not work. Thirdly – and this relates to the first – participants should have a clear concept of what SBR is really like. This does not mean that all people should have the matrix in mind but rather that the different parties involved with their own roles and interests should clarify these to each other in order to avoid a situation of distrust and confusion. SBR depends on the energy people involved in the process invest in it. Of course, a little pushing and pulling might help, but basically SBR is a voluntary act undertaken by a school in order to improve its functioning. Finally, the availability of support is necessary for effective SBR. 'Availability' is used on purpose, because SBR, being a school-based activity, needs some sort of tailor-made support available at the right time with the right means. This is a very difficult condition to fulfil. This condition may block a large-scale introduction of SBR but, nevertheless, I suggest that neglecting the school-based character of SBR is, by definition, the end of SBR.

Roles in school-based review

The SBR matrix defines roles and functions along the horizontal axis, without specifying activities. This is because different role patterns occur in different contexts: those involved in school evaluation will play different roles, even conflicting roles, and these roles may change during the process. It may be useful, however, to conclude this chapter with an overview of the favourable or unfavourable role patterns as they apply to practitioners, which is taken from our ISIP research (Bollen and Hopkins, 1987).

Although practitioners (i.e. teachers, headteachers, advisory teachers) like to occupy themselves with meaningful activities, they would be wise to think about the following:

- Is there a general feeling of not being well informed about what is going on in the school?
- Is there a general feeling that the school system should be improved in certain respects?
- Is there a general willingness to invest time and energy in improvement activities?
- Do at least a couple of key persons in school have the ability to manage a school development process?

Practitioners will have to make important decisions about their roles:

- Are they willing to be subject to review? In other words, are they – teachers as well as headteachers – willing to have their professional behaviours scrutinized?
- Who will actually do the review?
- Who will manage the review?
- Do they really accept a controlling body or person?

Practitioners will also have to make decisions about:

- whether to do an initial review;
- whether to ask for support (or if offered: to accept the support or not);
- whether to commit other groups like parents and pupils to SBR;
- the use of specific methods or procedures to gather data and come to valid conclusions;
- who will be informed about specific outcomes and who not;
- the evaluation criteria to be used to make decisions about whether to proceed or not at given times.

Practitioners should bear in mind that in a successful SBR strategy the following activities will take place:

- People will analyse their own activities, reflect upon them and communicate about them.
- People will, if necessary, plan for improvement and will carry out improvement activities.
- People will learn by doing, especially at the classroom level.

Finally, we remind practitioners of some of our findings:

- People do have different interests in SBR and behave according to those interests.
- SBR is a long-term rather than a short-term strategy.
- SBR will not work if it is not actively supported by the headteacher.
- Some of the benefits of SBR are indirect; such as an increased awareness of the need for cooperation and an enhanced problem-solving capacity at the individual and school level.
- SBR does not automatically bring about improvement but will provide impetus and direction for it.

Summary

In this chapter I have attempted to provide an overview of whole-school evaluation by describing a conceptual framework for school review (i.e. the matrix) and two particular approaches in some detail (i.e. GRIDS and IDP). Attention has also been given to other well-known approaches as well as to LEA-initiated schemes. Some of the conditions for successful review and role implications for practitioners were also noted. Up until recently, school-based review has been regarded as a discrete activity, but we are now in a position to see more clearly how it links with mainstream evaluation and to other school improvement efforts. SBR provides a methodology for more detailed and specific evaluation activities as was noted in the previous chapter. With the increasing importance of activities such as planning for school and staff development, curriculum review, teacher appraisal and managing an overload of change initiatives, a problem-solving approach along the lines outlined in this chapter provides a school level strategy for linking evaluation to development. The important point is that the whole-school evaluation strategy provides a vehicle or structure for carrying out and facilitating these other activities. In this respect, it is vital (a) that the initial review survey is appropriate to the school and focuses on relevant and important developmental issues, and (b) that the subsequent process fits into the rhythm of the school's organization.

9
Evaluating INSET

I have included a separate chapter on INSET because it is an issue which has been accorded much attention of late. The change in INSET funding nationally, the TRIST experience and the devolution of control to the consortia and school level imply different forms of delivery which have brought attendant demands for quality control. Yet there are problems with the evaluation of INSET. DES circulars talk about 'uncertainty in relation to monitoring and evaluation' and, although attempts are made to evaluate most INSET courses, these efforts often lack conviction. The problem seems to be three-fold: first, despite the rhetoric, the aims, purposes and effects of INSET remain hazy; secondly, and consequently, we do not seem to be evaluating the right things; and thirdly, an infrastructure to evaluate and consequently improve INSET at the LEA level seems in most cases to be missing. In this chapter I try to shed some light on the first two of these issues and give some examples of different INSET evaluation designs. The third issue is dealt with in Section IV. Although I am conscious of the subtleties of definition, for the ease of exposition I have in this chapter used the terms INSET, Professional Development and Staff Development interchangeably.

What is effective INSET?

In order to evaluate INSET effectively, one needs to know something about effective INSET. We are now in the fortunate position of having a number of research-based and analytic studies that give us a good idea of what makes for an effective INSET design.

So, for example, in a recent paper Bolam (1987) discusses the characteristics of the successful short INSET course and makes the following comments:

Issues associated with the design and implementation of good training courses have been the focus of several British research and development studies (e.g. Rudduck, 1981). A rough synthesis of their conclusions suggests that good courses have the following features:

- Collaborative planning involving course leaders, LEA sponsors and former or prospective participants;
- a clear focus upon participants' current and future needs;
- careful preparatory briefing for participants several weeks ahead of the course, with opportunities for pre-course work where appropriate;
- a programme which is structured but has enough flexibility to allow for modifications in the light of monitoring and formative evaluation;
- a programme which is oriented towards experience, practice and action, and using as appropriate, methods like action learning, action research, performance feedback and on-the-job assistance;
- 'sandwich' timetable including course-based and job-based experiences to facilitate this approach;
- careful de-briefing after the course and sustained support, ideally including on-the-job assistance where new skills are being implemented.

In a similar way, I tried to pull together much of the material that summarized our best knowledge to date on effective INSET in the synthesis book on the OECD INSET project. The following three extracts are from chapter nine of *Inservice Training and Educational Development* (Hopkins, 1986c).

Michael Fullan (in Hopkins, 1986c: 277–8) suggests that: there are a number of major specific guidelines for planning in-service:

1 The need for in-service to be integrated with and part and parcel of concrete programme change and problems experienced at the classroom and school level. It should have a project or programme focus.
2 Within these programmes, in-service should be intensive and ongoing.
3 The ongoing process of professional development must be linked to school building or organizational development efforts. Both teachers and administrators should be involved in in-service.
4 In-service training should be simultaneously directed at skill-specific and conceptual development over time.
5 Teachers may be the best source of skill and practical training, although consultants external to the school should be used for particular purposes.
6 Above all, one needs a plan at the school level, and at the school district level which systematically organizes and provides for (1) and (5) to happen in an interactive framework.

Bruce Joyce and Beverley Showers (1980) write that:

whether we teach ourselves or whether we learn from a training agent, the outcomes of training can be classified into several levels of impact:

awareness; the acquisition of concepts or organized knowledge; the learning of principles and skills; and the ability to apply those principles and skills in problem-solving activities.

Awareness. At the awareness level we realize the importance of an area and begin to focus on it. With inductive teaching, for example, the road to competence begins with awareness of the nature of inductive teaching, its probable uses, and how it fits into the curriculum.

Concepts and organized knowledge. Concepts provide intellectual control over relevant content. Essential to inductive teaching are knowledge of inductive processes, how learners at various levels of cognitive development respond to inductive teaching, and knowledge about concept formation.

Principles and skills. Principles and skills are tools for action. At this level we learn the skills of inductive teaching: how to help students collect data, organize it, and build concepts and test them. We also acquire the skills for adapting to students who display varying levels of ability to think inductively and for teaching them the skills they lack. At this level there is potential for action – we are aware of the area, can think effectively about it, and possess the skills to act.

Application and problem solving. Finally, we transfer the concepts, principles, and skills to the classroom. We begin to use the teaching strategy we have learned, integrate it into our style, and combine the strategy with the others in our repertoire.

Only after this fourth level has been reached can we expect an impact on the education of children. Awareness alone is an insufficient condition. Organized knowledge that is not backed up by the acquisition of principles and skills and the ability to use them is likely to have little effect.

Components of training

Most of the training literature consists of investigations in which training elements are combined in various ways, whether they are directed toward the fine-tuning of styles or the mastery of new approaches. From our analysis, we were able to identify a number of training components that have been studied intensively. Alone and in combination, each of these training components contribute to the impact of a training sequence of activity. (As we shall see, when used together, each has much greater power than when they are used alone.) The major components of training in the studies we reviewed are:

- Presentation of theory or description of skill or strategy;
- Modelling or demonstration of skills or models of teaching;
- Practice in simulated and classroom settings;
- Structured and open-ended feedback (provision of information about performance);

● Coaching for application (hands-on, in-classroom assistance with the transfer of skills and strategies to the classroom).

Bruce Joyce and Beverley Showers (1984) also write that:

research on training that investigates the relationship of coaching to transfer of learning is needed. If coaching should significantly boost the rate of implementation of new skills, strategies, and curriculum for long periods of time, it will be possible to measure much more meaningfully the effects of specific innovations on student learning.

In the meantime, we should operate on the best knowledge we have. In our opinion that means:

● The use of the integrated theory-demonstration-practice-feedback training programmes to ensure skill development.
● The use of considerable amounts of practice in simulated conditions to ensure fluid control of the new skills.
● The employment of regular on-site coaching to facilitate vertical transfer – the development of new learning in the process of transfer.
● The preparation of teachers who can provide one another with the needed coaching.

The Fullan extract is a more general systems level analysis, whereas the Joyce and Showers extracts are more specifically focused on programme design. Their seminal (Joyce and Showers, 1980) paper 'Improving inservice training' identifies as we have seen four levels of impact for INSET and five training components. This paper and the research which preceded and followed it (Joyce *et al.*, 1981; Joyce and Showers, 1988) suggest, as Ray Bolam (1987) has noted, an embryonic theory of skill training for teacher education. One can represent their ideas in the form of a matrix as shown in Table 9.1.

The point of this discussion is to emphasize the importance of linking INSET evaluation to effective INSET programme designs. So, for example, the design criteria implicit in Table 9.1 provide a basis for evaluating INSET courses. If the aim of the course is the acquisition of new and transferable teaching skills, then one could quite confidently frame one's evaluation questions around Joyce and Showers' training components. If the course design allowed for only description and modelling, then one could hypothesize that the acquisition and transfer of skills might well not occur. If this was the case then suggestions for the inclusion of practice, feedback and coaching components could be made in order to improve future course design. In a similar way, the second extract from Joyce and Showers is a summary of their findings on 'coaching' (see also Showers, 1985). Their research and theory suggests that coaching is a necessary strategy in facilitating system-wide acquisition of new teaching skills. If such a component is not present in the INSET design, then that begs some important evaluation questions and suggests some directions for development.

Table 9.1 The training matrix of Joyce and Showers (1980)

Training method/component	Level of impact			
	A General awareness of new skills	B Organized knowledge of underlying concepts and theory	C Learning of new skills	D Application on-the-job
1 Presentation/description (e.g. lecture) of new skills				
2 Modelling the new skills (e.g. live or video demonstrations)				
3 Practice in simulated settings				
4 Feedback on performance in simulated or real settings				
5 Coaching/assistance on-the-job				

Evaluating contemporary INSET: contexts, parameters and warnings

The radical change in the funding and structure of INSET in England and Wales, presaged by the TRIST experience, initiated by GRIST, and now institutionalized by LEATGS (LEA Training Grant Scheme) has produced a voluminous literature, much of which has focused on evaluation. This literature provides a more specific context for the evaluation of INSET and in this section I attempt a brief review of the main issues.

The first point is the radical change in context implied by the recent legislation. Despite its rhetorical tone, DES circular 6/86, which describes the LEA training grants scheme, firmly commits itself to school-focused in-service, a move which many have been arguing for for some time. The circular also stresses the planning of INSET and the identification of needs at the school, local and national levels; more effective management of the teaching force; and a commitment to the 'professional development of teachers'.

This marks a major shift in emphasis which is reflected in current INSET practice. Bolam (1987) describes the current state of the art as follows:

- greater reliance by LEAs on in-house provision;
- an increase in take-up for short courses, usually at the expense of long courses and secondments;
- the appointment by LEAs of full-time and part-time INSET co-ordinators, advisers, administrators and evaluators;
- considerable variation in the extent to which the GRIST budget is devolved to schools and growing recognition that substantial devolution may constrain LEA strategic planning and reduce its overall capacity to take up long courses;
- the creation of area-based clusters, especially for primary schools, to co-ordinate and manage GRIST;
- increasing recognition of the problems of strategic planning, administration and financial management arising from the annual GRIST process and budget;
- continuing frustration with the problems of inadequate supply cover and the associated problem of disruption to teaching and learning;
- a wide variety of practice in ways of using the five 'Baker' days; for example, as to whether LEA or schools should decide on their purpose, and how to deal with the resource, logistical and provider availability implications when schools take them simultaneously;
- growing recognition that, because these five days represent a major resource which in total can be larger than the GRIST budget, the two should therefore be managed together rather than independently.

The purpose of describing the context in such detail is to help focus more clearly the evaluation questions one asks, and provide one set of parameters in which the evaluation of INSET can occur.

Another set of parameters are provided by government, e.g. the DES note on the monitoring and evaluation of LEATGS. In this paper the DES outline 'five major questions [that] arise in planning monitoring and evaluation in LEAs':

   (i) who will use the results of monitoring and evaluation?
  (ii) for what purposes will they be used?
 (iii) what should be monitored and evaluated?
 (iv) how should the monitoring and evaluation be carried out? and
  (v) who should carry out the monitoring and evaluation?

The note then continues to amplify and generate further questions under these five headings which provide a potentially useful list of evaluation questions. This document therefore provides yet another context or set of parameters in which to consider the evaluation of contemporary INSET.

But before we become too optimistic about the utility of such questions in assisting our evaluations of INSET we must realize, as Joyce and Showers (1988: 111–12) remind us, that:

Designing the evaluation of staff development programs is difficult for a number of reasons. First, of course, the system is large and complicated. Second, the implementation of each event and program is heavily influenced by its context. The energy and interest of the schools and teachers amplify or diminish the effects of training events. Third, staff development influences its ultimate goal, student learning, through a chain of events. Content of high potential needs good training design if it is to come to life in the classroom to a degree that can achieve its potential. Measuring response to a series of training events by, for example, determining how participants liked them or whether initial skill and knowledge were developed provides only the beginning. If the skills are not employed and skillfully enough that student learning is affected, the chain is broken. The *entire* sequence has to be scrutinized. Fourth, the measurement of many of the important variables is technically difficult. For the implementation of training to be documented requires the collection of data by trained observers. Frequently tests of student behavior and learning have to be constructed − some of the most-used commercially-available instruments are not appropriate for all the objectives that we may have. Fifth, cost limitations almost always result in designs where a sample rather than the entire population is studied. We definitely favor the thorough study of a sample rather than a more superficial study of the entire population because the chain of events and moderating variables can only be tracked by the collection and analysis of high-quality data. Sixth, good evaluation runs against the normative practices that are termed 'evaluations'. The most common current practice is the use of opinionaires asking participants in training events to 'rate' the event and often the trainers and organizers. The opinions of personnel about training events, especially superficial ones, are very poor predictors of implementation. For example, a series of well-received lectures on a teaching practice will by themselves have relatively little effect on teaching practice. Other components are necessary to achieve an impact on practice. An 'evaluation' based on opinions about the lectures could be deceiving unless implementation is scrutinized also.

The central point that Joyce and Showers are making is that the evaluation of INSET needs to be viewed as a wholistic process and that an evaluation of individual parts of that process which disregard this wider perspective can contribute little to school improvement. So against this background of contexts and salutory warnings we turn in the following sections of this chapter to a consideration of some strategies for evaluating INSET and the techniques involved.

Strategies

I have become even more convinced of the necessity for a wholistic approach to the evaluation of INSET following the experience that Marilyn Evans and I had of evaluating an exemplary INSET course (Evans and Hopkins, 1988). During the evaluation we took the opportunity to examine not only the impact of the INSET programme on individual teachers' subsequent classroom behaviour, but also to relate that 'level of use' to the teachers' personality and the climate of the school. Our results suggested that variance in the use of the new ideas was accounted for by the prevailing school climate and the nature of the individual teacher. We found that those teachers operating in a more open democratic school climate, and at a higher psychological level, made greatest use of the ideas, strategies and skills acquired on the course.

I therefore agree with Joyce and Showers (1988: 114) when they suggest that in the evaluation of staff development there are four major sets of variables that fall under the categories Teacher, School and System, Staff Development Programme and Student (see Fig. 9.1). They describe these variables as follows.

1 *Individual teachers* bring to the staff development situation their current knowledge and skills, their teaching styles, and personal characteristics such as states of growth, conceptual levels, and concepts of selves. They also bring perceptions about their needs and preferences for certain kinds of staff development. The study of teachers can be designed to provide information that can have several uses. One is to determine *needs* as, for example, what teaching strategies are and are not in existing repertoires, and what knowledge about academic subjects is needed. Another is to provide baselines against which we can measure progress. A third is to generate information about variables that can moderate effects.
2 *Schools and school systems* can be characterized by types of leadership, the cohesion and synergy of their social system, the governance processes they employ, and their relationships with the communities they serve. These variables can also function as needs assessments, as baselines, and as moderators.

Figure 9.1   Teachers, schools, programs, students: The major variables in staff development systems (from Joyce and Showers 1988: 113).

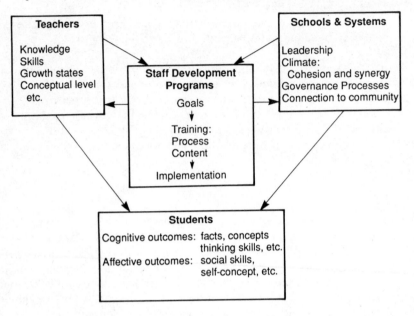

3 *Staff development programmes* can be defined by the goals and objectives they seek to accomplish, including the content and the processes employed in training, and the degrees of implementation intended. The goals are the source of the dependent variables of an evaluation, whether teaching skills and strategies, knowledge about academic content, student learning, or other designed outcomes of the programme or programme elements.
4 *Students* also bring to the educational setting existing knowledge, skills, and personal characteristics which can be studied to determine goals and programme structure, operate as baselines, and which also moderate treatments.

They continue to argue that such a framework provides a starting point for devising an INSET evaluation strategy.

A similar approach is followed by Michael Eraut and colleagues (1988) in their meta-evaluation of TRIST. In responding to the question 'were the intended outcomes achieved?', they comment (1988: 31):

This deceptively simple question conceals a number of important problems. One problem is that of perspective. Whose intentions are we considering, those of the inspector, provider, teacher or headteacher? Another is that of imprecision. People usually have a range of intentions, only some of which are clearly articulated or represented as INSET

Figure 9.2 Outcomes of an in-service course (from Eraut *et al.*, 1988: 31).

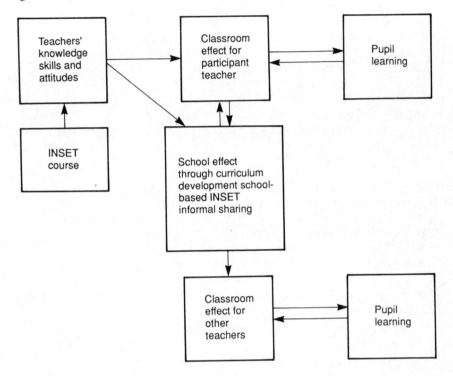

objectives. [From an external viewpoint, the outcomes of an in-service course can be depicted as shown in Fig. 9.2.]

INSET is intended to develop knowledge, skills and attitudes in teacher participants in order that they should (a) develop their own classroom practice and/or (b) create wider school effects through curriculum change, school-based INSET or informal sharing of their knowledge and experience with colleagues. In the case of (b) there may be expectations of consequent classroom change by teachers who did not attend the original course. These classroom changes are intended to affect pupils' learning in a manner that is consistent with the aims of the course.

This explanation of the model, however, is dangerously misleading. The organiser of an INSET course does not normally have any authority over school or classroom. Whether or not there is a 'school effect' will depend largely on decisions within the school itself, some no doubt made prior to the course and others during or after it; and these decisions may either promote or prevent changes of the kind discussed on the course. The likelihood of a classroom effect will also be influenced by many school factors – curriculum, timetable, resources – in addition to many teacher factors; and this affects participants' own classrooms as well as those of their colleagues.

Both Joyce and Showers, and Eraut are making the fundamentally important point that one cannot evaluate an INSET course *in vacuo*, and that it must be related to the system in which it is embedded. This complexity presents a formidable task for the evaluator, particularly as the questions so generated will vary in their level of penetration. One pragmatic solution to this problem is to order the evaluation questions within broad bands of enquiry. As David Oldroyd and Valerie Hall (1988: 89) noted:

> Eraut's study identified three categories of questions which might provide the starting point for generating more precise sub-questions as a basis for information gathering.

Questions about the programme:

● What did the various participants consider to be the main strengths and weaknesses of the course or activity?
● What changes would they recommend if it were to be repeated?
● Were they adequately briefed and prepared for it?
● To what extent were their expectations met?
● What are their views on the quality, importance and relevance of various activities?
● What kind of follow-up would enable them to get maximum benefit from the experience?

These questions are directed at participants and should be standard practice in formative and summative evaluation.

Questions about impact beyond the programme:

● What was the impact on teachers who participated?
● How useful was the activity in helping teachers to bring about anticipated or specified changes?
● Did teachers apply the acquired skills?
● Were there unintended outcomes, either positive or negative?

These questions about teacher performance require follow-up interviews and monitoring possibly by observation and thus are much more difficult to answer and demanding on time. Where information gathering goes beyond self-supporting, issues of sensitivity or relationships and confidentiality of information are raised.

Questions about broader effects within the institution:

● What has been the effect on the school and on classroom practice?
● What were the effects on pupils' learning?
● What was its effectiveness relative to other activities?
● Was it meeting a genuine need?
● Did it give value for money?

As noted above these questions take us into the area of the curriculum and institutional review.

Given the limited time and resources available for evaluation in most institutions, there will be an inevitable need to select from the large range

Table 9.2 Recommendations for the local evaluation of INSET (from Eraut *et al.*, 1988: 5–6)

1 Local evaluations of INSET programmes should ideally include both internal and external elements
2 Internal evaluators need good training in evaluation
3 Wherever possible, secondment for evaluation should be made on a full-time basis
4 Training should be provided in the management of evaluation
5 Training in professional monitoring should be provided for inspectors, advisers, advisory teachers and school INSET co-ordinators, with particular attention to their roles in INSET evaluation
6 The costs of professional monitoring should be born by the relevant INSET courses and activities, not charged to the evaluation budget
7 Professional monitoring of courses should be standard practice for all providers
8 An evaluation should have a clear initial brief
9 Each authority should establish a small committee or advisory group for INSET evaluation
10 The flow of information from professional monitoring of INSET should be co-ordinated and linked with the work of designated evaluators and their committees
11 Codes of practice for handling evaluation data should be established and observed
12 Procedures for reporting and feedback should be discussed during the early stages of an evaluation, to give guidance to evaluators and to ensure maximum utilization of their findings
13 Evaluators should seek multiple sources of evidence to 'triangulate' their findings and not rely on self-reports alone
14 Evaluators should elicit and formulate questions from stakeholders and negotiate which of them should be addressed and with what criteria in mind
15 Evaluators assessing the effectiveness of INSET activities should take into account differences in expectation, preparation and follow-up, and the school and classroom contexts of participants
16 Collecting evidence of changes in pupil attitudes and achievement should be the responsibility of school-based evaluation and of special research projects, not of INSET evaluations
17 INSET evaluation should focus on the link between INSET and teacher attitudes and behaviour, while school-based evaluation should focus on the link between school policy and practice and pupils' attitudes and achievement. Their aims and strategies should be mutually consistent
18 From a school or college standpoint, INSET evaluation should assess the match between INSET provision and the curriculum and staff development needs which they themselves have identified
19 INSET evaluations should give more attention to strategic questions and policy issues that are relevant to several programmes or to general patterns of INSET management and delivery
20 Evaluators should consider INSET programmes as appropriate targets for professional review, so that the combined effect of INSET activities can be examined in a coherent way
21 Strategic evaluation of INSET policies and programmes should re-examine their assumptions about INSET needs
22 The needs assessment process is so critical at both LEA and institutional levels that it also should be reviewed during INSET evaluation

Table 9.3 An illustration of evaluation possibilities for selected staff development outcomes (from Little, 1982: 30–31)

Can be evaluated by	Staff development that is designed to				
	Be satisfying to participants	*Build knowledge and skill*	*Foster actual use of new ideas and practices*	*Contribute to greater collegiality*	*Improve/alter students' performance, behaviour, attitudes*
Direct observation (performance-based evidence)	Participants' specific observations of the clarity of objectives, adequacy of instruction, opportunity for practice, usefulness of feedback Observers' records of frequency and nature of selected programme design components, e.g. instructors' modelling of intended behaviour	Staff developers supervisors' or peer observation of practice: • peer teaching • microteaching • other (e.g. team-building) Observation of actual implementation Criterion referenced knowledge or skill tests	Recorded classroom observation Teacher self-reports of nature and frequency of use (seminar 'debriefing', questionnaires, logs) Student reports of specific teacher practices	Direct observation of collaborative work (e.g. observation of team-building exercises; record of actual opportunities such as committee meetings) Participants' logs of actual work sessions	Classroom (or other) observation of specific performance, behaviours Student self-reports of behaviour; peer reports Criterion-referenced tests of knowledge, skill Norm-referenced tests of knowledge, skill Teacher logs, charts

Asking for perceptions, experiences	Participants' summary judgements of relevance and perceived utility of topic; participants' overall ratings of programme effectiveness Reviewers' judgements of programme prospects for achieving intended effects, based on review of design materials and activities	Participants' reports of main knowledge or skill gained Participants' anticipated gain on specific objectives of programme Others' reports of participants' gains	Teachers' and others' reported attitude toward (approval/disapproval) new practice Reported confidence; commitment to future use; support by peers and others; willingness to advocate to others, train others	Perceived sanctions for collaborative work Reported willingness to work with others Reported usefulness of working with others Perceived symmetry/equity in members' involvement, influence	Teachers' perceptions of student performance Students' perceptions, views, attitudes
Official records and other documentary evidence	Records of requests for new or follow-up participation			Collaboratively designed curriculum, lesson plans, other materials, classroom experiment, in-service sessions	Historical records of achievement, disciplinary referrals, etc., across time, groups, teachers, individual students, buildings

of possible evaluation questions. The criteria for such selection might well be:

- the potential usefulness of the answers in informing future action
- the feasibility of obtaining the required information
- the need to give an account of the effectiveness of the programme

Eraut *et al.*'s (1988) meta-evaluation of TRIST and their list of recommendations (see Table 9.2), are helpful in outlining a coherent strategy for the evaluation of INSET.

Techniques

The techniques used in the evaluation of INSET are generally the same as for other types of evaluation. Surveys, questionnaires, observations, interviews and document analysis are the stock in trade of the evaluator. An interesting approach to thinking about data collection techniques and INSET has been provided by Judith Little (see Table 9.3), and she links specific data collection techniques to particular staff development outcomes. This provides a very useful schema for designing an INSET evaluation and of beginning to face the different information needs at different system's levels noted above.

A range of data-gathering techniques have already been described in this book, but there are also a number of surveys or instruments that are particularly useful for the evaluation of INSET (Joyce and Showers, 1988: 119). Our own research on the effects of INSET (Evans and Hopkins, 1988) also contains a description of a number of relevant instruments and

Table 9.4   Levels of use of the innovation: Typical behaviours (after Hall *et al.*, 1975)

Level of use	Behavioural indices of level
VI. Renewal	The user is seeking more effective alternatives to the established use of the innovation
V. Integration	The user is making deliberate efforts to co-ordinate with others in using the innovation
IVB. Refinement	The user is making changes to increase outcomes
IVA. Routine	The user is making few or no changes and has an established pattern of use
III. Mechanical	The user is making changes to better organize use of the innovation
II. Preparation	The user is preparing to use the innovation
I. Orientation	The user is seeking out information about the innovation
O. Non-use	No action is being taken with respect to the innovation

techniques. One of the more reliable and useful instruments for evaluating the effects of in-service training is the Levels of Use of the Innovation (LOU) approach developed by Gene Hall and Susan Loucks (1977). The LOU categories (see Table 9.4) describe the behaviour of teachers as they become increasingly more familiar with and skilled in using particular curriculum or teaching approaches. It is a valid and reliable instrument with a well worked out administration and analysis process. It can also be used in developmental evaluations as it provides clear criteria for success. So, for example, if an LEA (or school) identified 'routine level of use' (LOU IVA) as the goal for teachers at the end of a pilot programme, then regular monitoring could measure progress towards that goal and encourage the redesign of the INSET support during the pilot in order to achieve it.

One of the approaches I have not mentioned so far is the most common INSET evaluation instrument, the self-report questionnaire on participants' opinion at the end of an INSET session. Joyce and Showers (1988: 121–2) are highly critical of 'opinionaires' which ask participants a variety of questions to which they respond on a 5-point scale. The questions tend to range from the attractiveness and/or effectiveness of the speaker and the training materials to the conditions of the training setting and refreshments. They argue that opinionaires tend to perpetuate the use of familiar offerings; produce the feeling that 'we know everything worth knowing'; and lose information about eventual use of knowledge or skill gained from training.

Such approaches are, however, inevitable and they are generally acceptable providing one realizes their limitations. Two examples of such questionnaires similar to the ones I use on my INSET courses are shown in Fig. 9.3.

Summary

I have tried in this chapter to sketch out some of the criteria, contexts, strategies and techniques for the evaluation of INSET. In drawing to a close I can do no better than to quote from Judith Little's (1982: 45) exemplary article on the requirements for a good staff development evaluation:

Range. The range of evaluation criteria should match the range of outcomes which the program publicly intends and which it is demonstrably and realistically designed to achieve.

Specificity. Program outcomes and program components or activities should be stated with sufficient specificity, concreteness, and precision to lend guidance to the formulation of evaluation criteria, the array of observable variables, and the selection of methods and measures.

Rigor. The rigor and stringency reflected in the evaluation design should adequately reflect the rigor and power of the program. Then, opportunities to pursue the strongest possible test of promising ideas will be deliberately cultivated.

Figure 9.3   Examples of INSET course members' evaluation questionnaire (from O'Sullivan *et al.*, 1988: 170 and 172).

EVALUATION SHEET I

SESSION TITLE: DATE AND TIME:

It would be of great assistance to the organizers of this session if you would be kind enough to complete this questionnaire.

1 List and comment upon any positive aspects of this session.

2 List and comment upon any negative aspects of this session.

3 Make any further comments or criticisms about the session and its relevance to your work. Any suggestions for improvements of content or presentation will be appreciated.

COURSE EVALUATION SHEET II

(a) Please use this sheet with a partner to review the course.

(b) You may wish to share your reactions as an LEA group as part of the final group session.

(c) The course organizers would find it extremely useful if you could complete this questionnaire individually and return it to us before the end of the conference.

PLEASE COMPLETE THESE SENTENCES:

1 The most useful part of this course was . . .
2 I expected that . . .
3 I did not expect that . . .
4 I liked . . .
5 I did not like . . .
6 Even though I did not expect to, I liked . . .
7 We needed more time to . . .
8 We spent too much time on . . .
9 There was not enough emphasis given to . . .
10 I felt the methods used were . . .
11 Work with partners was . . .
12 Work in groups was . . .
13 Sessions with the whole course together were . . .
14 The witness sessions were . . .
15 I felt the session on identifying training needs was . . .
16 My reactions to the school role play/simulation were . . .
17 I found the inter-LEA discussion groups on INSET design/delivery/support particularly . . .
18 My thoughts on the methods of evaluation used in the course are . . .
19 The presentation and talks were . . .
20 In addition I would like to say (including any suggestions for a repeat course) . . .

Relevance. Evaluation will be more valued by all if it is designed to provide useful information on recurrent issues and problems, if it preserves high standards while rewarding curiosity, and if it is designed to include teachers and administrators as informed partners in its design and conduct.

10
Project evaluation

Up to this point the evaluation role perspective adopted in the book has been a mix of internal–external with a slight bias to the former. In this chapter the balance shifts to the external evaluator. Although the internal evaluator will find some of the evaluation designs of interest – indeed each section in this chapter presents an evaluation strategy that can be used eclectically – the designs described below originated from 'outside' or external evaluators. As a consequence, perhaps they also tend to be a little more formal than those discussed in the three previous chapters. Individual components of these designs, however, have applications in a variety of evaluation for development settings.

The chapter begins with a discussion of some of the major issues surrounding project evaluation: the nature of the contract, the illusion of rationality, and the way in which the evaluation inevitably changes over time. The point being that evaluation research is an important but inexact science and recognition needs to be made of that fact not only by evaluators but also by those commissioning them. The following three sections of the chapter describe contrasting strategies for project evaluation with which I have recently been involved. The first example concerns TVEI, and is an attempt to develop an evaluation framework for curriculum developments that preserves the idiosyncracy and individuality of the local scheme. The second example is of an international multi-site case study of multicultural education. The third is a more structured multi-site evaluation of teacher appraisal in this country. The purpose of this chapter is to complement the discussion of strategies open to the developmental evaluator in previous chapters.

Some propositions concerning project evaluation

Some years ago Ray Bolam (1981) wrote a paper in which he discussed eight propositions that funding bodies and researchers should recognize and take account of as natural features of the evaluation of national projects. These practical issues provide a context in which to consider project evaluation.

Bolam's first two propositions are that *'the contract is crucial'* and that *'the evaluation task changes over time'*. The fact that these two propositions tend to be mutually exclusive creates significant problems for the evaluator. He or she has to set the parameters as clearly as possible, yet with the knowledge that the evaluation will most probably change or be extended during its life. There are no solutions to this predicament, but the inevitability of this situation needs to be anticipated.

Similarly inevitable is the third proposition, that *'the cast changes over time'*. These changes occur not only within the evaluation team but also in the funding body and the schools and LEAs providing the focus for the evaluation. This obviously affects the way in which the project is understood and put into practice. These changes in cast are sometimes mirrored by the fourth proposition that *'project policy changes significantly during the evaluation'*. Policy change can also be the result of external events such as economic recession or policy reinterpretation at the local level. Whatever the cause it often happens.

The fifth proposition, *'evaluative research designs balance rigour with practical realism'*, has been a continuing theme of this book, but its corollary (proposition 6) that *'implementation involves negotiation'* has only been implicit. The necessity for 'rigorous realism' is often not well understood by the non-evaluators involved in evaluation and they are often reluctant to relinquish ultimate control over the territory of the evaluation. This paradox creates difficulties for the evaluator in the implementation of the evaluation design. There are no solutions except experience and anticipation.

Bolam's final two propositions, that *'researchers affect the action'*(7), and *'evaluative research reports are not conclusive'*(8), tend only to be recognized by those non-evaluators involved in the evaluation once it is well under way. The implications of these propositions are less problematic in developmental evaluations because in these instances the evaluator purposefully adopts a formative role and the report is only one, although probably the most tangible, outcome of the evaluation.

There are four other issues I would add to Bolam's last two propositions. As they are related to the formative and implementation issues raised in Section raised in Section IV, I will only mention them briefly here, but they have important implications for the carrying out of project evaluation.

They are all to do with the reporting of evaluation. The first is that those who are subject to receiving an evaluation report take it more seriously than those who wrote it. And once it is in the public domain, there it remains. Consequently, great attention needs to be paid to language and style – casual drafting of an interim report can, as I have discovered to my cost, wreak havoc. Secondly, there are always different levels of interpretation of an evaluation report. Not everyone involved in an evaluation is interested in the same things. Not everyone will react to, or interpret, feedback in the same way. Be prepared for this and build into the evaluation safeguards against misinterpretation and also provide information for differing groups. Thirdly, although feedback does not inevitably lead to improvement, it does create energy. And, fourthly, this energy should be harnessed for development and improvement purposes.

Taken together, these propositions provide a useful set of issues that the project evaluator has to take account of before embarking on, and during, an evaluation. There are no obvious solutions to many of those predictable situations except that forewarned is forearmed!

A strategy for the evaluation of curriculum change at the local level

A few years ago a group of evaluators involved in the local evaluation of TVEI became concerned at the lack of systematic information emerging from these evaluation exercises. We wanted to find a way of conducting evaluations and of producing findings from across the local pilot evaluations that had some generalizable power but also preserved the individuality and idiosyncracies of the pilot schemes. I do not believe that we found a solution to the problem but we did come up with an evaluation framework that seemed to encapsulate the formative process that we felt characterized local evaluations of TVEI and other curriculum development initiatives. The description of the framework that follows is based on a paper I prepared for the then MSC TVEI unit. A fuller account of the framework can be found in Hopkins (1988a). The framework provides a relatively systematic strategy that has improvement and rationality as its *raison d'être*, and is useful to the range of people who may be cast in the role of evaluator. These characteristics need a little elaboration.

It must be recognized from the outset that the framework is a strategy rather than a technical guide. The framework is a way of conceptualizing the evaluation process and as such provides a guide to action. It does not, however, answer the 'how' questions; the focus is on 'why' evaluate and 'what' should be evaluated. In saying this I admit a bias, that in evaluation establishing the 'correct' question is as important as finding the 'correct' solution.

The framework is committed to development. The major purpose of local evaluations is to help improve the development of a particular curriculum development project – this is what is meant by formative evaluation. Summative evaluation, making a judgement on the worth of a thing, is not usually an important element in this process, although any description of a scheme inevitably involves some 'summative' judgements. Such analytical observations are an important part of a local evaluation, because the road to improvement travels through the landscape of description.

The main components of the framework (Fig. 10.1) are the three cells associated with policy (P), evaluation (E), and the formative process (F). I envisage a process that moves from policy formation and implementation, to evaluation, to formative discussion, which in turn leads to improved policy formation and implementation and another cycle of evaluation. Policy formation and implementation are usually the responsibility of the local education authority – the evaluation is inevitably the responsibility of the

Figure 10.1   A local evaluation framework for TVEI. Note that the arrows in the middle of the figure represent an ideal (idealized!) flow of action; other patterns of action are of course possible and indeed commonplace.

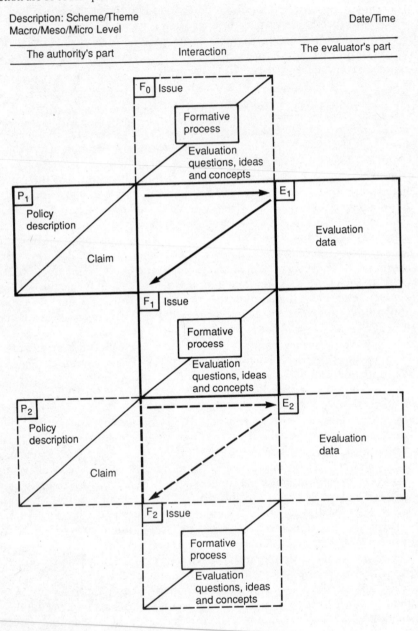

evaluator – but both need to interact if the formative process is to be successful. These separate and mutual roles are indicated in Fig. 10.1, as is the ideal flow of action.

It is initially very important that the evaluator clearly defines the situation he or she is getting into. I suggest that the framework is prefaced by a description of the scheme being evaluated, its major themes, and the consequent policy implications. This description is applicable at three levels: macro (project), meso (school/college) and micro (classroom). After completing the description of the scheme and theme to which the evaluation relates, one can turn to the three major elements or cells of the framework.

The '*P*' *cells* have two components. The first is the source/authority/ prescription/stated aim of the activity which is usually laid down by a policy maker rather than a practitioner. The second is the specific claim implied by the policy. The link between the two is more complex than may at first appear. This is for two reasons: first, because policy formation (i.e. the history of P) is a crucial factor in the evaluation; and, secondly, because the determination of a policy claim (i.e. what 'ought' to happen) from a policy statement is often problematic. Although a policy statement may not identify its claim (e.g. significant performance indicators), the claim may not be simply implicit. Projects may also issue claims that are orientated towards image rather than performance. As it is often possible to derive a number of (competing or inconsistent) claims from a policy statement the evaluator needs to:

- be sensitive to his or her own interpretation of a policy statement when 'identifying' its claims;
- be sensitive to participants' interpretations of a policy statement (i.e. what they think the policy is seeking to achieve);
- be sensitive to the interpretations others in the LEA may give a policy statement in the light of past experience;
- obtain further elucidation of the statement and its claims from the policy makers.

The '*E*' *cells* represent the evaluation data gathered in response to the claims made in the 'P' cells; it represents the collection of evidence that leads to evaluation. The data covers a wide range of information – in fact it can be anything that informs the situation under review. Documents, opinions, events, and policy statements are all data for evaluation, so in retrospect is the evaluation itself.

The '*F*' *cells* represent the formative process that occurs as a result of the evaluation data being analysed and interpreted in the light of project claims. This analysis and interpretation could be undertaken by a number of those involved in the project (e.g. evaluator, co-ordinator) either individually or collectively. Evaluators' questions which may be generalized across projects will usually emerge from this analysis. These evaluators' questions are normally of a different order to practitioners' questions which tend to be related to the day-to-day activities of the project. Evaluators' questions are usually to do with trends, ideas or concepts that transcend individual classroom concerns and relate to the wider implications of the scheme. These different order questions need to promote dialogue if an effective formative process is to occur. Policy and/or behaviour may or may not change as a result of this process; if it does, then that change is represented in subsequent P cells.

Cell P_2 represents the change occurring as a consequence of the formative process. This can be a shift of development in policy, or any change in emphasis or practice resulting from evaluation. The structure of this cell is similar to that of cell P_1 with a description of the policy and its implied specific claim. Cell E_2 represents the evaluation data gathered in response to the claim made in cell P_2. Cell F_2 represents the formative process.

Unfortunately, life is rarely as simple as this. To begin with, policy is not usually formed in a vacuum. Often there are antecedents, a history, and influences from other projects that inform or act upon the P_1 cell. These preconditions are illustrated in Fig. 10.1 as cell F_0. These influences may also act upon the E_1 cell in a subtle but still influential way.

The linkages between the P–E and E–F cells are also problematic. The movement from P to E begs many questions. Does policy specify its own evaluation? At what level is the policy to be evaluated? Who makes the decision to evaluate what? Are the evaluation techniques appropriate? Who decides the criteria for success?

Similarly, the link between E and F is not straightforward or inevitable and this also raises a number of questions. How is evaluation data fed into the formative process? Although very common, are written reports the most effective means of engaging participants in dialogue? What use is the formative process unless it involves practitioners, project authorities and evaluators?

The local evaluation framework is intended to suggest levels, sequences and organization of information gathering, processes, and analysis which will be useful to evaluators and enable them to meet more fully the needs of the many individuals involved in the project – whether they are aware of those needs or not. The framework can also be used by a variety of people engaged in curriculum evaluation. External evaluators can use it as a means of collating their data and planning feedback. Local authorities can use it to assess policy implementation. Co-ordinators can use it to track developments of the central themes of the curriculum. Teachers can use it as a basis for self-evaluation. All can use it as a common language to discuss and compare their various interests in a particular project or across a range of curriculum initiatives.

Models can often trap the user within the intention of its originator and so inhibit freedom of action. This framework is not prescriptive, yet its specificity will hopefully provide not only a basis for thinking about curriculum practice and policy, but also a systematic and commonsense structure for doing evaluation. As such, the framework is less a straitjacket and more an exhortation to action. Because it is a means of understanding, planning, comparing, discussing and thinking about curriculum development, the framework has potential value.

Figure 10.2 The multi-site case study approach (taken from Yin, 1984: 51).

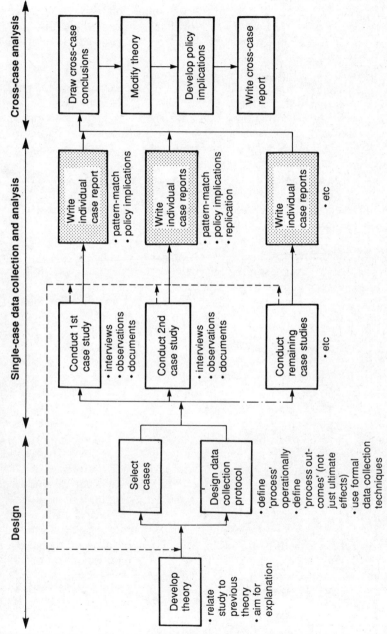

A multi-site multicultural case study approach

I am currently assisting the OECD to develop a case study evaluation strategy for its Educational and Cultural and Linguistic Pluralism (ECALP) Project. What follows are extracts from a paper on a multi-site case study that I prepared for those responsible for producing the national case studies. It provides another example of a large-scale multi-site evaluation design that has a formative and qualitative bias.

The purpose of the ECALP project is to study innovation strategies which have resulted in particularly successful forms of education for the children of immigrants or ethnic minority groups. The detailed analysis of these innovations is likely to be of interest to all those who are involved in multicultural education. It will draw attention to some effective and exemplary practices and also identify useful criteria for the formulation of new policies in this area. A case study approach is especially well suited to the goals of the project, since inclusion in the sample is dictated by the uniqueness or creativity of the strategy rather than on the number of such cases.

Unfortunately, the case study approach is often associated with certain methodological problems. Among these are: a lack of clarity about the nature of the innovation; the absence of theoretical frameworks against which to consider the innovation; a variety of sources of data and the way in which they are handled; a vagueness about analytical procedures and their link to issues such as validity and reliability; and how this analysis can lead to the generation of theory and the formation of policy. In order to help overcome some of these problems the ECALP project is adopting an explicit process for its multi-site case study strategy together with the use of a case study protocol as a means of structuring national case studies and facilitating cross-case comparison.

Figure 10.2 is a flow diagram which represents the multi-site case study approach adopted by the ECALP project. The process progresses through three stages: design, single case data collection and analysis, and cross-case analysis. The design stage includes the first phase of the ECALP project that identified a series of parameters that provide the 'theoretical' bases for this the second phase of the project. At the time of writing, the cases have (in most instances) been identified and case study protocols are being developed. The second stage of the project, the production of the individual national cases, will be completed within 18 months and follow the flow outlined in the middle part of Fig. 10.2. The final stage of the project, the cross-case analysis, again following the steps outlined in Fig. 10.2, will be completed by the following year.

The foundation of an effective multi-site case study design is the formulation of a series of case study protocols for each individual case study. The case study protocol being used in the ECALP project is composed of four sections (see Table 10.1). A description of how to develop a protocol is found in Yin (1984: 64–74). The unique feature of the ECALP protocols is that they are uniform yet idiosyncratic, in that they represent both the aspirations of the ECALP project while characterizing the uniqueness of the individual case. The major similarities and differences between the individual case study protocols need some elaboration.

Table 10.1   The Case Study Protocol (adapted from Yin, 1984: 64)

Section 1   Overview of the case study project (both ECALP and individual), e.g. objectives, issues and background

Section 2   Field procedures, e.g. case study sites, data sources, ethics, time lines

Section 3   Case study design, i.e. its propositions, the case study questions, its unit(s) of analysis, the logic linking data to propositions, and criteria for interpretation

Section 4   Guide for case study report, e.g. outline, analytical procedures, format for narrative, documentation, grounded theory

In section 1, the ECALP project overview is common, whereas the content of the individual cases obviously varies and requires articulation in order to establish an agreed statement for the field workers and provide information for the reader. The field procedure outlined in section 2, while inevitably being similar in approach, will be unique to each particular case study. The second section of the protocol therefore focuses on the 'nuts and bolts' issues related to the access to school sites, the variety of data sources, the ethics of data collection and ownership, and the time lines established for the production of the case study.

Case study design issues are the focus of section 3. It is here where the overlap between the ECALP project concerns and the particular issues related to each case is most pronounced. The five features of a case study research design (Yin, 1984: 29) are as follows:

1 the case study propositions;
2 its questions;
3 its unit of analysis;
4 the logic linking data to propositions; and
5 criteria for interpretation.

These features are best considered under two general headings: conceptual framework (features 1–3) and data gathering and analysis (features 4 and 5).

The conceptual framework for the case study design is comprised of the case study's propositions, its questions and the unit(s) of analysis. There will probably be two types of proposition, those pertaining to the individual case and those shared by the project. The parameters described in ECALP (1988) comprise the project's propositions. These parameters are: cultural/linguistic incorporation, community participation, pedagogy, assessment, technology and pre-school education. Although these parameters provide a theoretical context for the project they need not apply to each case study. The assumptions underlying them, however, will be an important aspect of cross-case analysis.

The case study questions are initially derived from the propositions, but will also reflect the concerns of the project and the individual case. Five types of case study questions can be distinguished: (i) to individuals; (ii) to cases; (iii) across cases; (iv) to the entire study; and (v) about policy issues and conclusions. Questions (i) and (ii) are more case-specific and questions (iii), (iv) and (v) tend to be more related to the project. They do, however, build on and inform each other. A comprehensive range of questions that form the basis of this section of the protocol can also be found in ECALP (1988).

The unit of analysis is an often neglected aspect of case study research. What is the focus of the case study? Is it the school? The classroom? The school district? National policy? Or the innovation itself? Not only does the focus of the case study need clear identification and description but its implications for the questions asked and its relationship to the parameters needs also to be defined. The unit of analysis has also to be related to various other levels in the education system.

These three elements of the case study design, i.e. propositions, questions and unit of analysis, provides a framework for the field of enquiry of the case study. Although this framework is comprehensive, each case study is unique and will generate its own individual map of enquiry. The interaction of these three elements of the case study design provide a context in which the individual case can be defined.

The final two elements of the case study design, the logic linking data to propositions and the criteria for interpretation, are obviously interlinked and focus on issues related to data gathering and analysis.

Writing the case study report comprises the fourth and final part of the case study protocol. Some specific advice about the preparation of the cases is given in ECALP (1988). This advice concerns the length, timing, methods and role of those involved in the case study. As regards the actual format of the case study, this can follow a number of different patterns, e.g. the linear analytic, the comparative, the chronological or theory building case study. The *linear analytic* case study which follows a systematic pattern, such as the list of questions or issues contained in the protocol, is the most common format and for a number of reasons is to be preferred. The *comparative* case study either repeats the portrayal of the innovation from different perspectives, or replicates the innovation in a series of different situations; the *chronological* case study adopts a narrative format; and the *theory building* case study commits itself to supporting or elucidating a particular theoretical position.

In summary, this brief review of the case study approach adopted by the ECALP project has concentrated on the multi-site case study approach and the production of the case study protocol. The case study protocol, although only the initial part of the overall process, provides a fundamental foundation stone which lays the basis for the production of authentic individual case studies and valid cross-case comparisons. Consequently, it is necessary to give careful and sufficient attention to the preparation of the protocol in the early stages of the project, particularly when the case studies are being prepared by a variety of people (project workers, researchers, policy makers) in a number of different countries, none of whom are responsible for producing the cross-case analysis.

Evaluation of the School Teacher Appraisal Pilot Study

An example of the application of a qualitative methodology to a large-scale, multi-site project is provided by the evaluation of the School Teacher Appraisal Pilot Study. This description is taken from a more technical discussion of our approach to qualitative methodology (Hopkins *et al.*, 1989). In this project, the scope of the evaluation was defined by the size and nature of the pilot study and by the 'evaluation contract'. Essentially, the evaluation task involved three key areas: (1) monitoring and reporting of the progress in each of the six LEA's piloting appraisal, (2) presenting an overview of the pilot study in order to identify and be able to comment on general issues, and (3) reviewing literature and research on appraisal. Ultimately, all three tasks have been justified by the need to collect data from the pilot study in order to inform the development of national guidelines for appraisal.

While there were precedents for this type of evaluation, some of the data-handling issues were innovative. In essence, the aim was to bring rigour into qualitative approaches. The basic methodological model used was influenced by the ideas of Miles and Huberman (1984a, b). The evaluation has followed the general tenor of their advice in making procedures and thought processes explicit and has been influenced by their approach to data handling.

In operationalizing this model for an evaluation team of six members a number of stages were followed. First, the evaluation team drew up a *data collection matrix* to provide a guide as to what information to collect. The matrix was based on an analysis of the ACAS Appraisal/Training Working Group Report which set out a framework and principles for teacher appraisal, and on the submissions for inclusion in the pilot study of the participating LEAs. The matrix took the form of the stages an appraisal scheme might go through and tabulated related issues. It has informed the design of all subsequent evaluation instruments, such as questionnaires or interview schedules, thus enabling a consistent approach.

Secondly, a *data analysis framework* was devised (see Fig. 5.1, p. 71). This has three stages: (1) data collection, (2) data reduction and analysis, and (3) data preparation. Data collection has been accomplished in a variety of ways. In the original evaluation proposal, four approaches to gathering data were stressed – using questionnaires, interviews, observation and the analysis of documents. Subsequently, as the work of evaluation developed, more emphasis has been given to the use of case studies, cameos and the use of self-reporting by those involved in the pilot study. The various approaches to data gathering have complemented and drawn on each other (and thus aid the validation process) and have been informed by the matrix drawn up in the light of ACAS principles and LEA plans. The system has allowed for additional data-gathering instruments to be brought in as the evaluation progresses.

At the data reduction and analysis stage, new data has been cross-checked for internal consistency and consistency with other data. It has then been transferred on to summary sheets, which have themselves been based on the data collection matrix. In practice, this has meant that the data which appear on these summary sheets will have (i) emerged from several sources, (ii) been compared with other data, (iii) been collected by more than one evaluator, and (iv) been re-checked with sources in the field. This data has been stored on a word processor by issue and LEA and indexed by headings drawn from the matrix.

At the data presentation stage, reports of a more or less formative nature have been prepared and issues identified for further investigation. Hypotheses have both emerged and begun to be established. In view of the cyclical nature of the evaluation model, such reports, issues and hypotheses have also been recorded on the word processor to allow for further cross-checking, analysis and updating.

The matrix and the framework are, as has been indicated, interrelated and built on each other during each of these stages. The system has worked best when there has been a full flow of data enabling adequate cross-checking. When there has not been a full flow of data, inferences drawn from the data could only be regarded as provisional.

The criteria used in any evaluation are always problematic. In this evaluation the team have not used their own model of appraisal against which to assess data. At the data collection stage, the evaluators have gone into the field to collect and analyse data which have usually emerged as an analytical description. At this stage there have been no criteria, simply a methodology. What have emerged are the validated responses or attitudes of, for example, a Head or teachers. The second stage has involved the interpretation of the data by reference to explicit, extant criteria. These criteria have come from three sources: the principles set out in the ACAS document, LEA policy and relevant literature. As the pilot study and the evaluation have gathered momentum the intention has been to produce evaluation reports that are descriptive and analytical, interpreted by the sort of criteria referred to above, and illuminated by cameos or mini case studies.

The methodology adopted has provided a means of resolving a number of typical evaluation dilemmas. Some of these have been of a technical nature; for example, how to carry out a multi-site evaluation without injustice to particular individual experience. Other dilemmas have concerned the different possible roles open to evaluators and the various possible uses of evaluation. Given the sensitivity of appraisal, and the moves to establish it as national policy, the political dilemmas of the evaluation could not be ignored.

These dilemmas and the context of the pilot have served to make this evaluation a useful case study for those engaged on similar exercises. In particular, the scale, political dimension and fixed frame of reference have all placed heavy demands on the evaluation methodology. This had to not only process information, but also had to stand up to a sometimes very rigorous public scrutiny.

In summary, the chief characteristics of the approach have been:

1 The cross-checking of data from different sources, gathered by different evaluators.

2 The interpretation of data in the light of explicit criteria, provided by others.
3 The way the methodological framework provides a stable procedural structure for handling data but is capable of being supplemented with new instruments as the evaluation develops.
4 The way the methodological framework provides a basis for reconciling the individual working practices of team members in order to achieve a 'common front'.
5 The way the presence of such a rigorous and explicit approach to methodology serves accountability purposes.

Summary

This chapter has considered project evaluation, and in contrast to other chapters in this section has adopted more of a large-scale and external perspective. A series of propositions concerning the somewhat ambivalent and changing nature of project evaluation and problems associated with feedback were first considered. This overview was followed by descriptions of three large-scale evaluation projects that adopted different strategies to achieve similar ends. Although these accounts have been of specific evaluations, the strategies described are adaptable to a range of evaluation settings. Consequently, I hope that this discussion complements the smaller-scale approaches to evaluation discussed in previous chapters of this section on developmental approaches.

Section IV
Making an impact

11
Making evaluation formative

The phrase 'evaluating for development' implies a formative approach: an approach that produces evaluation data and reports that help participants or policy makers improve practice or programmes. Although the distinction between formative and summative evaluation is superficially clear – a guide to improvement as against evidence for judgement – in practice it often breaks down. Often formative evaluations are little more than a series of mini summative reports; and, similarly, summative evaluation reports are often used to encourage development. I have also found formative evaluation extremely difficult to do. Often I try very hard to make an evaluation improve a programme; I do all the right things, yet it still just comes apart in my hand. But occasionally a hastily prepared report will have enormous impact. Formative evaluation can be an uncomfortable and unpredictable business. This is particularly the case in the evaluation of categorically funded projects where time is at a premium and sponsors appear to require judgements on partially implemented programmes. In this chapter, therefore, I begin by examining some of the paradoxes surrounding formative evaluation, which is followed by an extended discussion of some of the problems involved. In the final section I discuss a number of ways in which evaluation data can be reported or fed back to participants or policy makers.

The paradox of formative evaluation

At a recent seminar David Bridges (1988) set out a paradox for formative evaluation. His central point, the paradox, is that the more formative an evaluator becomes the less independent he or she can be in practice. He makes the argument by reference to the issues outlined in Table 11.1, which are self-explanatory. Bridges' thesis is that on the dimensions associated with reporting, values, status, prescription and engagement, the closer and more

Table 11.1   What conditions help to make professional evaluation 'formative'? (from Bridges, 1988)

	← *Towards greater formative influence and less independence*	*Towards greater independence and less formative influence* →
Reporting	Continual formal and informal dialogue with managers and decision makers	Written document produced long after practice is established
Values	Common basis of values shared between evaluator(s) and developer(s)	Evaluator(s) values different from those of developer(s)
Status	Evaluator perceived as more or less equal in status to developer	Evaluator perceived as having different (and in particular) lower status
Description/ prescription	Evaluator will enter into discussion about alternative strategies or even recommended action	Evaluator describes analyses and reports only
Engagement/ distance	The evaluator wants the initiative to succeed and feels some responsibility for its success	The evaluator has a stance of detached curiosity, scepticism or opposition

committed the formative evaluator is to the project the less independent he or she becomes. Whether the formative evaluator is necessarily lacking in independence or 'too cosy' is a moot point. I would like to believe that an evaluation can be both formative and independent. There is, however, a logic to Bridges' argument which cautions the evaluator not to fall into the trap of collusion while attempting to make his or her evaluation more formative.

At the same seminar as Bridges talked about his formative-independence paradox, I reflected on an ongoing formative evaluation I was involved with. Despite my commitment to a formative approach I felt that I was getting nowhere. Over the 4 years of the evaluation, reports became shorter and the period of feedback increased, but still with minimal effect. The problem as I saw it was five-fold and I summarized the points in these questions:

- What to evaluate?
- What is formative evaluation?
- Beware the enclave?
- How does one give feedback?
- How does one facilitate action?

These apparently simplistic questions belie more profound issues. Usually, the evaluation focus is negotiated at entry. In this particular evaluation the focus was often left to me, but even then I had to be certain at the outset that the most appropriate issues had been selected. Is this the issue that is going to provide the most useful data for developmental purposes? If not, what is and how do I get access to it? Coupled to this is the question of formative evaluation *per se*. Is it simply a succession of short summative reports? Or, does it have a distinctive character of its own? How do I do it? What does it look like? What effect does it have?

'Beware the enclave?' is an exhortation as well as a question and is similar to the concerns expressed earlier. Objectivity tends to suffer when one gets too involved and their problems become your problems. It is an issue of a different order from the others and perhaps the most difficult to resolve.

The fourth question – 'How does one give feedback?' – screamed at me when faced with a library full of teachers not knowing why they were there but expecting some sort of 'talking (down?) to'. How does one facilitate mutual dialogue in the library before the bell rings? Or how, when in the committee room of the County Hall, does one get the politicians and policy makers to engage with substantive issues rather than asking for marks out of 10, before the bar opens? Sure it's feedback . . . of a sort, but does it do any good? And why are these situations so predictable?

This leads to the final question, 'How does one facilitate action?'. Given that feedback is difficult to facilitate, then action as a result often appears a non-starter. How does one prepare the evaluation report or video or whatever, in such a way as to provide the impetus, energy and time to move into constructive action? Why are we so much better at talking about things than doing something?

How can evaluation become formative?

It was these rather dismal thoughts that prompted my reflection on the formative process. I came away with no real solutions, but at least the reflection produced some promising ideas. In my search for answers there were three sources of inspiration.

The first was from my colleagues Rob Fiddy and Ian Stronach (1987) who graphically expressed similar concerns and experiences. They argue that in contemporary evaluation democratic approaches put too much pressure on the client to interpret the data. They argue that we need to move from theories of transmission to theories of reception in the utilization of evaluation data. Why is it, they ask, that we, as evaluators and researchers into educational practice, are so uninterested in the pedagogical relations between ourselves and our clients? Especially since the evidence seems to be that our clients learn little from us, and value us still less. Their responses are illuminating: they argue for the abandonment of external critique, the rejection of models for formative evaluation, the end to writing reports, the development of pedagogy (rather than methodology), new kinds of educational research, and for the reintegration of evaluation and development.

The second influence was that of Ken Leithwood and colleagues who have been exploring similar territory. In a recent review of the utilization of evaluation data, Cousins and Leithwood (1986: 360) concluded that evaluation results are utilized most effectively when:

- evaluations were appropriate in approach, methodological sophistication, and intensity;
- the decisions to be made were significant to users and of a sort considered appropriate for the application of formally collected data;
- evaluation findings were consistent with the beliefs and expectations of the users;
- users were involved in the evaluation process and had a prior commitment to the benefits of evaluation;
- users considered the data reported in the evaluation to be relevant to their problems;
- a minimum amount of information from other sources conflicted with the results of the evaluation.

The third influence is a paper by Matthew Miles (1987) on 'Practical guidelines for school administrators: How to get there'. His goal is to describe the path from knowledge to action, to develop a model for how knowledge could affect action, seen from the knowledge-user's point of view.

Here in his words (Miles, 1987: 2–3) is a cut at what might be required. Let's assume that some valid 'knowledge' has been generated by a researcher. What key conditions must be present if someone (a 'user') is to take some action congruent with the knowledge?

Clarity: The knowledge must be understood clearly – not be fuzzy, vague or confusing.

Relevance: The knowledge is seen as meaningful, as connected to one's normal life and concerns – not irrelevant, inapplicable, impractical.

Action images: The knowledge is or can become exemplified in specific actions, clearly visualized. Without such images, knowledge-based action is unlikely.

Will: There must be motivation, interest, action orientation, a will to do something with the knowledge.

Skill: There must be actual behavioral ability to do the action envisioned. Without skill, the action will either be aborted or done incongruently with the knowledge undergirding it.

Miles (1987: 3–4) makes some further comments about this model:

though there's a rough sequence from clarity to skill, the conditions are interactive. For example, seeing clear action images may result in an

Table 11.2 Questions for reviewing (evaluating) evaluations (from Harlen and Elliot, 1982: 303–304)

1 Did the evaluation serve to inform the decisions or judgements for which it was originally intended?
2 What decisions have been taken as a consequence of the evaluation?
3 Was the evaluation task interpreted and carried through consistently as intended?
4 Was the information which was gathered appropriate to the purpose of the evaluation?
5 What steps were taken to allow for bias, unrepresentativeness, and low reliability in the information gathered?
6 Were the actual evaluators in the best position to carry out the evaluation?
7 Were the methods used appropriate to the kind of information which was required?
8 Were the methods systematic and explicit?
9 Did those involved in supplying the information approve of the methods used for collecting it?
10 Was there sufficient time allowed in the evaluation for the necessary data to be collected?
11 Was the evaluation carried out at the best time to serve its purpose?
12 What were the side-effects, positive and negative, of the evaluation process?
13 Were satisfactory procedures used to protect the interests of those who supplied information?
14 Were the criteria by which judgement or decisions were made appropriately drawn and explicitly stated?
15 Was the evaluation reported in a way which communicated effectively with the intended audience?
16 What reactions did the report provoke in the participants and in the decision makers?

increased sense of relevance. Or added skill may increase will, since a good outcome is expected.

Furthermore, it is sad but true that plenty of school improvers think that skill can be developed through reading, lectures, or watching videotapes. It can't. Improving skill requires doing, practice, getting feedback, reshaping the doing until your doing makes sense, is smooth and gets you where you want. We know this about skiing, tennis, and golf, but not quite, it seems, about the behaviors involved in educational change. There are good skill-development models around (e.g. Joyce and Showers), but they often don't get used when it comes to day-to-day doing.

One can conclude from the foregoing discussions that formative evaluation:

● pays explicit attention to the change process;
● focuses on users' issues;
● involves users in the process;
● develops a pedagogy for learning from evaluation;

- utilizes a methodology consistent with its purpose; and
- integrates evaluation and development.

Guidelines and criteria for preparing reports

There are a number of guidelines and criteria that people have produced that are helpful in formulating one's evaluation report. Such a list of questions for evaluating an evaluation was given by Harlen and Elliott (see Table 11.2).

As regards the nature of evaluation reports, Oldroyd and Hall (1988: 96) confirm much of the advice given in this chapter when they say:

> Effective reports need to focus on what the specified audience really needs to know. There is little point in asking busy professionals to spend time producing documents which have no practical use. Good quality evaluation reports depend on clear evaluation questions, authentic information rather than impression, and clear conclusions based on explicit criteria and linked to specific recommendations. The more concise and clear they are, the more likely they are to be read and to influence decision-making.

Eraut (1985: 24) expands on this point when he comments:

> Yet evaluation is more than a report or a series of reports. The basic purpose of evaluation is to underpin the learning process for all those associated with course provision. It helps communication, extends understanding and deepens the linkage between all involved; and these processes will be served by verbal interaction as well as by the written word.

He then makes some specific suggestions (Eraut, 1985: 25):

> The goal of evaluation is to ensure that it leads to appropriate action. So not only what is written, but also the pattern of reporting, should be aimed at generating action-related thinking. The evaluator must target on those who need to know because they have responsibility for acting rather than those who would merely find the information useful.
>
> Thus some reporting needs to be *task specific*. For instance:
>
> (i) early feedback to the course team about course members' perceptions;
> (ii) listing of issues or concerns for the attention of particular people;
> (iii) specification of needs by a particular group such as LEA officers or the course members;
> (iv) specific short papers illuminating a particular matter needing attention;
> (v) exemplars of 'good practice', for the course team, NDC, LEA or schools;
> (vi) summary of outcomes, for the providing institution, NDC, LEA or councillors.

The form of such reports will be *action specific*, for example:

(i) an item for the attention of the Course Committee may need to be discussed with the Chairman and/or others to ensure adequate presentation and coverage on the agenda;

(ii) a matter may need discussing with an LEA adviser or officers to determine the evidence needed to take it forward within the Education Office;

(iii) feedback to particular individuals in the providing institution about a significant issue needing attention may begin with a memo.

Taken together this rather eclectic collection of advice provides some indication of the character of formative reports, although as is implicit in all that has been written, such reports are of necessity idiosyncratic.

Preparing evaluation reports

One of the approaches I often use in preparing evaluation reports is to follow the descriptive analysis approach referred to when discussing Stake's matrix in Chapter 2. The report is typically short, preceded by an executive summary, with the main body of the text being a description of my response to the evaluation questions being as 'value free' and 'objective' as I can. This description has been subject to the analytical process outlined in Chapter 5. The report typically concludes with an interpretation of the descriptive data from the viewpoint of various 'up front' criteria and may or may not include a set of recommendations. This sort of approach has proved to be quite successful, particularly in the focused, and time and resource limited evaluations that are so common nowadays.

There are, however, some serious pitfalls inherent in this approach for the formative evaluator. Formative implies a sense of collaboration and shared goals, but when the report is placed on the table it tends to distort this relationship. The most common reaction on the part of the 'client' is a 'how well have we done' attitude which is often followed by defensiveness in response to perceived criticism. This has been an all too regular an occurrence for me recently, particularly at the early stages of an evaluation, where the handling of the first report is an important element in the 'learning from evaluation' process.

Although this predictable crisis is often overcome, it is rarely without cost, and can distort the formative relationship for some time. I have found that four strategies in particular have tended to help. The first is to give feedback as you go along. Attempt to establish a critical dialogue so that both the project and the evaluation learn from the experience. Establish early on the principle of 'off the record' discussion. The second is to discuss the contents of the evaluation report verbally with the 'client' before submitting the final report – in particular format, general content and any possibly contentious issues. This makes the report less of a surprise. Thirdly, allow the client a right of reply, especially on matters of fact. Establishing this as a principle of procedure early on in the evaluation allays fears that the evaluation report is cast in stone. Fourthly, pay careful attention to the use of language. The most innocuous phrase can be misinterpreted and lead to a vitriolic reaction. So re-read the draft carefully, look for ambiguities and try and place yourself in the client's position by reading it from his or her perspective. Remember that they often perceive their reputations as being on the line in the report.

This advice is of course no panacea, but the discussion should serve to highlight the fundamental point that the written evaluation report often assumes irrational importance for some; it should therefore be prepared very carefully.

Case studies

Robert Stake (1986b: 94) talks about case studies as providing vicarious experiences for 'readers who are not placed to observe for themselves, but who when realising the descriptive account, can experience vicariously the various perplexities and efforts to remedy'. We can understand far better if we have concrete images to relate to, and in formative evaluation, case studies or cameos (briefer more discrete descriptions of instances) often provide such concreteness. As Adelman *et al.* (1976: 148–9) note:

Case studies have a number of advantageous characteristics that make them attractive to educational evaluators or researchers:

(i) Case study data, paradoxically, is 'strong in reality' but difficult to organise. This strength in reality is because case studies are down-to-earth and attention holding, in harmony with the reader's own experience, and thus provide a 'natural' basis for generalisation.

(ii) Case studies allow generalisations either about an instance or from an instance to a class. Their peculiar strength lies in their attention to the subtlety and complexity of the case in its own right.

(iii) Case studies recognise the complexity and 'embeddedness' of social truths. By carefully attending to social situations, case studies can represent something of the discrepancies or conflicts between the viewpoints held by participants.

(iv) Case studies, considered as products, may form an archive of descriptive material sufficiently rich to admit subsequent reinterpretation. Given the variety and complexity of educational purposes and environments, there is an obvious value in having a data source for researchers and users whose purposes may be different from our own.

(v) Case studies are 'a step to action'. They begin in a world of action and contribute to it. Their insights may be directly interpreted and put to use for staff or individual self-development, for within institutional feedback, for formative evaluation, and in educational policy making.

(vi) Case studies present research or evaluation data in a more publicly accessible form than other kinds of research report, although this virtue is to some extent bought at the expense of their length. The case study is capable of serving multiple audiences. It reduces the dependence of the researcher upon unstated implicit assumptions (which necessarily underlie any type of research) and makes the research process itself accessible.

Nisbet and Watt (1984) make some suggestions about how to design and do a case study, which is similar to the ideas discussed in Chapter 5. They suggest that a case study should start with an open phase, a general review without prejudgement. Then you must focus on those aspects which you identify as of crucial importance. The third stage involves putting on paper in draft form your interpretation. Before you can put this into its final form, you must check your interpretations with your informants, to take account of (but not necessarily accept) their critical comments. They also make some suggestions on procedure:

1 *Cross-checking*. In order to guard against being misled, either in interview, or by documents, you must check one informant against another, and test what they say against any documents which exist. Similarly, observations in one context must be checked against others in comparable situations. This process is called *triangulation*. The basic principle in data collection for case studies is to check your data across a variety of methods and a variety of sources.
2 *A conceptual framework*. When it comes to analysing your data, trying to fit all the varied information into a coherent story or picture, you will have to decide on a framework of concepts. Again, you have a difficult balance to maintain, avoiding the two extremes of forcing the data to fit your preconceptions (or omitting the awkward bits that do not fit) and presenting the information in such a disorganized form that it is impossible to make sense of it.

There are a number of other ways in which case study methodology can be made more valid. One is the comparative case study, where instead of spending x amount of time on a single case study the researcher spends x/2 time at two roughly comparable (rather than diverse) sites. If the researcher was looking at the role of the chartered librarian in enhancing study skills for example, such a design would arguably produce more valid information. This design can be illustrated in the following way where x is the event and O the observation:

$$\frac{x \; O_1}{x \; O_2}$$

The exemplary case study, therefore, will have a number of characteristics. It will be *significant*, i.e. the case itself will be of general interest and the issues it raises will be of some importance. It will be *complete*, in so far as the

Figure 11.1   A formative evaluation cartoon (Fiddy and Stronach, 1987).

boundaries of the case are explicit and justifiable, that the evidence collected is sufficient to cover the substance of the case, and that the case study ran its full course. It will *consider alternative perspectives* in so far as it considers rival explanations and is critical and evaluative in style. It will *display sufficient evidence* (often in appendices and footnotes) to enable the reader to reach an independent judgement regarding the merits of the analysis. Finally, it will be *composed in an engaging manner*, which means a clear writing style, a logical presentation and a seductive and entertaining narrative drive (Yin, 1984).

Other formats for reporting on formative evaluations

There are any number of formats that one can use to feedback formative evaluation data. As long as the principles of procedure outlined in Chapters 4 and 5 are followed, then imagination is the only limit on the possibilities. Here are four examples.

1 *Cartoons.* Fiddy and Stronach (1987) used a cartoon (see Fig. 11.1) to present the data with as much impact as possible.
2 *Data displays.* Another way of presenting evaluation data to make the maximum impact is to use a matrix format. For example, Matthew Miles used his formative feedback model described earlier with the key findings from his school improvement research. The matrix displayed the various stages and interpretation of his data in a most convincing and accessible way. Similarly, Marilyn Evans and I displayed the data from our INSET research (see Chapter 9) using data display tables as shown in Table 11.3. This approach allows large amounts of data to be displayed economically and could be accompanied by another page of questions and explanation that highlighted the main issues.
3 *Fiction* is another approach that can be used to report evaluation data. Rob Walker (1981) made the argument for this approach in his amusingly entitled paper 'On the uses of fiction in educational research (and I don't mean Cyril Burt)'. The following example is part of a summary of 29 interviews with modern language teachers (from Rudduck and Hopkins, 1984: 72–3):

French conversation piece
This section is an imaginary discussion by teachers on library use and independent study, based on 29 verbatim interview transcripts from the LASS archive.

The scene was a teachers' college, one of those beautifully elegant and ornate Georgian buildings that used to be the country seat of some member of the landed gentry but which in later years served as a seat of learning for young women who aspired to become teachers. It preserved its façade of elegance and decorum until quite recently, but then, in response to economic and political pressures, it began to cater for a much wider range of students. The austerity associated with the institution disappeared, and use of the buildings was encouraged for short courses

Table 11.3 An example of a data display (from Evans and Hopkins, 1988)

Profile of School A depicting: (a) school climate, (b) psychological state of the individual teacher and (c) the individual teacher's utilization of educational ideas

School climate		The psychological state of the individual teacher						The individual teacher's utilization of educational ideas		
		Rating					Descriptive analysis	Rating		Descriptive analysis
Rating	Descriptive analysis	Gregorc (1982)	Telford (1970)	Georgiades (1972)	Maslow (1962)			LoU	Imp. score	
116.3	1 Goal focus. The development of literacy and numeracy within a conducive atmosphere.	**Teacher 1.**								
	2 Communication adequacy. Ease of communication attributed to smallness of staff group. Formal mechanics of communication in evidence. Staff meetings held on a regular basis. External support welcome. Parental involvement actively encouraged.	AR	213	30	4		Very confident; assured of own worth and value. A definite orientation towards achievement; constantly striving for perfection. This abstract-random's approach to change is subject to the intensity of her interest. Capable of learning in a holistic manner, and has strong recollection ability.	IVA	83	Sound knowledge of aesthetic philosophy. Actively seeking out new ideas and collaborating with experts. Planning occurred at routine level. Assessment at mechanical level. Classroom performance at routine level. No difficulties reported in use. Overall use assessed at routine level.
	3 Optimal-power utilization. A collegial form of school management.	**Teacher 2.**								
	4 Resource utilization. (a) Effective use of scale post holders as curriculum leaders. INSET was greatly valued as an	CS	208	28	4		Shows interest in growth and new experience; seeking further achievement. Stresses personal worth, while maintaining a sense of belonging to the group. Once an idea proves viable to this concrete-sequential individual he strives for perfection. Change	III	61	Mechanical knowledge base. Actively involved in organized workshops. Seeking out further information. Planning and performance at mechanical level. No continuity or sequence established. Assessing remained at level of orientation. Overall

educational tool. (b) Small school capitation allowance proved a limiting factor, but staff worked together in an attempt to maximize resource utilization.

5 *Cohesiveness*. The staff were perceived to be functioning as a 'whole' as regards curriculum matters.

6 *Morale*. The atmosphere was indicative of a feeling of well being and satisfaction.

7 *Innovativeness*. Innovative and realistic. Time, discussion and the provision of resources viewed as essential components.

8 *Autonomy*. Staff free to explore various educational ideas within their own classrooms.

9 *Adaption*. Staff flexible in approach, and able to adapt to new demands.

10 *Problem solving*. Staff functioned as a group in formulating school policies.

Teacher 3.
CS   179   15   3+   III   40

must be structured and sequential.

An orientation towards belonging; striving to increase personal competence. This concrete-sequential individual required time to adapt to new situations. Change must come in slow, deliberate and incremental steps. Faith placed in specialists to explain phenomena which are not personally verifiable.

use assessed at mechanical level.

Knowledge base at level of preparation. Actively involved in organized workshops. Planning and assessing remained at low level. Performance at mechanical level; lack of confidence shown in offering child appropriate guidance. Overall use assessed at mechanical level.

and weekend conferences. Conference members now have the experience of wandering the slightly dowdy gardens and lawns, enjoying sunshine and views, and wondering how many others have trodden these paths before.

Outside it was one of those balmy, listless days, but inside, behind those august walls, in a well appointed meeting room, a discussion was going on. Twenty-nine modern language – mainly French – teachers were meeting to discuss, with a group of researchers, the topics: library use, independent study, and the teaching of French in the sixth form. The researchers were explaining the purpose of their study. Let us eavesdrop for a while.

> We are carrying out this study – it's called Library Access and Sixth Form Study – carrying out interviews with lots of people in schools. We've chosen three areas, history, biology and French, to talk to members of staff about, about the library and the sixth form, and about the way in which a pupil moves from being an instructed pupil to being a student . . . (8.B.80).

> One of the topics we are interested in is how students make the transition from directed learning, where they're given all the information, to independent learning, where they have to go out and find some information for themselves, or select from different kinds of information. Maybe you could talk about how you see this happening in French . . . (15.B.38).

The question hung in the air for a few moments, and then the discussion began:

> I feel a lot of people think that the sixth form is very different from the rest of language teaching, that when students get past O-level and arrive back in September they are different people altogether, that all of a sudden they have magically acquired study skills and responsible attitudes, which simply isn't the case. I think that the A-level syllabus is a watered-down degree. It no longer, in my view, reflects the utility orientation of the O-level and CSE syllabuses. We are asked as language teachers to reach a fair standard in the major skills of translating in both directions, comprehension and essay writing, and, if that weren't enough, then we've also got to add on literary skills. My aim at the end of an A-level course is to have in front of me a group of young people who can converse happily in French on complex topics, who can write accurate French, can translate from French into English accurately because that's a skill which people need to use, and who get some satisfaction out of translating English into French accurately (13.B.31–3).

It seemed that there was a reasonable consensus among participants on the difference between O- and A-level and the researchers now began to question the nature of this difference:

So, at sixth form level, is there something different in the way you approach. . . .?

Well, certainly, in that the students are expected to do a lot more reading round their own subject. They can use the library for any critical works, or any works in English, for example, that are relevant to what they're studying in French. My present A-level group are studying *L'Alouette* by Anouilh and there are several versions of the Joan of Arc story, by Shaw. . . .

After analysing the interviews I felt that they contained a particular 'message' and so attempted to present that information in an appropriate medium. The setting was fictional but the message was authentic. The codes following the quotations reference the extract to its location within the case record. All the interview extracts used in the piece were representative and had been selected according to the analytic procedures outlined in Chapter 5.

4 *Data reduction* is another way of presenting formative evaluation data. Again in their paper on formative evaluation, Fiddy and Stronach (1987) take a series of teacher's comments about the management of a pilot project and juxtapose them with the management's comments and from this reduced data make some comments about possible action. Reducing and presenting the data in this way allows the reader to see everyone's views as well as the logic of the analysis and advice being given by the evaluator. Further discussion on communicating evaluation findings is found in Morris *et al.* (1987).

Feedback and problem solving

Much of this chapter has been about the form of evaluation reports. I should also add a few words about how these reports, data or information can be used within the school for problem solving. One example of how to do this has already been provided by the methodology of the GRIDS project; another is the STP model of Schmuck and Runkel (1985). The theory and tradition of data feedback is long and quite complex (Hopkins, 1982), but suffice it to say that feeding back information creates energy within an institution and this energy needs to be directed through some form of action plan if development is to occur.

Having established valid conclusions from the evaluation it is necessary to find ways of organizing the information into a development or action plan. The STP model organizes information to define a problem and to resolve or manage conflict that occurs in creating a solution. Information is organized into three interrelated dimensions. The *situation* is defined by the data gathered from the specific review, the *target* is defined by the establishment of criteria and the gap provides the impetus for the formulation of *action plans* as shown in Table 11.4.

The use of a problem-solving cycle provides one approach to formulating action plans. Most problem-solving cycles follow a sequence similar to this (Schmuck and Runkel, 1985: 198–9):

Table 11.4   The S-T-P model of problem analysis (adapted from Schmuck and Runkel, 1985)

The *situation*	Dimension: Information about (a) the essential features of the current state and (b) the forces that facilitate and that impede moving to a more desired state
The *target*	Dimension: The desired state. What we want to accomplish and to avoid. Targets are chosen because those working on the problem value and desire them; they are not imposed. (Imposed requirements are part of the situation dimension)
The *action plan*	Dimension: Specific action proposals aimed at changing the current state into the desired state. 'Who will do what by when?' Any proposal for action always implies some view of the situation and of the target

Here are some common expressions and terms that fit into the three dimensions.

Situation	*Target*	*Action plan*
Starting point	Termination	Path from S to T
Facts, opinions, explanations about current conditions, predictions about efforts to change	Goals, aims, ends, values, purposes, objectives	Means, plan, strategy, implementation, procedure
Environment as the group perceives it	Outcome desired by the group	The group's behaviour

1 *Agree on the problem.* Effective problem-processing demands attention to two kinds of questions at the outset: Where are we now (the situation, S)? and Where do we want to be (target, T)? An effective group must reach a working agreement early about what constitutes its S and T.

2 *Generate alternative paths.* The group chooses a target and tries to think of steps or paths or plans (P) to get from the existing situation (S) to the target (T). Brainstorming is often used in this phase.

3 *List helping and hindering forces.* Once the group has agreed firmly on the desirability and feasibility of a target (and by considering Ps helps to clarify the desirability and feasibility), it can move into considering the forces that will work for and against its efforts.

4 *Choose action steps.* The group assigns people to the various agreed-upon actions and assigns schedules using PERT charting.

5 *Act.* This is the phase of committed action.

6 *Monitor and recycle.* Meetings are scheduled at which progress will be reviewed. Working toward a target tests how well the situation has been understood.

Summary

In this chapter I have tried to discuss some of the problems of making evaluation formative and suggest possible lines of action. The discussion is incomplete in places which reflects the problematic nature of formative evaluation. Many of these problems are to do with writing up research and evaluation reports, but writing up is only half the problem. The other side of the formative coin is ensuring that action occurs as a result. Some strategies for doing that and for linking evaluation to school improvement are discussed in the final chapter.

12
Evaluation and school improvement

In this final chapter I want to bring the discussion back to the central theme of the book, evaluation for school development, and attempt briefly to put it into a school improvement context. In order to do this I will first define what I mean by school improvement, extend the discussion begun in Chapter 2 about various approaches to evaluation and school improvement, and conclude with a model for evaluation and school improvement and some practical advice about how to achieve it.

School Improvement

My own attitude and approach to school improvement has been strongly influenced by my association with the OECD International School Improvement Project (ISIP) (van Velzen et al., 1985; Hopkins, 1987a). The purpose of this project and the developmental work associated with it was to identify strategies and processes at various levels of the educational system that improve the quality of schooling. This essentially qualitative approach to improving school effectiveness has been complemented by a more research-oriented and quantitative approach that has identified the characteristics of effective schools (Rutter et al., 1979; Purkey and Smith, 1983).

It is generally agreed, for example, that 'effective schools' are characterized by factors such as:

1 Curriculum-focused school leadership.
2 Supportive climate within the school.
3 Emphasis on curriculum and teaching.
4 Clear goals and high expectations for students.

5 A system for monitoring performance and achievement.
6 Ongoing staff development and in-service.
7 Parental involvement and support.
8 LEA support.

These are characteristics that predispose schools towards effectiveness. Although school effectiveness research is continuing to refine the nature of these characteristics, it has largely ignored the process that gives rise to such factors. In general, this research approach is concerned with identifying characteristics, whereas school improvement is about the implementation of processes and strategies for enhancing quality at the school and LEA levels. Although the school effectiveness and school improvement approaches are complementary, as Clark and his colleagues (1984) have illustrated, there is much work still to be done in drawing the two approaches together.

School improvement is defined in ISIP (van Velzen *et al.*, 1985: 48) as:

> a systematic, sustained effort aimed at change in learning conditions and other related internal conditions in one or more schools, with the ultimate aim of accomplishing educational goals more effectively.

This definition is rather abstract and needs some explanation. In so doing, I draw on the elaboration made previously in *Improving the Quality of Schooling* (Hopkins, 1987a: ch. 1). Much practical and research experience in the past decade has supported three main conclusions. First, achieving change is much more a matter of implementation of new practices at the school level than it is of simply deciding to adopt them. Secondly, school improvement is a carefully planned and managed process that takes place over a period of several years; change is a process, not an event. Thirdly, it is very difficult to change education – even in a single classroom – without also changing the school as an organization; the cooperation of fellow teachers and the endorsement of the headteacher are usually necessary too.

School improvement is therefore more than just classroom change; it also presupposes attention to other 'related internal conditions' such as the curriculum, the school organizational structure, local policy, school climate, relations with parents, and so on. If change is only aimed at the improvement of 'learning conditions' (i.e. the immediate activities students experience) in a particular classroom, it is not included in the definition nor is the isolated training of individual teachers. But when a school pays attention to the conditions necessary for improvement on both classroom and institutional levels, that is school improvement according to the definition. Thus without ignoring the classroom there must be a 'classroom exceeding' perspective.

School improvement is therefore about curriculum development, strengthening the school organization, the teaching–learning process and a developmental approach to evaluation. This approach focuses attention on the process of strengthening the schools' capacity to deal with change.

Evaluation of school improvement

'Evaluations of' are usually concerned with evaluating the outcomes of an improvement effort (e.g. How well does this new reading programme work? Is TVEI having any effect?, and so on). These are implementation questions. Michael Fullan has written extensively about implementation (e.g. Fullan, 1982) and also about evaluation. In 'Evaluating program implementation' (Fullan, 1983), he asked 'what can be learned about accomplishing and evaluating program implementation?' and argues that there are two ways forward – determining the degree of implementation and identifying the factors necessary for explaining the degree of implementation. What is required first, he argues, is a definition of the change being promulgated. It is important for innovators (and presumably evaluators) to know 'what aspects of current practice would change, if this program were to be used effectively'. According to Fullan, this 'base line' knowledge allows for the measurement of actual practice to determine how it compares with the original intended practice.

However, Fullan admits that such approaches to assessing implementation tend to be promoted 'from a fidelity perspective, i.e. the extent to which users employ the practices intended by the model developers'. This stands in contrast to the 'mutual adaptation' perspective, i.e. how far the change is adapted to the particular needs and character of the school. It is important not to neglect the mutual adaptation approach, for as Miles (1987) has observed:

> Some prior research has emphasised 'fidelity' pressures as important to successful implementation. However, many of these studies have been of programs, e.g. quite concrete, self-contained activities, that have relatively minimal impact on the basic structure of the school, or its objective. In this study we are dealing with something very different, something approaching a reform. An adaptive, evolving approach seems more useful. . . .

To explain the degree of implementation, Fullan (1983) refers to four clusters of factors: attributes of the programme itself, implementation strategies, LEA and school factors, and 'extraneous factors' (my version of his list is given in Table 12.1). Presumably, given this orientation, change evaluators would delve into these four areas to explain the degree of success of implementation. In so doing, Fullan contends, evaluators bring 'more intelligence to the debate', can confirm or disconfirm the 'validity of the program', and facilitate a 'discussion of worth'.

When faced with the task of assessing the degree of implementation, Fullan (1983) suggests instruments such as the 'levels of use' schema (Hall *et al.*, 1975), the Concerns Based Adoption Model (CBAM) (Hord, 1987) or the 'practice profile' drawn up by Loucks-Horsley and Crandall (1982, 1986). 'Evaluations of' also tend to be concerned with a school's climate or leadership style. Examples of these instruments are found in Dalin's IDP scheme (Dalin and Rust, 1983) and Cohen's (1976) collection of approaches that includes

Table 12.1 Factors relating to implementation as a basis for the evaluation of school improvement (based on Fullan, 1983)

Characteristics of the innovation
1 Need for the change
2 Clarity, complexity and scope of the change
3 Quality and availability of materials
4 Nature of initiation decision

Characteristics at the local level
5 History of innovative attempts
6 Expectations of and training for Heads
7 Teacher professional development
8 External support
9 Planning, including time line and monitoring
10 Overload

Characteristics at the school level
11 Heads' actions
12 Teacher–teacher relations and actions
13 Parental and community involvement

Factors external to the school system
14 Teacher strikes
15 Demographic factors
16 Changes in funding

Implementation strategies
17 In-service training
18 Monitoring and feedback
19 Attention to components of implementation
20 School development plan and school-based review

Halpin and Croft's (1963) Organizational Climate Description Questionnaire (OCDQ) and Finlayson's (1973) School Climate Index. Two other recent approaches discussed in Chapter 8 are DION and FOCUS. The point at issue is that change evaluators will need to utilize such schemes – or develop similar approaches – to the analysis of climatic and cultural factors within institutional life. The eclectic approach we adopted (Evans and Hopkins, 1988) in our study of the impact of an in-service course on change in educational practice that assessed school climate, leader personality and level of work, is such an example.

Evaluation for school improvement

As I stated earlier, the sense of what is meant by evaluation for school improvement is perhaps best captured in the commonly understood phrase 'formative evaluation'. It is evaluation conducted for the purpose of bringing about improvements in practice. An example of this approach is given by the current local evaluations of the Technical and Vocational Education Initiative (TVEI) in the United Kingdom (Hopkins, 1986a, 1989). These local evaluations of a major curriculum innovation have evolved a distinct role and purpose which is to help and develop the implementation of the initiative in particular local education authorities. The critical feature of this evaluation approach is that its prime focus is on facilitating change.

There are two major issues raised in the literature that relate to the effectiveness of evaluation for school improvement. The first is a lack of appreciation of the change or implementation process, and the second is the problem of communicating or utilizing evaluation data. Fullan (1981) has argued that formative evaluation has generally been unhelpful in improving practice because it has neglected to gather information on the change process, preferring to focus on variables such as student outcomes or attitudes. Berman and McLaughlin (1976: 500) concluded in their massive study on the impact of federally sponsored programmes in education in the United States that:

> Although student outcomes might be the ultimate indicator of the effectiveness of an innovation . . . projects must go through the complex and uncertain process of implementation before they can affect students, it makes sense to put first things first and to measure the effectiveness of implementation before examining potential student impacts.

In short, lack of implementation data makes the interpretation of the outcome data misleading or meaningless, particularly if we do not know what has been implemented or even if anything has been implemented at all.

In order to do 'evaluation for' properly, therefore, data needs to be gathered on elements of the change process itself. There are two aspects to this: defining the change itself and assessing the factors influencing the change. Change is not unidimensional and any educational innovation will involve to a greater or lesser degree change on each of the following dimensions:

1 Alterations in structure (e.g. timetabling, grouping in the classroom).
2 Use of new materials (e.g. textbooks, high-tech resources).
3 Acquiring new knowledge (e.g. use of high-tech equipment, new subject areas).
4 Practising new teaching styles (e.g. student-centred learning, discussion).
5 Internalizing new beliefs (e.g. accepting the worthwhileness of a new approach, realizing that a new approach works better).

These components of implementation have been thoroughly described by Fullan (e.g. Fullan and Park, 1981) and need to be incorporated in any evaluation design that purports to facilitate improvement. Failure to do so runs 'the risk of appraising non-events' (Charters and Jones, 1973) or drawing conclusions from data on student outcomes when the programme has not been implemented in the first place. Data on the implementation components just described, therefore, also provide a framework for effective development.

The second issue concerns the utilization of evaluation data. The fruits of evaluation are usually the written report, and yet that is a particularly inappropriate medium for communicating about development. This is a problem, as we saw in the previous chapter, that 'applied researchers' and 'change evaluators' have been grappling with for some time. An example of evaluation for school improvement was given in Chapter 10 with a discussion of a framework for enhancing the formative capacity of TVEI local evaluations. Such evaluations have a predominantly formative function and have developed a unique character. The aim in developing the framework was to preserve the integrity and idiosyncracy of, while allowing some generalization across, TVEI local evaluations and so strengthen their formative capacity.

Evaluation as school improvement

This somewhat tautological phrase attempts to convey the idea that the process of evaluation and development is one and the same thing. As I have outlined in some detail in Chapters 7 and 8 some ways of doing this, I will not rehearse these strategies here. One should note, however, that GRIDS and the other approaches described in Chapter 8 are not the only ways of doing school-based review. GRIDS and SBR are not the only approaches to evaluation as school improvement either. The teacher-researcher or action research movement mentioned earlier and exemplified in the work of Lawrence Stenhouse and John Elliott, and the vitality of the Classroom Action Research Network are all examples of this trend. So too are the various school management courses sponsored and developed by the National Development Centre in the UK, the school leader courses in other European countries and the various school improvement 'partnerships' of the type described by ISIP.

Based on the research literature and my own and others' experience, it appears that evaluation as school improvement becomes increasingly effective when it:

- is linked to a particular task at the school level;
- emphasizes a clear perception and definition of process and role;
- receives external support;
- is 'owned' at the school level;
- is free from accountability overtures; and
- utilizes a systematic and self-conscious methodology.

Evaluation and school improvement

It is becoming increasingly clear that fundamental curriculum change will not occur in schools unless these efforts are also linked to attempts to alter organizational and institutional factors. As I have written elsewhere (Hopkins, 1984: 15), 'many potentially powerful educational reforms have floundered because little attention was given to the organisational context in which they were to occur'. Strategies for school improvement need to address directly the culture of the school.

This book has been specifically concerned to outline an approach to school development through evaluation *or* an approach to evaluation that results in school development. If, however, one also harbours aspirations for school improvement, evaluation by itself is not enough. It also has to be linked to other staff development, organizational development and planning strategies within the school as well as demands for accountability, curriculum reform, and bureaucratic regulation from the outside.

I have sketched out a 'concept map' that describes the complexity involved and builds on the ideas and strategies discussed in previous chapters. My attempt can be seen in Fig. 12.1. The bottom half of the figure is already familiar territory. It is the evaluation process described in Chapter 7 and emphasizes again the links between school self-evaluation and curriculum development.

The central feature of Fig. 12.1 is the school development plan. In their simplest form school development plans are a set of curriculum and organizational targets with implementation plans and time lines set by the school on an annual basis within the context of local and national aims. The plans are usually based on a 3-year cycle with details for the first year and contingent aspirations for the subsequent 2 years. Optimally, they will include details of performance indicators, staff development needs, organizational developments and resource (both human and financial) implications.

School development plans are a relatively new phenomena in the UK (Hargreaves *et al.*, 1989). The Education Reform Act and a number of the other recent curriculum and organizational initiatives, however, have required or will require the use of school development plans in one form or another. The LEA Training Grants Scheme, TVEI Extension, the National Curriculum, Teacher Appraisal and Local Management of Schools, are examples of initiatives that require overt planning at the school level. Besides being a blueprint for implementation, these plans also provide a basis for evaluation and monitoring both at the school and LEA levels.

The school development plan reflects not only the school's aspirations but also the local and national context. In a similar way, school development is buttressed by the external support structure and school autonomy is mediated through the monitoring function of the Inspectorial and Advisory service among others. The role of school governors and the community at large are also involved in monitoring and setting school aims. The internal–external interface is in reality a fluid dimension and alters over time and within specific contexts. This apparent tension can be very creative, because a school's autonomy needs ultimately to be relative and responsible.

The top half of Fig. 12.1 is less familiar and reflects the concerns of this particular chapter. If we are to take seriously the messages of the educational change and school improvement literature and experience, then school-level planning needs also to take seriously both teacher and school development.

Figure 12.1 Evaluation for school development: a concept map

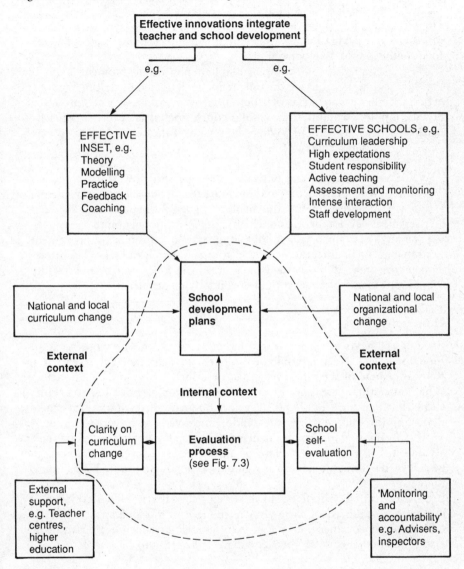

Figure 12.1 identifies some of the key ideas about teacher and school development that have already been discussed in this book. Teacher development occurs partly as a result of effective INSET designs and Fig. 12.1 refers to Joyce and Showers' training approach. School development occurs when schools strive towards an organizational structure that promotes high student outcomes. Some of these characteristics have been identified by the effective

schools research and they too are included in Fig. 12.1. The point being that insights such as these should also form part of a school development plan. Quality education is predicated on the integration or synthesis of school improvement, evaluation and curriculum development strategies that find a focus in the school development plan.

These ideas are new and complex and I am not for one moment saying that Fig. 12.1 is complete, but we can only refine such models by linking theory and action together in the praxis of school improvement. By way of summarizing this section, let me quote some similar conclusions from a recent paper from Michael Fullan (1988a: 30), where he reviewed the recent literature on the change process in secondary schools:

> Whatever the particulars, powerful strategies for powerful change are required, which restructure and integrate teacher development, principal and school development, student development, and accountability and assessment development, and which cross institutional boundaries.
>
> Finally, it is no accident that long term institutional improvement strategies end up integrating organizational research and school improvement research. Without such integration the focus tends to be on the solutions themselves rather than the underlying problems.

How to Begin

Although I have no doubt that the message of the previous section is fundamentally correct, it would be foolhardy to claim that it is easy to attain. Radical change of the type I have just described is very difficult to achieve. What I am arguing for is not simply that evaluation becomes less of a 'bolt on extra', but that the school and LEA develop a complementary infrastructure that supports and nurtures the school improvement process. Within this process, evaluation for development is a necessary but not necessarily sufficient condition. This vision of the relatively autonomous and creative school cannot be achieved overnight. Is there any guidance on how to proceed? Fortunately, there is.

So how can a school or LEA develop a capacity for developmental evaluation? At the risk of parodying the thoughtful and sophisticated literature on school improvement, let me give six guidelines which are based on and elaborated in the work of Michael Fullan (1982, 1988b). They are:

1 Reduce overload by searching for common factors and then prioritize.
2 As far as possible fit developments into local needs and the rhythm of the school.
3 Start small, think big and break into phases.
4 Work through *ad hoc* representative groups.
5 Reduce early costs and increase early rewards.
6 Provide ongoing INSET and support.

Overload is the most pressing problem in schools today. 'Overload', as

Fullan (1988b: vi) comments, 'fosters dependency'. Dependency is created by the continual bombardment of new tasks and results in one's actions being predominantly shaped by the events, actions or directions of others. One way to take charge in this situation is to look for common factors in these changes. Teaching/learning and assessment, for example, are common threads running through many curriculum changes and, having identified them, prioritize. Do a few things as best as you can and do the others as well as you would have anyway. There are few penalties in the education system for such strategic action. In the specific case of evaluation, do not try to evaluate everything at once.

Secondly, try and link your priority area to a well-known or identifiable need at the school level and fit into the rhythm of the school. For example, if the school is currently concerned with records of achievement then evaluate that rather than a curriculum or organization area in which there is little current interest. Similarly, make certain that as far as possible the strategies you adopt fit into the rhythm of the school and build on what the school is doing already. Only bring totally new ideas and strategies to the school when it is absolutely necessary.

Thirdly, and in a similar vein, start small and think big, and also break into phases. Although the Head's vision may be of a completely self-evaluating institution, this goal may best be achieved by sub-dividing the process into a number of smaller steps each of which builds on the other. By doing this success is being created at an early stage and that experience and success acts as a springboard for future developments. So, for example, begin self-evaluation with a group of staff who are enthusiastic or on a topic or issue that is comparatively easy to evaluate.

The fourth guideline is to work through *ad hoc* or temporary groups. At the start of an innovation the history of the group responsible for the new developments is often a hindrance. They may have been involved in activities that did not succeed or were unpopular. It is often better, therefore, to create groups for specific purposes such as evaluation, particularly if they are representative of the range of experience and opinion in the school.

'Reduce early cost and increase early reward' is the fifth guideline. This refers more to psychological than monetary costs and rewards. The exhortation not to make the change too threatening, particularly in its early stages, echoes earlier guidelines. The risk of failure, i.e. not succeeding immediately at a new activity, is a major threat to teachers who live and work in schools whose climates are not attuned to experimentation. 'Early rewards' are to do with positive reinforcement, or with acknowledging a teacher's efforts by providing a pleasant environment in which to do INSET; or above all providing real opportunities for the experience of professional judgement. Most teachers find the exercise of professional expertise a very motivating and rewarding experience. Despite the importance of financial gain, it is the empowerment and feeling of efficacy that comes with professional growth and the exercise of professional judgement that is the most rewarding for most teachers. For too long we have neglected this professional potential within our educational system.

The final guideline is ongoing INSET and external support. The various characteristics of effective INSET have already been discussed, and it is combinations of such strategies that is being referred to here. Obviously, INSET needs to be tailored to specific situations and, if possible, to be 'front-end loaded', but also with a sustained and ongoing commitment. External support refers to the system that provides INSET and other technical advice. Unfortunately, this system is not as well developed in the UK as it is in other European countries or North America. What is required are specific inputs that are ongoing and provide psychological as well as technical support in an atmosphere of professional dialogue rather than bureaucratic accountability.

These rather simplistic and commonsense lists of guidelines refer to the implementation of any innovation, not specifically a capacity for evaluation at the school and LEA levels. The point being that a capacity for evaluation is necessary but not sufficient within a general strategy for school improvement.

Coda

It is appropriate that I conclude this chapter and the book with a coda rather than a summary. The purpose of both has been to make an argument for an approach to evaluation that has a developmental or school improvement focus. The coda or sub-text to the argument is the need to empower teachers, school leaders, advisers and others who work in and support schools. The improvements in the quality of schooling that are implied in these pages occur not through legislative fiat, but through the exercise and development of the professional judgement of those within the system. We do not become more effective by slavishly following administrative memoranda or external models, but by acquiring skills and strategies, through understanding, reflection and through the refinement and exercise of judgement. This was principally the message of my book on classroom research (Hopkins, 1985a), but I am now more than ever persuaded that such an ethic although important is also insufficient. We improve schools not by teachers individually enhancing their professional and personal efficacy, but by teachers *collectively* doing so within a supportive school organization. The classroom exceeding perspective I referred to earlier is the essential foundation stone for school improvement.

As I sit thinking and searching for the right exhortatory words to conclude this book, I hear the voices of dissent: it's too romantic, unrealistic, he doesn't know (or more kindly has forgotten) what it is all about. That is all as may be, but the dependency culture created by the overload of change that we have all experienced in the past decade is subtly but powerfully de-powering and de-energizing. As an antidote I point to what for me are the most exciting aspects about the school improvement and effective schools research: first that schools and teachers do make a difference, and second that the characteristics of effective schools are related to their properties as social systems rather than being contingent on external factors such as resources and government legislation. To put it another way, irrespective of external factors, the staff of a school can by their own efforts make the place a more effective and productive teaching environment for the students within it. This is not simply an optimistic and romantic exhortation, but one that is grounded in research and experience.

I do not believe for one moment that this book is a panacea. What I do believe, however, is that the only way to increase the quality of schooling within our system is to encourage teachers to develop their professional abilities as educators, to become collectively more self-conscious and systematic about the exercise of their own and colleagues' professional judgements, and to establish an infrastructure at the school and LEA levels for so doing. Evaluation for development is one of those ways.

Further reading

I have tried as far as possible to avoid excessive lists of citations in the text. However, the interested reader may find it helpful to have some indication of areas for further reading. In making these suggestions I have generally followed the sequence of chapters in the book.

Contrasting definitions of evaluation can be found in Eisner's (1979) *The Educational Imagination*, Popham's (1988) *Educational Evaluation* and Guba and Lincoln's (1981) *Effective Evaluation*, as well as in Scriven (1967), Nevo (1986) and Cronbach *et al.* (1980). As regards the specific character of British evaluation in the 1970s, two groups were identified in Chapter 1: those associated with the Schools Council and those with CARE.

Of the writings from the former group, three volumes are of particular interest and their titles give a good indication of their various emphases: *Evaluation in Curriculum Development: Twelve Case Studies* (Schools Council, 1973), *Curriculum Evaluation Today* (Tawney, 1976) and *Evaluation and the Teacher's Role* (Harlen, 1978).

Among the writings of those associated with CARE, a number of papers stand out: MacDonald's (1976) seminal article on 'Evaluation and the control of education', Walker's (1980) paper on the conduct of case study, and Hamilton's (1977) scholarly survey of the field of curriculum evaluation. Among the themes explored by the group were the evaluation of curriculum innovation (e.g. MacDonald and Walker, 1974), strategies for action research in classrooms (e.g. Elliott and Adelman, 1976), the ethics of educational evaluation (e.g. Adelman, 1984), strategies for school evaluation (e.g. Simons, 1987), the use of case study and case records in evaluation (e.g. Rudduck, 1985) and alternative approaches to reporting evaluation data (e.g. Jenkins, 1977).

Two of the better known books on evaluation published during the early 1980s are Maurice Holt's (1981) *Evaluating the Evaluators* and Malcolm Skilbeck's (1984) *Evaluating the Curriculum in the Eighties*. They both chart the increasingly political nature of evaluation, as does David Smetheram's (1981) *Practising Evaluation*. Marten Shipman's (1979) *In School Evaluation* presents a managerialist view of school evaluation, while the GRIDS Handbooks (McMahon *et al.*, 1984) specify a more and developmentally oriented approach. Finally, the work of the Open University's 'Curriculum Evaluation and Assessment' Course team as manifest in Course E364, provided many teachers with access to the issues surrounding, and techniques involved in doing, curriculum evaluation. The course was supplemented by an excellent reader, *Calling Education to Account* (McCormick 1982), and an admirable text on *Curriculum Evaluation in Schools* by two of the course team members, Bob McCormick and Mary James (1988, 2nd ed.).

It is difficult to document the contemporary evaluation scene adequately but Murphy and Torrance's (1987) reader is a useful source. Another brave attempt was made by Colin McCabe (1987) in a recent paper 'The external evaluator: Inspector or management consultant?' In the paper he surveys the recent literature on evaluation and suggests the following sources as being representative of the current state of the art in the UK.

Eraut, M. and Burke, J. (1986). *Improving the Quality of YTS*. Brighton: University of Sussex.

Fiddy, R. and Stronach, I. (1986). *TVEI Working Papers 1*. Norwich: University of East Anglia.

Holly, P. (ed.) (1986b). *Cambridge Journal of Education*, 16 (2).

Hopkins, D. (ed.) (1986a). *Evaluating TVEI: Some Methodological Issues*. Cambridge: Cambridge Institute of Education.

McCabe, C. (ed.) (1986b). *TVEI: The Organisation of the Early Years*. Clevedon, Avon: Multilingual Matters.

Stoney, S. M., Pole, C. J. and Sims, D. (1986). *The Management of TVEI: A Summary*. Windsor: NFER.

Colleagues and myself have also commented on the problems of contemporary evaluation in a recent article (Hutchinson *et al.*, 1988) and book *TVEI at the Change of Life* (Hopkins, 1989).

The emphasis in Chapter 2 was on the different approaches to and models for evaluation. Surveys of the main issues and overviews of the models are found in the OU text by David Jenkins (1976) and the books by Worthen and Sanders (1987, *Educational Evaluation*), Stufflebeam and Shinkfield (1985, *Systematic Evaluation*), Madaus *et al.* (1983, *Evaluation Models*), Eisner (1985, *The Art of Educational Evaluation*) and House (1986, *New Directions in Educational Evaluation*). The agricultural botany versus illuminative evaluation debate is documented in Hamilton *et al.* (1977) and Rudduck and Hopkins (1985).

Issues associated with the design of evaluation (Chapter 3) are comprehensively covered in the *Program Evaluation Kit*, edited in nine volumes by Joan Herman (e.g. Herman *et al.*, 1987); and to a lesser extent in the handbook on *Evaluation in the Voluntary Sector* (Ball, 1988) and in Eraut *et al.*'s (1988) *Local Evaluation of INSET*. The ethical dimension has also been comprehensively covered by evaluators in the UK. MacDonald's (1976) democratic model is essentially about the ethics of evaluation; this is also the case with Helen Simons' *Getting to Know Schools in a Democracy* (1987), which is an interesting case study in the ethics of evaluation. Her 'Suggestions for a school self evaluation based on democratic principles' also contains a helpful discussion on and suggestions for ethical procedures (1982). Clem Adelman's (1984) book *The Politics and Ethics of Evaluation* is similarly useful.

As regards data collection (Chapter 4), *Doing Your Research Project* (Bell, 1987) and *Conducting Small Scale Investigations* . . . (Bell *et al.*, 1984), Robert McCormick and Mary James' (1988) *Curriculum Evaluation in Schools*, Louis Cohen and Lawrence

Manion's (1980) *Research Methods in Education*, Rob Walker's (1985) *Doing Research*, Bob Burgess's (1984) *In the Field* and my own *A Teachers' Guide to Classroom Research* (Hopkins, 1985a) are all useful introductions. They are not only practical but also give an overview of the field and a guide to the more technical literature.

The literature on data analysis (Chapter 5) is burgeoning, particularly the contributions from the USA (Hopkins *et al.*, 1989). The most important recent contribution to the development of qualitative research is by Miles and Huberman, who articulated the methodology they used in their school improvement case studies conducted for the DESSI project in 'Drawing valid meaning from qualitative data: Toward a shared craft' (1984a) and *Qualitative Data Analysis: A Sourcebook of New Methods* (1984b). The link between various aspects of validity and reliability and particular techniques in qualitative methodology are discussed in Egon Guba's (1981) paper 'Criteria for assessing the trustworthiness of naturalistic inquiries', but it is written in quite technical language. The book on case study by Robert Yin (1984) is more accessible; also helpful in this regard are the papers by Skrtic (1985) and Hammersley (1987). Other books that address these issues are Strauss' (1987) excellent *Qualitative Analysis for Social Scientists*, Lincoln and Guba's (1985) *Naturalistic Inquiry*, Patton's (1987) *Creative Evaluation*, Hammersley and Atkinson's (1983) *Ethnography*, House's (1980) *Evaluating with Validity* and van Maanen's (1983) *Qualitative Methodology*.

Initial further reading on evaluation roles (Chapter 6) and the evaluation of specific curriculum or school areas (Chapter 7) are most easily found in the readers on evaluation published by the Open University, i.e. McCormick (1982), Murphy and Torrance (1987) and the associated course material (e.g. OU Course E364 and the new MA module on Educational Evaluation). Lewy and Nevo's (1981) *Evaluation Roles in Education* and some of the textbooks already mentioned are also helpful.

Besides the references to the specific approaches to whole-school evaluation in Chapter 8, I have recently reviewed the whole area in *Doing School Based Review* (Hopkins, 1988b). Our work on school evaluation in ISIP may also be of some interest (Hopkins, 1985b; Bollen and Hopkins, 1987). Two reviews of the British experience are found in Desmond Nuttall's (1981) Schools Council booklet and Phil Clift *et al.*'s (1987) *Studies in School Self Evaluation*.

It was suggested in Chapter 9 that the recent research on effective INSET contributes to a framework of ideas against which INSET designs can be evaluated. Arguably, the work of Joyce and Showers is the most important, not only the articles quoted from in the chapter, but also their recent book *Student Achievement Through Staff Development* (1988). Other books that provide very helpful insights into the design of INSET programmes are: Eric Hoyle and Jacquetta Megarry's (1980) *Professional Development of Teachers*, Jean Rudduck's (1981) *Making the Most of the Short Inservice Course*, Ray Bolam's (1982) *School Focused Inservice Training*, Marv Wideen and Ian Andrew's (1987) *Staff Development for School Improvement*, Susan Loucks-Horsley *et al.*'s (1987) *Continuing to Learn*, and Fergus O'Sullivan, Ken Jones and Ken Reid's (1988) *Staff Development in Secondary Schools*. Other useful advice, other than that quoted here, on developing strategies for the evaluation of INSET can be found in Colin McCabe's (1980) book on *Evaluating In-service Training for Teachers*, the whole issue of the *Journal of Staff Development*, 3 (1), April 1982, Michael Eraut's (1985) NDC booklet on the *Evaluation of Management Courses*, and Peter Holly *et al.*'s (1987) Delta Project report *The Experience of TRIST*.

Project evaluation, which was discussed in Chapter 10, is another issue that is not often addressed directly in the literature. Bolam's (1981) paper mentioned in the chapter and Fullan's (1983) article on programme implementation are notable exceptions. This is also the case with formative evaluation and most of the useful references have already been quoted in the chapter. Some other references which may help in writing up evaluation are Sapsford and Evans (1984) and Woods (1985).

The school improvement (Chapter 12) literature is vast, and it is inappropriate to review it here. Good starting points, however, are found in Fullan's (1982) *The Meaning of Educational Change*, Joyce *et al.*'s (1983) *The Structure of School Improvement*, Miles and Huberman's (1984) *Innovation up Close*, Loucks-Horsley and Hergert's (1985) *An Action Guide to School Improvement*, and our own *Alternative Perspectives on School Improvement* (Hopkins and Wideen, 1984) and *Improving the Quality of Schooling* (Hopkins, 1987a). The first book in the ISIP series by van Velzen *et al.* (1985), *Making School Improvement Work*, also provides a good introduction to the field. A useful handbook that discusses strategies and activities that link evaluation to school improvement is Schmuck and Runkel's (1985) *The Handbook of Organisation Development in Schools*.

This further reading list is necessarily limited by my own interests and experience. It certainly does not claim to be exhaustive, but I do hope that it will be of some use to the reader who is keen to pursue further some of the ideas discussed in the book.

References

Abbott, R. *et al.* (1988). *GRIDS Handbook*, 2nd edn (Primary and Secondary School versions). York: Longman for the SCDC.

Abbott, R. *et al.* (1989). *External Perspectives in School Based Review*. York: Longman for the SCDC.

Acheson, K. and Gall, M. (1980). *Techniques in the Clinical Supervision of Teachers*. New York: Longman.

Adelman, C. (1984). *The Politics and Ethics of Evaluation*. London: Croom Helm.

Adelman, C. *et al.* (1976). Rethinking case study: notes from the second Cambridge Conference. *Cambridge Journal of Education*, **6**, 139–50.

Atkinson, P. and Delamont, S. (1986). Bread and dreams or bread and circuses? A critique of 'case study' research in education. In Hammersley, M. (ed.), *Controversies in Classroom Research*. Milton Keynes: Open University Press.

Ball, M. (1988). *Evaluation in the Voluntary Sector*. London: Forbes Trust.

Barrow, R. (1985). Context, concepts and content: Prescriptions for empirical research. Vancouver: Simon Fraser University (mimeo).

Barrow, R. (1986). Empirical research into teaching: The conceptual factors. *Educational Research*, **28** (3).

Becker, H. S. (1958). Problems of inference and proof in participant observation. *American Sociological Review*, **28**, 652–60.

Bell, J. (1987). *Doing Your Research Report*. Milton Keynes: Open University Press.

Bell, J. *et al.* (1984). *Conducting Small Scale Investigations in Education Management*. London: Harper and Row.

Berman, P. and McLaughlin, M. (1976). Implementation of educational innovation. *Educational Forum*, **40**, 345–70.

Birchenough, M. *et al.* (1989). *Reviewing School Departments*. York: Longman for the SCDC.

Bolam, R. (1981). Evaluative research: A case study of the Teacher Induction Pilot Schemes project. *Journal of Education for Teaching*, **7** (1), 70–83.

Bolam, R. (1982). *School Focused Inservice Training*. London: Heinemann Educational.

Bolam, R. (1987). What is effective INSET? Paper presented to NFER Annual Members Conference, 1987. Windsor: NFER (mimeo).

Bollen, R. and Hopkins, D. (1987). *School Based Review: Towards a Praxis.* Leuven, Belgium: ACCO.

Bridges, D. (1988). What conditions help to make evaluation formative? Cambridge: Homerton College (mimeo).

Burgess, R. (1984). *In the Field.* London: George Allen and Unwin.

Campbell, D. T. and Stanley, J. C. (1963). Experimental and quasi-experimental designs for research on teaching. In Gage, N. L. (ed.), *Handbook of Research on Teaching.* Chicago: Rand McNally.

Charters, W. and Jones, J. (1973). On the risk of appraising non-events in program evaluation. *Educational Researcher,* 2 (11), 5–7.

Clark, D. *et al.* (1984). Effective schools and school improvement. *Educational Administration Quarterly,* 20 (3), 41–68.

Clift, P. (1987). LEA initiated school based review in England and Wales. In Hopkins, D. (ed.), *Improving the Quality of Schooling.* Lewes: Falmer Press.

Clift, P. *et al.* (1987). *Studies in School Self Evaluation.* Lewes: Falmer Press.

Cohen, L. (1976). *Educational Research in Classroom and Schools: A Manual of Materials and Methods.* London: Harper and Row.

Cohen, L. and Manion, C. (1980). *Research Methods in Education.* London: Croom Helm.

Cousins, J. B. and Leithwood, K. A. (1986). Current empirical research on evaluation utilization. *Review of Educational Research,* 56 (3), 331–64.

Croll, P. (1986). *Systematic Classroom Observation.* Lewes: Falmer Press.

Cronbach, L. (1963). Evaluation for course improvement. *Teachers College Record,* 64 (8), 672–83.

Cronbach, L. *et al.* (1980). *Toward a Reform of Program Evaluation.* San Francisco: Jossey Bass.

Dalin, P. (forthcoming). *School Improvement.* Windsor: NFER/Nelson.

Dalin, P. and Rust, V. (1983). *Can Schools Learn?* Windsor: NFER/Nelson.

Dalin, P. *et al.* (1987). *The School Development Guide.* Windsor: IMTEC/NFER.

ECALP (1988). Guidelines for the preparation of case studies. Paris: OECD/CERI (mimeo).

Eisner, E. W. (1979). *The Education Imagination.* London: Macmillan.

Eisner, E. (1985). *The Art of Educational Evaluation.* Lewes: Falmer Press.

Elliott, J. and Adelman, C. (1976). *Innovation at the Classroom Level: A Case Study of the Ford Teaching Project.* Unit 28, Open University Course E203: Curriculum Design and Development. Milton Keynes: Open University Press.

Elliott-Kemp, J. and William, G. (1980). *The DION Handbook.* Sheffield Polytechnic: PAVIC Publications.

Elliott-Kemp, J. and West, B. (1987). *SIGMA: A Process Based Approach to Staff Development.* Sheffield Polytechnic: PAVIC Publications.

Eraut, M. (1985). *Evaluation of Management Courses.* Bristol: National Development Centre for School Management Training.

Eraut, M. and Burke, J. (1986). *Improving the Quality of YTS.* Brighton: University of Sussex.

Eraut, M. *et al.* (1988). *Local Evaluation of INSET.* Bristol: National Development Centre for School Management Training.

Evans, M. and Hopkins, D. (1988). School climate and the psychological state of the individual teacher as factors affecting the utilisation of educational ideas following an in-service course. *British Educational Research Journal,* 14 (3), 211–30.

Fiddy, R. and Stronach, I. (1986). *TVEI Working Papers No. 1.* Norwich: CARE, University of East Anglia.

Fiddy, R. and Stronach, I. (1987). How can evaluation become formative? Norwich: CARE, University of East Anglia (mimeo).

Finlayson, D. S. (1973). Measuring school climate. *Trends in Education,* April.

Fisher, R. (1935). *The Design of Experiments.* Edinburgh: Oliver and Boyd.

FitzGibbon, C. (1986). The roles of the TVEI local evaluator. In Hopkins, D. (ed.), *Evaluating TVEI: Some Methodological Issues.* Cambridge: Cambridge Institute of Education/MSC.

FitzGibbon, C. and Morris, L. (1987). *How to Design a Program Evaluation.* London: Sage.

Flanders, N. (1970). *Analysing Teaching Behaviour.* Reading, Mass.: Addison-Wesley.

Foucault, M. (1976). *Birth of the Clinic.* London: Tavistock.

Fullan, M. (1981). The relationship between evaluation and implementation. In Lewy, A. and Nevo, D. (eds), *Evaluation Roles in Education.* London: Gordon Breach.

Fullan, M. (1982). *The Meaning of Educational Change.* Toronto: OISE Press.

Fullan, M. (1983). Evaluating program implementation. *Curriculum Inquiry,* **13,** 214–27.

Fullan, M. (1988a). Change processes in secondary schools: Towards a more fundamental agenda. Toronto: University of Toronto, Faculty of Education (mimeo).

Fullan, M. (1988b). *What's Worth Fighting for in the Principalship?* Toronto: Ontario Teachers Federation.

Fullan, M. and Park, P. (1981). *Curriculum Implementation.* Toronto: Ministry of Education.

Galton, M. (1978). *British Mirrors.* Leicester: University of Leicester School of Education.

Glaser, B. and Strauss, A. (1967). *The Discovery of Grounded Theory.* New York: Aldine.

Guba, E. C. (1981). Criteria for assessing the trustworthiness of naturalistic inquiries. *Educational Communication and Technology Journal,* **29,** 75–91.

Guba, E. C. and Lincoln, Y. S. (1981). *Effective Evaluation.* San Francisco, Calif. Jossey-Bass.

Hall, G. and Loucks, S. (1977). A developmental model for determining whether the treatment is actually implemented. *American Educational Research Journal,* **14,** 236–76.

Hall, G. *et al.* (1975). Levels of use of the innovation. *The Journal of Teacher Education,* **26** (1), 52–6.

Halpin, A. W. and Croft, D. B. (1963). *The Organisational Climate of Schools.* Chicago: Midwest Administration Centre, University of Chicago.

Hamilton, D. (1976). *Curriculum Evaluation.* London: Open Books.

Hamilton, D. (1977). Making sense of curriculum evaluation. In Shulman, L. (ed.), *Review of Research in Education,* Vol. 5. London: Peacock.

Hamilton, D. *et al.* (eds) (1977). *Beyond the Numbers Game.* London: Macmillan.

Hammersley, M. (1987). Some notes on the terms validity and reliability. *British Educational Research Journal,* **13** (1), 73–81.

Hammersley, M. and Atkinson, P. (1983). *Ethnography: Principles in Practice.* London: Tavistock.

Hargreaves, D. *et al.* (1989). *Planning for School Development.* London: HMSO.

Harland, J. (1987). The TVEI experience: Issues of control, response and the professional role of teachers. In Gleeson, D. (ed.), *TVEI and Secondary Education: A Critical Appraisal*. Milton Keynes: Open University Press.

Harlen, W. (1978). *Evaluation and the Teacher's Role*. London: Macmillan.

Harlen, W. and Elliott, J. (1982). A checklist for planning or reviewing an evaluation. In McCormick, R. (ed.), *Calling Education to Account*. London: Heinemann Educational.

Heller, H. (1985). *Helping Schools Change*. York: Centre for the Study of Comprehensive Schools, University of York.

Herman, J. *et al.* (1987). *Evaluators Handbook*. London: Sage.

Holly, P. (1986a). Developing a professional evaluation. In Holly, P. (ed.), *Cambridge Journal of Education*, 16 (2).

Holly, P. (ed.) (1986b). Symbolism and synergism: curriculum evaluation for the 1980s. Guest editor of the special edition of the *Cambridge Journal of Education*, 16 (2).

Holly, P. and Hopkins, D. (1988). Evaluation and school improvement. *Cambridge Journal of Education*, 18 (2), 221–45.

Holly, P. *et al.* (1987). *The Experience of TRIST*. London: Manpower Services Commission.

Holt, M. (1981). *Evaluating the Evaluators*. London: Routledge and Kegan Paul.

Hopkins, D. (1982). Survey feedback as an organisation development intervention in educational settings: A review. *Educational Management and Administration*, 10 (3), 203–215.

Hopkins, D. (1984). Change and the organisational character of teacher education. *Studies in Higher Education*, 9 (1), 37–45.

Hopkins, D. (1985a). *A Teacher's Guide to Classroom Research*. Milton Keynes: Open University Press.

Hopkins, D. (1985b). *School Based Review for School Improvement*. Leuven, Belgium: ACCO.

Hopkins, D. (ed.) (1986a). *Evaluating TVEI: Some Methodological Issues*. Cambridge: Cambridge Institute of Education/MSC.

Hopkins, D. (1986b). Sex role stereotyping and self fulfilling prophecies in local TVEI evaluation. *TVEI Working Papers*, 2, 16–22.

Hopkins, D. (ed.) (1986c). *Inservice Training and Educational Development*. London: Croom Helm.

Hopkins, D. (ed.) (1987a). *Improving the Quality of Schooling*. Lewes: Falmer Press.

Hopkins, D. (1987b). Enhancing validity in action research. *British Library Research Paper*, 16.

Hopkins, D. (1988a). Evaluating for development. *Evaluation and Research in Education*, 2 (1), 1–10.

Hopkins, D. (1988b). *Doing School Based Review*. Leuven, Belgium: ACCO.

Hopkins, D. (ed.) (1989). *TVEI at the Change of Life*. Clevedon, Avon: Multilingual Matters.

Hopkins, D. and Leask, M. (1989). Performance indicators and school development. *School Organisation*, 9 (1), pp. 3–20.

Hopkins, D. and Wideen, M. (eds) (1984). *Alternative Perspectives on School Improvement*. Lewes: Falmer Press.

Hopkins, D. *et al.* (1989). Growing up with qualitative research and evaluation. *Evaluation and Research in Education*, 3 (2).

Hord, S. (1987). *Evaluating Educational Innovation*. London: Croom Helm.

House, E. (1980). *Evaluating with Validity*. London: Sage.

House, E. (ed.) (1986). *New Directions in Educational Evaluation*. Lewes: Falmer Press.

Howard, J. and Hopkins, D. (1988). Information skills in TVEI and the role of the librarian. *British Library Research Paper*, **51**.

Hoyle, E. and Megarry, J. (1980). *Professional Development of Teachers*. London: Kogan Page.

Hutchinson, B. *et al.* (1988). The problem of validity in the qualitative evaluation of categorically funded curriculum development projects. *Educational Research*, 30 (1), 54–64.

ILEA (1983). *Keeping the School Under Review* (Primary, Secondary and Special School Versions). London: ILEA Learning Resources Centre.

Jenkins, D. (1976). *Curriculum Evaluation*. Units 19 and 20, Open University Course E203: Curriculum Design and Development. Milton Keynes: Open University Press.

Jenkins, D. (1977). 'Saved by the bell' and 'Saved by the army'. In Hamilton, D. *et al.* (eds), *Beyond the Numbers Game*. London: Macmillan.

Joyce, B. and Showers, B. (1980). Improving inservice training: The messages of research. *Educational Leadership*, 37, 379–85.

Joyce, B. and Showers, B. (1984). Transfer of training: The contribution of coaching. In Hopkins, D. and Wideen, M. (eds), *Alternative Perspectives on School Improvement*. Lewes: Falmer Press.

Joyce, B. and Showers, B. (1988). *Student Achievement Through Staff Development*. New York: Longman.

Joyce, B. *et al.* (1981). *Flexibility in Teaching*. New York: Longman.

Joyce, B. *et al.* (1983). *The Structure of School Improvement*. New York: Longman.

Kemmis, S. and McTaggart, R. (1981). *The Action Research Planner*. Victoria, Australia: Deakin University Press.

Kirk, J. and Miller, M. (1986). *Reliability and Validity in Qualitative Research*. London: Sage.

Lawton, D. (1980). *The Politics of the School Curriculum*. London: Routledge and Kegan Paul.

Lawton, D. (1983). *Curriculum Studies and Educational Planning*. London: Hodder and Stoughton.

Leask, M. (1988). Teachers as evaluators. Unpublished M.Phil. Thesis, University of East Anglia.

Lewy, A. and Nevo, D. (eds) (1981). *Evaluation Roles in Education*. London: Gordon Breach.

Lincoln, Y. and Guba, E. (1985). *Naturalistic Inquiry*. London: Sage.

Little, J. (1982). Making sure: Contributions and requirements of good evaluation. *Journal of Staff Development*, 3 (1), 25–47.

Loucks, S. and Crandall, D. (1982). The practice profile. Andover, Mass.: The Network (mimeo).

Loucks-Horsley, S. and Crandall, D. (1986). *Analyzing School Improvement Support Systems*. Leuven, Belgium: ACCO.

Loucks-Horsley, S. and Hergert, L. (1985). *An Action Guide to School Improvement*. Andover, Mass.: The Network.

Loucks-Horsley, S. *et al.* (1987). *Continuing to Learn*. Andover, Mass.: The Network.

Madaus, G. *et al.* (eds) (1983). *Evaluation Models*. Dordtecht: Kluwer-Nijhoff.

McCabe, C. (1980). *Evaluating Inservice Training for Teachers*. Windsor: NFER.

McCabe, C. (1986a). How to choose your evaluator. In Hopkins, D. (ed.), *Evaluating TVEI: Some Methodological Issues*. Cambridge: Cambridge Institute of Education/MSC.

McCabe, C. (1986b). *TVEI: The Organisation of the Early Years.* Clevedon, Avon: Multilingual Matters.

McCabe, C. (1987). The external evaluator, inspector or management consultant? *Evaluation and Research in Education,* 1 (1), 1–8.

McCormick, R. (ed.) (1982). *Calling Education to Account.* London: Heinemann Educational.

McCormick, R. and James, M. (1988). *Curriculum Evaluation in Schools,* 2nd edn. London: Croom Helm.

MacDonald, B. (1976). Evaluation and the control of education. In Tawney, D. (ed.), *Curriculum Evaluation Today.* London: Macmillan.

MacDonald, B. (1978). *The Experience of Innovation.* Norwich: CARE, University of East Anglia.

MacDonald, B. and Parlett, M. (1973). Rethinking evaluation: Notes from the Cambridge Conference. *Cambridge Journal of Education,* 3 (2), 74–82.

MacDonald, B. and Sanger, J. (1982). Just for the record? Notes towards a theory of interviewing in evaluation. Norwich: CARE, University of East Anglia (mimeo).

MacDonald, B. and Walker, R. (1974). *Innovation, Evaluation Research and the Problem of Control.* SAFARI Project/CARE, University of East Anglia.

McMahon, A. *et al.* (1984). *The Grids Handbook* (primary and secondary school versions). York: Longman for the Schools Council.

Merton, R. and Kendall, P. (1946). The focused interview. *American Journal of Sociology,* 50, 541–57.

Miles, M. (1987). Practical guidelines for school administrators. Paper presented at AERA, April 1987. New York: Centre for Policy Research (mimeo).

Miles, M. B. and Huberman, M. A. (1984a). Drawing valid meaning from qualitative data: Toward a shared craft. *Educational Researcher,* 13 (5), 20–30.

Miles, M. B. and Huberman, M. A. (1984b). *Qualitative Data Analysis: A Sourcebook of New Methods.* Beverly Hills, Calif.: Sage.

Morris, L. *et al.* (1987). *How to Communicate Evaluation Findings.* London: Sage.

Murphy, R. and Torrance, H. (eds) (1987). *Evaluating Education.* London: Harper and Row.

Nevo, D. (1986). Conceptualisation of educational evaluation. In House, E. (ed.), *New Directions in Educational Evaluation.* Lewes: Falmer Press.

Nisbet, J. and Watt, J. (1984). Case study. In Bell, J. *et al.* (eds), *Conducting Small Scale Investigations in Education Managements.* London: Harper and Row.

Nuttall, D. (1981). *School Self Evaluation: Accountability With a Human Face.* London: Schools Council.

Oldroyd, D. and Hall, V. (1988). *Managing Professional Development and INSET.* Bristol: National Development Centre for School Management Training.

Open University (1981). Course E364. *Curriculum Evaluation and Assessment in Educational Institutions.* Milton Keynes: Open University Press.

O'Sullivan, F. *et al.* (1988). *Staff Development in Secondary Schools.* London: Hodder and Stoughton.

Parlett, M. and Hamilton, D. (1972). Evaluation as illumination: A new approach to the study of innovative programmes. Occasional Paper No. 9, Centre for Research in the Educational Sciences, University of Edinburgh. Reprinted in Hamilton, D. *et al.* (eds) (1977). *Beyond the Numbers Game.* London: Macmillan.

Patton, M. Q. (1980). *Qualitative Evaluation Methods.* London: Sage.

Patton, M. Q. (1982). Reflections on evaluating staff development. *Journal of Staff Development,* 3 (1), 6–24.

Patton, M. Q. (1987). *Creative Evaluation,* 2nd edn. London: Sage.

Popham, J. (1988). *Educational Evaluation*, 2nd edn. Englewood Cliffs, N.J.: Prentice Hall.

Powney, J. and Watts, M. (1987). *Interviewing in Educational Research*. London: Routledge and Kegan Paul.

Purkey, S. and Smith, M. (1983). Effective schools: A review. *Elementary School Journal*, 83, 427–52.

Rudduck, J. (1981). *Making the Most of the Short Inservice Course*. London: Methuen Educational.

Rudduck, J. (1985). A case for case records? In Burgess, R. (ed.), *Strategies of Educational Research*. Lewes: Falmer Press.

Rudduck, J. and Hopkins, D. (1984). *The Sixth Form and Libraries*. London: British Library.

Rudduck, J. and Hopkins, D. (1985). *Research as a Basis for Teaching*. London: Heinemann Educational.

Rutter, M. *et al.* (1979). *Fifteen Thousand Hours*. London: Open Books.

Sapsford, R. and Evans, J. (1984). Evaluating a research report. In Bell, J. *et al.* (eds), *Conducting Small Scale Investigations in Education Management*. London: Harper and Row.

Schools Council (1973). *Evaluation in Curriculum Development*. London: Macmillan.

Schmuck, R. and Runkel, P. (1985). *The Handbook of Organization Development in Schools*. Palo Alto, Calif.: Mayfield.

Schwandt, T. A. and Halpern, E. S. (1988). *Linking Auditing and Meta-Evaluation: An Audit Model for Applied Research*. Beverly Hills, Calif.: Sage.

Scriven, M. (1967). The methodology of evaluation. In Stake, R. E. (ed.), *AERA Monograph Series on Curriculum Evaluation*, No. 1. Chicago: Rand McNally.

Shipman, M. (1979). *In-School Evaluation*. London: Heinemann Educational.

Showers, B. (1985). Teachers coaching teachers. *Educational Leadership*, 42 (7), 43–8.

Simons, H. (1980). *Towards a Science of the Singular*. Norwich: CARE, University of East Anglia.

Simons, H. (1982). Suggestions for a school self evaluation based on democratic principles. In McCormick, R. (ed.), *Calling Education to Account*. London: Heinemann.

Simons, H. (1987). *Getting to Know Schools in a Democracy*. Lewes: Falmer Press.

Skilbeck, M. (1984). *Evaluating the Curriculum in the Eighties*. London: Hodder and Stoughton.

Skrtic, T. S. (1985). Doing naturalistic research into educational organisations. In Lincoln, Y. S. (ed.), *Organisational Theory and Inquiry*. Beverly Hills, Calif.: Sage.

Smetheram, D. (ed.) (1981). *Practising Evaluation*. Driffield: Nafferton Books.

Stake, R. (1967). The countenance of educational evaluation. *Teachers College Record*, 68, 523–40.

Stake, R. (1986a). Evaluating educational programmes. In Hopkins, D. (ed.), *Inservice Training and Educational Development*. London: Croom Helm.

Stake, R. (1986b). An evolutionary view of program improvement. In House, E. (ed.), *New Directions in Educational Evaluation*. Lewes: Falmer Press.

Steadman, S. *et al.* (1989). *Setting Standards in Schools*. York: Longman for the SCDC.

Stenhouse, L. (1975). *An Introduction to Curriculum Research and Development*. London: Heinemann Educational.

Stenhouse, L. (1980). *Curriculum Research and Development in Action*. London: Heinemann Educational.

Stoney, S. *et al.* (1986). *The Management of TVEI: A Summary*. Windsor: NFER.

Strauss, A. L. (1987). *Qualitative Analysis for Social Scientists*. Cambridge: Cambridge University Press.

Stronach, I. (1981). Beyond dispute. Clydebank evaluation, Jordanhill College of Education, mimeo.

Stronach, I. (1986). Practical evaluation. In Hopkins, D. (ed.), *Evaluating TVEI: Some Methodological Issues*. Cambridge: Cambridge Institute of Education/MSC.

Stufflebeam, D. and Shinkfield, A. (1985). *Systematic Evaluation*. Dordrecht, Netherlands: Kluwer-Nijhoff.

Tawney, D. (1976). *Curriculum Evaluation Today*. London: Macmillan.

Tyler, R. (1949). *Basic Principles of Curriculum and Instruction*. Chicago: University of Chicago Press.

van Maanen, J. (ed.) (1983). *Qualitative Methodology*. London: Sage.

van Velzen, W. *et al*. (1985). *Making School Improvement Work*. Leuven, Belgium: ACCO.

Walker, R. (1980). The conduct of educational case study: Ethics, theory and procedures. In Dockerell, W. and Hamilton, D. (eds), *Rethinking Educational Research*. London: Hodder and Stoughton.

Walker, R. (1981). On the uses of fiction in educational research (and I don't mean Cyril Burt). In Smetherham, D. (ed.), *Practising Evaluation*. Driffield: Nafferton Books.

Walker, R. (1985). *Doing Research. A Handbook for Teachers*. London: Methuen.

Wideen, M. (1986). The role of the evaluator. In Holly, P. (ed.), *Cambridge Journal of Education*, 16 (2).

Wideen, M. and Andrews, I. (1987). *Staff Development for School Improvement*. Lewes: Falmer Press.

Wiseman, S. and Pidgeon, D. (1972). *Curriculum Evaluation*. Windsor: NFER.

Woods, P. (1985). New songs played skilfully: Creativity and technique in writing up qualitative research. In Burgess, R. (ed.), *Issues in Educational Research*. Lewes: Falmer Press.

Worthen, B. and Sanders, J. (1987). *Educational Evaluation: Alternative Approaches and Practical Guidelines*. London: Longman.

Yin, R. (1984). *Case Study Research*. London: Sage.

Zigarmi, P. and Loucks, S. (eds) (1982). Special issues on evaluation. *Journal of Staff Development*, 3 (1).

Index